The Right to Food

Francis Adams

The Right to Food

The Global Campaign to End Hunger and Malnutrition

palgrave
macmillan

Francis Adams
Department of Political Science and Geography
Old Dominion University
Norfolk, VA, USA

ISBN 978-3-030-60254-3 ISBN 978-3-030-60255-0 (eBook)
https://doi.org/10.1007/978-3-030-60255-0

Cover illustration: kenkuza_shutterstock.com

This Palgrave Macmillan imprint is published by the registered company Springer Nature Switzerland AG
The registered company address is: Gewerbestrasse 11, 6330 Cham, Switzerland

To my beloved boys, Jayden and Adryan

Preface

The world's problems can feel overwhelming. As I complete work on this book, the spread of a novel respiratory infection is threatening the lives of people across every continent. The current global pandemic only adds to a lengthy and foreboding list of economic, social, and environmental threats to our collective well-being. While these threats are serious and must be recognized, attention should also be accorded to the response to these threats. Every day international institutions, local governments, community groups, and committed individuals are working to build more equitable, healthy, and sustainable communities. By highlighting this work, which often goes unnoticed, this book challenges the all too common narrative of endless crisis.

The global campaign to end hunger and malnutrition, which is the focus of this project, is a prominent example of collective action in response to an urgent humanitarian need. Because this campaign is led by the United Nations, I am also challenging another commonly accepted narrative. The UN is often considered either unable or unwilling to effectively address the world's major challenges. Yet each year the food assistance agencies of the UN save countless lives from the scourge of hunger and malnutrition in every corner of the globe. By highlighting these efforts, which also go largely unnoticed, I am challenging the prevailing narrative of a United Nations without power or purpose.

During the course of this project, I benefitted from the support of various individuals to whom I would like to express my gratitude. I am especially grateful to Anca Pusca, Balaji Varadharaju, and Sham Anand who were exceedingly helpful in guiding this project to a successful conclusion. I would also like to acknowledge the support I received from people at Old Dominion University. Kent L. Sandstrom, Dean of the College of Arts and Letters, was a consistent source of assistance and encouragement. I also received the continued support of my colleagues in the Department of Political Science and Geography and the Graduate Program in International Studies.

Although I could not have completed this project without the support of these individuals, its shortcomings are solely my responsibility.

Norfolk, VA, USA
August 2020

Francis Adams

Contents

Acronyms

ADB	Asian Development Bank
AoA	*Agreement on Agriculture*
APFC	Asia-Pacific Forestry Commission
ARNS	Africa Regional Nutrition Strategy
ASAP	Adaptation for Small Holder Agriculture Program
AU	African Union
CA	Conservation Agriculture
CAADP	*Comprehensive Africa Agriculture Development Program*
CaFAN	Caribbean Farmers Network
CARDI	Caribbean Agricultural Research and Development Institute
CBT	Cash-Based Transfers
CELAC	Community of Latin American and Caribbean States
CESCR	Committee on Economic, Social and Cultural Rights
CFA	Comprehensive Framework for Action
CFS	Committee on World Food Security
CFSVA	Comprehensive Food Security and Vulnerability Analysis
CODA	Conditional on-Demand Assistance
CPI	Corruption Perceptions Index
CSA	Climate Smart Agriculture
CSD	Commission on Sustainable Development
CSO	Civil Society Organization
DESA	Dietary Energy Supply Adequacy
DFA	Depth of the Food Deficit
ECOSOC	Economic and Social Council
ECOWAS	Economic Community of West African States

ECTAD	Eastern Caribbean Trading and Agricultural Development Organization
EEZ	Exclusive Economic Zone
EFSA	Emergency Food Security Assessment
EMOP	Emergency Operation
ENSO	El Niño Southern Oscillation
ETC	Emergency Telecommunications Cluster
EU	European Union
EWEA	Early Warning Early Action
FAC	*Food Assistance Convention*
FAO	Food and Agriculture Organization
FFA	Food-for-Assets
FFS	Farmer Field School
FFT	Food-for-Training
FFW	Food-for-Work
FIAN	Food First Information and Action Network
FIES	Food Insecurity Experience Scale
FITTEST	Fast IT and Telecommunications Emergency and Support Team
FIVIMS	Food Insecurity and Vulnerability Information and Mapping System
FNS	Farmer Nutrition School
FSIN	Food Security Information Network
FtMA	Farm to Market Alliance
G8	Group of 8
GAM	Global Acute Malnutrition
GATT	*General Agreement on Tariffs and Trade*
GCC	Gulf Cooperation Council
GCF	Green Climate Fund
GEF	Global Environmental Facility
GHG	Greenhouse Gas
GHI	Global Hunger Index
GIPB	Global Partnership Initiative for Plant Breeding Capacity Building
GM	Genetically Modified
HAS	Humanitarian Staging Area
HFLACI	*Hunger-Free Latin American and Caribbean Initiative*
HGSF	Home-Grown School Feeding
HLPE	High Level Panel of Experts
HLTF	High-Level Task Force
HRC	Human Rights Council
HRF	Humanitarian Response Facility
ICARDA	International Center for Agricultural Research in the Dry Areas
ICARRD	International Conference on Agrarian Reform and Rural Development

ICCPR	*International Covenant on Civil and Political Rights*
ICESCR	*International Covenant on Economic, Social and Cultural Rights*
ICN2	Second International Conference on Nutrition
ICPD	International Conference on Population and Development
IDP	Internally Displaced Person
IFAD	International Fund for Agricultural Development
IFPRI	International Food Policy Research Institute
IFSA	International Food Security Assessment
IGA	*International Grains Arrangement*
IGWG	Intergovernmental Working Group
ILAC	*Latin American and Caribbean Initiative for Sustainable Development*
ILC	International Land Coalition
IMF	International Monetary Fund
IMR	Infant Mortality Rate
IOM	International Organization for Migration
IPC	Integrated Food Security Phase Classification
IPCC	Intergovernmental Panel of Experts on Climate Change
IPOA-IUU	*International Plan of Action to Prevent, Deter and Eliminate Illegal, Unreported and Unregulated Fishing*
IPR	Intellectual Property Rights
IRC	International Rescue Committee
IRRM	Integrated Rapid Response Mechanism
IUU	Illegal, Unreported and Unregulated
LDN	Land Degradation Neutrality
LIFDC	Low-Income Food Deficit Country
LRIMS	Land Resources Information Management System
LRP	Local And Regional Purchases
MAFAP	Monitoring and Analyzing Food and Agricultural Policies
MAM	Moderate Acute Malnutrition
MDD	Minimum Dietary Diversity
MDER	Minimum Dietary Energy Requirement
MDG	Millennium Development Goals
MPA	Marine Protected Area
MRV	Monitoring, Reporting, and Verification
NAFTA	*North American Free Trade Accord*
NEPAD	*New Partnership for African Development*
NERICA	New Rice for Africa
NGO	Nongovernmental Organization
ODA	Official Development Assistance
OECD	Organization for Economic Cooperation and Development
P4P	Purchase-for-Progress
PHL	Post-Harvest Loss

PoU	Prevalence of Undernourishment
PRRO	Protracted Relief and Recovery Operations
REDD+	Reducing Emissions from Deforestation and Forest Degradation
REVA	Refugee Influx Emergency Vulnerability Assessment
RFLP	Regional Fisheries Livelihood Programme
RITA	Relief Item Tracking Application
RTE	Ready-to-Eat
RUFIN	Rural Finance Institution Building Program
RUSF	Ready to Use Supplemental Food
SAM	Severe Acute Malnutrition
SAP	Structural Adjustment Program
SDG	Sustainable Development Goals
SPFS	Special Program for Food Security
SSA	Sub-Saharan Africa
TAPS	Technical Assistance for Project Start-Up Facility
TFR	Total Fertility Rate
TI	Transparency International
TPDS	Targeted Public Distribution System
TSFP	Targeted Supplementary Feeding Program
UN	United Nations
UNCCD	*United Nations Convention to Combat Desertification*
UNCLOS	*United Nations Convention on the Law of the Seas*
UNDFF	United Nations Decade of Family Farming
UNDP	United Nations Development Programme
UNECA	United Nations Economic Commission for Africa
UNECLAC	United Nations Economic Commission for Latin America and the Caribbean
UNEP	United Nations Environmental Programme
UNESCAP	United Nations Economic and Social Commission for Asia and the Pacific
UNHAS	United Nations Humanitarian Air Service
UNHCR	United Nations High Commission for Refugees
UNHRD	United Nations Humanitarian Response Depots
UNICEF	United Nations Children's Fund
UNRWA	United Nations Relief and Works Agency
UNSCN	United Nations System Standing Committee on Nutrition
UNU	United Nations University
VGGT	*Voluntary Guidelines on Responsible Governance of Tenure of Land, Fisheries and Forests in the Context of National Food Security*
WASH	Water, Sanitation, and Hygiene
WEAI	Women's Empowerment in Agriculture Index
WFC	World Food Council
WFP	World Food Programme

WFS	World Food Summit
WHO	World Health Organization
WSSD	World Summit for Social Development
WSSD	World Summit on Sustainable Development
WTO	World Trade Organization
WUE	Water Use Efficiency
WWF	World Wildlife Fund
ZHC	Zero Hunger Challenge

CHAPTER 1

Introduction

Today's world is marked by a tragic injustice. Although the total amount of food produced can easily feed all people, hunger and malnutrition remain widespread. More than a billion people, mostly in the developing world, lack regular access to safe, sufficient, and nutritious food.[1] Children are often the first to suffer. A quarter of the world's children are malnourished and thousands of children die each day simply because they do not have enough food to eat.

This book examines the global campaign to end hunger and malnutrition. Focus is placed on the work of the United Nations (UN) which has led international efforts to improve food security in the world's poorest countries. This includes both a long-term project to establish food as a universally recognized human right as well as the work of three affiliated agencies—the World Food Programme (WFP), Food and Agriculture Organization (FAO), and International Fund for Agricultural Development (IFAD)—in each region of the developing world.[2]

Hunger, Malnutrition, and Food Insecurity

The terms *hunger*, *malnutrition*, and *food insecurity* are referred to repeatedly throughout this volume and require careful definition. Hunger occurs when a person's average daily caloric intake is less than their minimum dietary energy requirement (MDER).[3] A continued and severe

F. Adams, *The Right to Food*,
https://doi.org/10.1007/978-3-030-60255-0_1

imbalance between caloric intake and energy expenditure will eventually lead to illness, organ failure, and mortality.[4] In addition to total caloric intake, it is also important to consider the nutritional content of the food consumed.[5] Malnutrition occurs when a person does not consume sufficient vitamins, minerals, proteins, carbohydrates, and other essential micronutrients to meet their basic nutritional needs.[6] Because malnutrition weakens the body's immune system, the risk of contracting communicable and parasitic diseases is heightened.[7]

Hunger and malnutrition are typically caused by food insecurity. FAO defines food insecurity as a "... lack of secure access to sufficient amounts of safe and nutritious food for normal human growth and development and an active and healthy life."[8] A distinction is also drawn between moderate and severe food insecurity. A person is considered moderately food insecure if they have been forced to reduce the quality and/or quantity of food they consume while a person is considered severely food insecure if they have completely exhausted their food supplies.[9] Food insecurity is caused by one or more of the following four factors: a lack of food **availability** due to shortages in domestic production or imports; a lack of food **access** due to an inability to procure food; a lack of food **utility** due to poor nutritional content; and a lack of food **stability** due to recurrent shortages.[10] Food insecurity can be transitory (occurring at a time of crisis), seasonal (occurring during certain times of the year), or chronic (occurring on a continuing basis).

Food insecurity is more common for women than men for a number of reasons discussed below. Women who are pregnant or nursing are especially susceptible to malnutrition. During these periods, women need to consume significantly more vitamins, minerals, and other micronutrients. Iron-Deficient Anaemia during pregnancy, for example, endangers a woman's health and increases the risk of adverse maternal and neonatal outcomes.[11] Anemia is extremely common among women of reproductive age in the developing world.[12]

Meeting the nutritional needs of women throughout pregnancy is also critical for the health of their babies.[13] A lack of Folic Acid can lead to cerebral and spinal birth defects, a lack of Iodine can impair the baby's nervous system, a lack of Calcium can impede development of the baby's heart, muscles, and nerves, and a lack of Vitamin D can compromise growth of the baby's bones. If a woman is malnourished during pregnancy, there is a greater likelihood of restricted intrauterine growth and low birth weight of the baby.[14] The risk of death for an infant born at two-thirds of normal weight is ten times greater than for a infant born at normal weight. Low birth weight also slows the development of the baby's immune system and thus heightens the risk of contracting illnesses.[15]

Malnutrition during childhood can be highly debilitating over the course of an entire lifetime.[16] When children are poorly nourished, their growth, health, and cognitive skills are all compromised.[17] Iron and Iodine deficiency impedes physical and cognitive development, Vitamin A deficiency can cause blindness, Vitamin D deficiency endangers bone health and increases the risk of diabetes, and Zinc deficiency impairs overall growth. When children do not consume sufficient protein, they risk developing Kwashiorkor (which causes a distended stomach and swollen feet) and Marasmus (which causes skin to be damaged and loosen). Because malnutrition weakens the immune system, children are far more susceptible to illness and infectious diseases. Nearly half of child mortality in the developing world is due to malnutrition or malnutrition-related diseases.[18]

Malnutrition can cause children to be too short for their age, a condition known as stunting, or too thin for their height, a condition known as wasting.[19] Stunting impairs physical and cognitive development and can lead to immune system disorders that increase the risk of developing chronic diseases. The consequences of stunting are largely irreversible regardless of nutritional intake in later years. At present, approximately 150 million children, roughly a quarter of all children under five in the developing world, are stunted.[20] Wasting causes delayed cognitive development, reduced muscular strength, and lower bone density.[21] When children suffer from wasting much of their body energy is directed toward continually fighting off infections and disease. For girls, wasting is associated with adverse pregnancy outcomes later in life, including delivery complications, preterm birth, and low birth weight of their babies.[22] At present, over fifty million children, approximately eight percent of all children under five in the developing world, are wasted.[23] A third of these children are severely wasted.[24]

Food Insecurity Measurements

A number of measurements have been developed to assess the prevalence and severity of food insecurity. The Integrated Food Security Phase Classification (IPC), developed by FAO, is among the most commonly used measurements. IPC identifies the following five phases of food insecurity: IPC 1, *Generally Food Secure*, when more than eighty percent of households can meet their basic food needs without resorting to atypical coping strategies; IPC 2, *Borderline Food Insecure*, when food consumption is reduced for at least twenty percent of households but is minimally adequate; IPC 3, *Acute Food and Livelihood Crisis*, when at least twenty percent of households have significant food consumption gaps and levels of acute malnutrition are above normal; IPC 4, *Humanitarian Emergency*, when at least twenty percent of households face extreme food consumption gaps, resulting in high levels of acute malnutrition; and IPC 5, *Famine/Humanitarian Catastrophe*, when at least twenty percent of households face a complete lack of food, acute malnutrition exceeds thirty percent of the population, and starvation is evident.

FAO also employs a range of additional instruments to assess the level of food insecurity in a country. The Prevalence of Undernourishment (PoU) indicator estimates the proportion of the population whose habitual food consumption is insufficient to provide the dietary energy levels that are required to maintain an active and healthy life.[25] The measurement is based on national estimates of dietary energy supply, minimum dietary energy requirements for an average individual, and the distribution of food within a country. While the PoU compares food availability to estimated needs, it does not identify which population groups are the most food insecure. The Depth of the Food Deficit (DFD) estimates the overall food shortage of a country. Researchers first determine the number of calories the average individual would need to meet their energy requirements. The difference between the average energy requirement and average caloric consumption is then calculated. This food deficit is then multiplied by the number of undernourished individuals and then divided by the total population of the country. The Dietary Energy Supply Adequacy (DESA) measurement also focuses on whether the dietary energy supply of a country is able to meet the dietary energy requirements of all people. A country's supply of calories is normalized by the average energy requirement estimated for its population. Like PoU and DFD, this measurement assesses whether undernourishment is primarily due to a lack of food availability. The Food Insecurity Experience Scale (FIES) estimates the percentage of people who have serious constraints on their ability to access nutritious food.[26] This measurement relies on the responses of people at the individual and household level to a series of questions regarding their direct experiences of food insecurity. The questions focus on behaviors when respondents encounter difficulties meeting their basic food needs due to a lack of money or other resources.[27] Because FIES disaggregates at sub-national levels and across different population groups, it identifies the geographic distribution of people who face serious constraints obtaining sufficient food. Similarly, the Food Insecurity and Vulnerability Information and Mapping Systems (FIVIMS) assembles information about food insecurity at both national and global levels. FIVIMS draws upon a range of data sources related to household food security and nutritional availability to assess where and why people are food insecure.

Three additional measurements have been developed to assess food insecurity. The WFP's Comprehensive Food Security and Vulnerability Analysis (CFSVA) draws upon household interviews, feedback from focus groups, and secondary data to measure the nutritional status of various segments of a population. The Global Hunger Index (GHI) combines the following four indicators into a single score: the share of the population that is undernourished, the percentage of children under five who are stunted, the percentage of children under five who are wasted, and the mortality rate of children under five. Countries are ranked on a 100-point GHI Severity Scale, where 0 is the best score and 100 is the worst. The GHI Severity Scale indicates whether the level of hunger in a country is low, moderate, serious, alarming, or extremely alarming.[28] Lastly, the World Health Organization (WHO) employs the Global Acute Malnutrition (GAM) measurement to assess the nutritional status of children during protracted humanitarian crises. The measurement is based on the weight and height of children between 6 and 59 months of age. The average weight-to-height ratio of a representative group of children in crisis is compared to a reference group of children not experiencing nutritional deficits. Children in the first group who weigh less than eighty percent of the minimum weight of children with the same height in the reference group are classified as GAM. A further division is made between Moderate Acute Malnutrition (MAM) for children within the seventy and seventy-nine percent range and Severe Acute Malnutrition (SAM) for children who fall below seventy percent. If at least fifteen percent of children in a given population group fall into one of these two categories for more than a year, the situation is classified as Persistent GAM.

Causes of Food Insecurity

Although the global community has long called for marshaling all available resources to combat hunger and malnutrition, devising effective strategies to meet this challenge is an exceedingly complex and highly contested process. A comprehensive understanding of the central causes of food insecurity is essential. Although these causes vary considerably between and within countries, food insecurity is almost always the product of multiple factors—economic, political, environmental, and international—operating simultaneously within the context of a specific time and place. These factors typically interact with each other in ways that compound and intensify food insecurity.[29]

Economic Causes

Poverty is the primary cause of chronic hunger and malnutrition most everywhere in the world. While food might be available in local markets, it is often beyond the reach of the poorest households.[30] In fact, hunger and malnutrition frequently exist within the context of food surpluses. Not only do the poor struggle to purchase sufficient food, but they rarely have the land, water, seeds, tools, technology, and other resources needed to grow food for themselves and their families. The food that is consumed is generally of lower quality and lacks the vitamins, minerals, and other micronutrients needed to maintain good health. Because poor communities spend a larger portion of their income on food than wealthy communities, price increases have a more adverse and destabilizing impact. Poverty and hunger are mutually reinforcing outcomes: poverty causes hunger by depriving people of the means to buy or produce sufficient food while hunger causes poverty by limiting the ability of people to work to their fullest potential.[31]

Food insecurity is almost always higher in the countryside than in cities.[32] On average, people living in rural areas are almost three times more likely to be impoverished than those living in urban environments. The rural poor also have less access to safe water, sanitation, health care, and other critical public services. Seventy-five percent of the world's poor live in rural areas and obtain part or all of their income from some form of agriculture. However, many of these people do not have formal titles for the lands that they work. Because governments rarely recognize communal or customary rights, small-scale farmers can easily be displaced through land acquisitions by more powerful domestic and foreign actors.[33] Land ownership has become increasingly concentrated throughout the developing world.[34] Although approximately eighty percent of the world's farms are small, they occupy just twelve percent of the world's agricultural land.[35]

Food insecurity can also be linked to ethnic and gender inequalities. While ethnic divisions have a long and troubled history in most societies, they were often intensified during the colonial period when European powers drew arbitrary boundaries and favored some ethnic groups over others. Marginalized ethnic groups continue to have less access to nutritious food, clean water, health care, education, and other public resources.[36] It is also important to recognize that women are typically more food insecure than men.[37] Women living in urban areas tend to be concentrated in low-paid jobs with long hours, poor working conditions, and limited social protections. Gender differences are even more pronounced in rural areas.[38] Although women do at least half of all agricultural work, they often lack the resources needed to improve their incomes and living conditions. Legal restrictions and societal norms work against the interests of women, especially with respect to owning land or obtaining the credit, tools, technology, and extension services needed to become more food secure. When men migrate to urban areas in search of employment, the number of female-headed households in the countryside increases and these households typically have the highest levels of food insecurity.[39]

Political Causes

Governments also contribute to food insecurity. Because rural communities have little political influence, public sector policies are rarely structured to meet their needs. Most public resources flow to cities rather than the countryside. A long-standing bias against agriculture often leaves rural communities without the tools, technology, and basic infrastructure needed to increase food production or generate higher incomes. Small-scale farmers are invariably characterized by low levels of productivity and glaring inefficiencies in the use of critical inputs. Agricultural sectors are also characterized by high levels of post-harvest loss. About a quarter of all crops produced in the developing world are lost because of inadequate harvesting techniques, storage facilities, and distribution systems.[40] There are also sizable losses in the fishing sector due to poor refrigeration, inadequate processing facilities, and difficulty reaching wholesale markets within reasonable time periods.

When governments do invest in agriculture, they generally favor the cultivation of commercial crops for export over staple crops for domestic consumption. Over the course of the past two decades, the most fertile agricultural lands in developing countries have become increasingly used for the cultivation of crops that are used for the production of biofuels, especially maize, palm oil, sorghum, soybeans, and sugarcane.[41] Farmlands are also being set aside for the grazing of livestock as the worldwide demand for meat consumption increases. The attraction of exports is readily apparent. Exports help generate the foreign exchange needed to purchase critical raw materials, energy supplies, capital goods, and manufactured items from abroad. It is important to recognize, however, that export agriculture almost always leads to a greater concentration of land ownership as small-scale farmers are displaced by large landowners and agribusinesses. Because the cultivation of export crops is more environmentally hazardous, this transition also jeopardizes the long-term sustainability of agricultural production and rural economies.

Public sector corruption also contributes to food insecurity. Political systems throughout the developing world generally function as patronage machines where the private interests of a few outweigh the public welfare of many.[42] The deleterious consequences of corruption are manifold. Because corrupt behavior tends to favor those with the greatest resources, it further intensifies inequality. Moreover, by distorting public policy and diverting resources, social protection programs, including nutrition, agricultural, and rural development programs, are underfunded. While corruption is a universal phenomenon and by no means limited to the developing world, many of the conditions that engender corrupt behavior are especially pronounced in poor countries. Corruption is more likely to occur when government officials have considerable discretion over the allocation of resources, institutional accountability and transparency are limited, and a lack of effective oversight mechanisms makes the disclosure and punishment of illegal acts unlikely.

Corruption can be especially pronounced in countries that are endowed with an abundance of natural resources, a phenomenon known as the "resource curse."[43] Because governments generate enormous revenues from natural resource exports, there is less need to maintain popular support through the redistribution of resources or funding of basic needs. The income generated from natural resource rents enables governments to repress political opponents and forestall public sector reform. With few restraints on public sector actors, the revenues that flow to governments are often squandered on unproductive investments or lost to corruption. The resource curse is economically detrimental in other respects. Because governments derive most of their revenues from natural resources, there is less need to diversify domestic economies and few new employment opportunities are created. Large inflows of foreign capital into natural resource sectors typically cause a country's currency to appreciate, making it harder for domestic producers to sell their goods on external markets. Civil conflict is also more likely due to the intense competition over access to lucrative minerals, metals, and hydrocarbons.[44]

Civil conflict is certainly a major cause of food insecurity in many parts of the developing world.[45] Such conflicts destroy land, crops, livestock, equipment, and physical infrastructure. As agricultural output falls, the food available in local markets declines and food prices increase. Opposing factions often prevent the distribution of food supplies to specific regions of a country. Conflict also causes people to flee to other parts of their country or to neighboring countries. When people are forced to abandon their homes, possessions, and sources of income, their food insecurity dramatically increases.[46] These people often resort to negative coping strategies, such as selling productive assets, mortgaging land, abandoning livestock, contracting high interest loans, or exploiting natural resources, that further compromise their long-term food security. Countries experiencing high levels of political violence typically have neither the resources nor the will to meet domestic food needs and neighboring countries can be quickly overwhelmed by large numbers of refugees streaming across their borders. Sixty percent of all people who are currently food insecure live in countries that have high levels of civil conflict or are recovering from conflict.

Environmental Causes

An imbalance between a country's population size and its natural resource base also causes food insecurity. A country's natural resources, especially its land, water, forests, and fisheries, may be insufficient to meet the nutritional needs of a rapidly expanding population. Countries with the highest population growth are often unable to meet the increasing demands placed on their food systems.[47] In fact, population growth is generally highest precisely in those countries with the most severe resource constraints.[48]

The natural resources required to meet escalating food needs have steadily deteriorated in most parts of the developing world. In many of the poorest countries, the need for fertile agricultural land is rapidly outpacing the availability of such land. As poverty levels increase, smallholder farmers often cultivate lands more intensely and use agricultural methods that are more environmentally hazardous.[49] The productivity of large tracts of land is also declining. The expanded use of chemical fertilizers, herbicides, and pesticides is causing widespread deterioration of soil quality. Nearly forty percent of the world's agricultural lands are now degraded and an additional twelve million hectares are lost to soil erosion, land degradation, or desertification each year.[50] Forty percent of the world's people live in areas marked by high levels of land degradation.[51]

There is also a growing scarcity of water resources in the developing world.[52] Freshwater withdrawal as a percentage of renewable freshwater is rapidly increasing in most countries. The world's demand for water has tripled over the last half century and most people live in countries where water tables have fallen over an extended period of time. The intensive and often wasteful use of water resources is drying up rivers, lakes, watersheds, and coastal estuaries. While three-quarters of the world's accessible freshwater originates in forested watersheds, approximately forty percent of all watersheds have lost more than half of their original tree cover. Pollution is also a major threat to freshwater resources. Approximately eighty percent of wastewater is dumped directly into water bodies and one-third of rivers in developing countries contain severe pathogenic pollution. Regulations to curtail pollution from agriculture, industry, and mining are limited and the regulations that do exist are poorly enforced. As water resources decline, agriculture—which consumes about seventy percent of the world's freshwater—is increasingly at risk.[53]

The developing world is also home to high levels of deforestation. Millions of hectares of forests are cut down, degraded, or fragmented each year, especially in the Amazon, Congo Basin, and Southeast Asia.[54] Although illegal logging operations contribute to deforestation, most forest loss is due to the conversion of forest areas for farming, ranching, or mining. Forests provide ecosystem services that are critical for sustainable food production, including purifying the air, regulating water cycles, protecting watersheds, replenishing soils, stabilizing the climate, and the maintaining essential habitats for plant and animal life.[55]

Climate change is intensifying the loss of natural resources in developing countries.[56] As the earth's air, surface, and ocean temperatures rise, the health, productivity, and nutritional content of many crop species declines.[57] Higher temperatures and inter-seasonal climate variability have delayed or shortened growing seasons and increased soil erosion.[58] Heat and dryness significantly reduce crop yields. Thermal expansion of seawater and the melting of polar ice caps, ice sheets, and glaciers, especially in Greenland and Antarctica, are causing sea levels to rise. Saline intrusion is damaging previously fertile lands. The increased variety and number of insects that thrive at higher temperatures are causing widespread destruction to crops.[59] Elevated carbon dioxide levels are also contributing to the spread of weeds that reduce the growth of crops. The adverse impacts of climate change have already contributed to lower productivity in the cultivation of major food crops, including wheat, rice, and maize.

Climate change is also impacting the availability of freshwater resources in the developing world. In areas where there is less precipitation and greater evaporation, lakes and other inland water bodies are drying up, thus reducing the water supply available for agricultural and livestock production.[60] The melting of mountain glaciers, especially in the Andes and the Himalayas, is also limiting the water available for agricultural cultivation in the valleys below. A quarter of the world's population currently resides in regions where water resources are insufficient to meet overall food needs.

Climate change is also reducing fish populations in the developing world. Oceans absorb the vast majority of the heat that is trapped by greenhouse gas (GHG) emissions. As ocean temperatures rise, fish tend to migrate toward cooler waters away from the tropics. Moreover, climate change induced ocean acidification, salinity, oxygen depletion, and the spread of pathogens, as well as the degradation, bleaching, and loss of coral reefs, are all decreasing food supply for fish and damaging their breeding habitats. Warmer temperatures have caused the extinction of some marine species, shifted the habitat of others, and contributed to the spread of disease throughout the food chain. Because warmer waters are especially harmful to fish embryos, the reproduction of some species has declined. Inland fisheries and aquaculture have also declined due to changes in water temperature, precipitation, and evaporation.

Rising temperatures are causing the increased frequency and intensity of extreme weather events. Droughts, heat waves, forest fires, storms, hurricanes, cyclones, typhoons, floods, and other natural hazards are contributing to the loss of crops, arable lands, livestock, water resources, forests, and rural infrastructure.[61] The number of extreme climate-related disasters has more than doubled since the early 1990s.[62] The quantity, quality, and safety of food supplies are all compromised by the disruption of agricultural production and post-production processes. People who are already food insecure are the least able to endure the shocks caused by a warmer earth and more frequent natural disasters.[63]

International Causes

There are also factors associated with the structure of the global economy that contribute to food insecurity in the developing world. The trade in agricultural commodities, for example, frequently works against the interests of small-scale farmers. Because North American and European countries heavily subsidize their agricultural sectors, farmers in these countries can sell their grains on global markets at lower prices than would otherwise be the case. The dumping of agricultural products at artificially low prices undermines farmers in poor countries, where subsidies are either considerably smaller or nonexistent.[64] The Agreement on Agriculture (AoA), negotiated under the auspices of the World Trade Organization (WTO), was presented as an important step toward reducing subsidies to agricultural producers. However, wealthy countries retain many of their farm subsidies by employing different forms of exemption that are allowed under the accord. In addition, WTO rules have permitted global agribusinesses to appropriate indigenous knowledge of food production by obtaining intellectual property rights (IPR) over the genetic material of seeds and livestock breeds. Under the new rules, global agribusinesses have expanded their influence over how food is produced, processed, marketed, and delivered to consumers around the world.[65]

Large-scale acquisitions of land by foreign countries or agribusinesses also undermine food security in the developing world.[66] Land acquisitions have been entered into with countries in the Persian Gulf and East Asia that have significant food deficits.[67] These acquisitions typically take place in areas where land governance is weak and customary tenure arrangements are not respected. Although most of these acquisitions have been completed in sub-Saharan Africa, they have also occurred in parts of South America and Southeast Asia. The lands acquired are used to produce food or animal feed that is in short supply at home. Land acquisitions, which typically involve leases of twenty-five to fifty years, rarely compensate local farmers who are pushed off of lands that their communities may have cultivated for generations. The lands acquired by foreign interests are then used to grow crops for consumption in their home countries or to be sold on world markets. As noted above, the increased use of biofuels is raising the global demand for maize, palm oil, sorghum, soybeans, and sugarcane. The cultivation of crops grown for biofuel production, which requires larger tracts of land than traditional farming, has driven land acquisitions in a number of countries.

Land acquisitions by foreign countries or global agribusinesses are defended by governments in the developing world as an effective means of attracting foreign exchange, increasing investment in domestic agriculture, expediting the transfer of technology, improving local infrastructure, and creating new employment opportunities. However, these presumed benefits are rarely realized, at least not at the levels anticipated. The negative consequences of these arrangements are far more common. When the most fertile agricultural lands are used to produce crops that are shipped abroad, food insecurity increases at home. Subsistence farmers who are left with marginal lands find it harder to produce the food needed for their families or to sell on local markets. Outside interests are also less likely to adequately preserve the land and local ecosystems. Areas where large-scale land acquisitions have taken place are marked by increased topsoil erosion, aquifer depletion, water pollution, deforestation, and biodiversity loss.

Foreign fishing fleets also contribute to food insecurity.[68] Fish and seafood have long been important sources of animal protein and minerals in the diets of people in the developing world. However, long-distance fishing fleets are causing a significant decline in fish populations. Vessels owned by American, Chinese, European, Japanese, Korean, and Russian companies engage in illegal, unreported, and unregulated (IUU) fishing in the exclusive economic zones (EEZ) of developing countries.[69] These deep-water fleets, which are heavily subsidized by their home governments, often take advantage of weak control, regulation, and surveillance capacities to operate illegally off the coast of Latin American, African, and Asian countries.[70] Coastal fish populations are being exploited at rates well beyond their biological capacities for regeneration. An estimated eighty-five percent of global fish stocks are over-exploited, depleted, fully exploited, or in recovery from exploitation. Declining fish stocks are reducing per capita fish consumption in the developing world and undermining coastal communities that depend on fishing as their primary source of income.[71]

Foreign fishing fleets often engage in highly destructive practices, such as bottom trawling, which involves dragging long nets along the ocean floor and scooping up most everything in their path. The bycatch that is trapped in these nets is then discarded, causing the needless loss of millions of fish. These nets also damage the coral reefs and natural habitats that are necessary for the survival and reproduction of fish populations. Damage to marine ecosystems requires an extremely long time to recover. Even when fishing vessels operate outside the EEZ, they often use prohibited techniques to catch far more fish than permitted.

The external debts of many developing countries also contribute to food insecurity. For countries with large external debts, simply making annual interest payments can absorb a significant percentage of foreign exchange earnings. Resources that could have been used for social protection programs or investments in agrarian development are absorbed by these interest payments. Moreover, the governments of highly indebted countries often expand export agriculture, lease agricultural land and territorial waters to foreign interests, and exploit fragile natural resources in order to generate the foreign exchange needed to service their debts. Each of these measures increases food insecurity at home.

Countries with large external debts frequently turn to the International Monetary Fund (IMF) for support. The structural adjustment agreements that these countries enter into with the IMF, which are ostensibly designed to stabilize macroeconomic conditions and reduce budget deficits, require cutbacks in public sector spending and deregulation of domestic economies. These agreements also mandate trade liberalization, including the reduction of tariffs and non-tariff barriers to agricultural imports, thus exposing domestic farmers to an influx of foreign grains. Because structural adjustment agreements also require reducing restrictions on foreign investment, this typically results in more land being acquired by global agribusinesses.

Food Aid and Food Assistance

Reducing food insecurity in developing countries is among the greatest challenges in the world today. The international community provides both food aid and food assistance throughout Latin America, Africa, the Middle East, and Asia. Although "food aid" and "food assistance" are often used interchangeably, it is important to define each term separately. Food aid refers to emergency food relief to people with urgent needs and is typically extended at times of humanitarian crisis. Such aid can be provided either in-kind or through cash-based transfers and commodity vouchers. In-kind aid refers to the direct provision of food to people in need. Bags of rice dropped from cargo planes over drought-stricken lands or loaves of bread thrown from the back of flatbed trucks to outstretched hands in overcrowded refugee camps are examples of in-kind aid. Alternately, cash-based transfers and commodity vouchers allow people to purchase food in local markets. In times of natural disaster or civil conflict, food aid is absolutely essential and saves countless lives.[72]

Food assistance, on the other hand, goes beyond short-term emergency relief to address the root causes of food insecurity. WFP defines food assistance as "… a full range of instruments, activities, and platforms that empower vulnerable and food-insecure people and communities so they can regularly have access to nutritious food."[73] Food assistance is thus structured to build the local resources, knowledge, and capacities needed to ensure people can either produce or purchase sufficient food for themselves and their families. This typically involves longer-term efforts to increase agricultural productivity, promote rural development, and preserve natural environments.[74] *The ultimate goal of food assistance is to eliminate the need for food aid.*

The United Nations has led the campaign to end hunger and malnutrition in the developing world. This includes a long-term effort to ensure food is universally recognized as a basic human right as well as the allocation of both food aid and food assistance to poor communities in Latin America, Africa, the Middle East, and Asia. Three UN-affiliated agencies—the World Food Programme, Food and Agriculture Organization, and International Fund for Agricultural Development—provide food aid in response to humanitarian emergencies as well as broader food assistance to address the root causes of hunger and malnutrition. Food assistance is often structured to improve agricultural productivity through the distribution of improved seeds, equipment, irrigation, and extension services, the defense of land rights, or support for farmers associations[75] Resources have also been deployed to foster broader rural transformation, including the expansion of non-farm employment, diffusion of financial services, construction of infrastructure, and development of wider markets for the products of small enterprises.[76] These agencies have also sought to preserve natural resources and local ecosystems, especially the land, water, forests, and fisheries that are critical for sustainable food production.

Chapter Outline

This book begins with international efforts to establish access to safe, sufficient, and nutritious food as a universally recognized human right before turning to the work of the three United Nations food agencies in each region of the developing world. Chapter 2 chronicles the evolution of the right to food regime beginning with the *Universal Declaration of Human Rights* in the early days of the United Nations and ending with the recent *Right to Food* resolution of the Human Rights Council. The major institutional mechanisms that have been established to promote and defend the right to food are also identified. The latter part of this chapter describes the purpose, structure, and major programs of the three United Nations food agencies.

Chapters 3–6 examine food insecurity in Latin America, Africa, the Middle East, and Asia. The first part of each chapter outlines the nature and central causes of food insecurity in each region. These chapters then survey the work of UN agencies in providing emergency food aid, promoting agricultural productivity, advancing rural development, and preserving natural environments. The projects identified are representative of the work undertaken within recent years but are by no means an exhaustive review of all the activities that these agencies have supported.

Although Latin American countries have made progress in reducing hunger and malnutrition, nearly 200 million people continue to be food insecure. Chapter 3 first outlines the parameters of malnutrition in Latin America and then turns to the economic, political, and environmental causes of food insecurity. The last section reviews multilateral efforts to meet the nutritional needs of poor communities in the region. Although some countries continue to receive emergency food aid, most assistance is structured to improve agricultural productivity, promote rural development, and preserve natural environments.

Africa has the highest proportion of people who suffer from hunger and malnutrition of all world regions. Chapter 4 offers a broad outline of food insecurity in Africa before turning to its central causes. International efforts to meet the nutritional needs of poor communities are then considered. The United Nations provides emergency food aid to people impacted by natural disasters and civil conflicts, as well as broader assistance to address the underlying causes of food insecurity.

Most Middle Eastern countries, which are the focus of Chapter 5, have seen food insecurity dramatically worsen in recent years. Civil conflicts have caused enormous damage to food production, destroyed physical infrastructure, and forced millions of people to flee their homes. In addition to civil conflict, a number of other factors that contribute to hunger and malnutrition in the region are identified in the first part of this chapter. The chapter then reviews international efforts to improve food security. Although the majority of this work involves the provision of emergency food aid to people suffering from civil conflict, UN agencies have also promoted agrarian and rural development, as well as the preservation of natural environments.

Asia is the focus of Chapter 6. Despite a decline in the percentage of people who are food insecure, this region is home to the largest number of malnourished people in the world. More than 500 million people, largely concentrated in South and Southeast Asia, are unable to secure safe, sufficient, and nutritious food on a daily basis. This represents half of all malnourished people in the world. This chapter describes conditions in Asia, identifies the central causes of food insecurity, and reviews international efforts to meet the nutritional needs of poor communities. While food aid is provided in emergency situations, especially in response to natural disaster, most assistance is structured to address the root causes of food insecurity.

The concluding chapter considers ways to strengthen food aid and assistance in the years to come. A series of recommendations are advanced to improve food aid as well as restructure food assistance to more effectively promote agricultural productivity, rural development, and environmental preservation. Many of these recommendations reflect lessons learned from the actual experience of food aid and assistance described in this volume.

It is hard to imagine a more fundamental human right than the right to food. Beyond the moral imperative that no woman, man, or child should suffer from hunger or malnutrition, food insecurity imposes enormous economic, political, and environmental costs on the entire world. Hunger and malnutrition cause the loss of labor productivity, decline of rural areas, unsustainable rural-urban migration, political instability, civil conflict, refugee crises, and environmental destruction. These problems threaten the collective well-being of all people. Food aid remains imperative at times of humanitarian emergency while food assistance is needed to make such emergencies less frequent. The world clearly has the resources and capacity to feed all people. Our common future depends on ensuring this ideal becomes an enduring reality.

Notes

1. According to FAO, nearly 1.9 billion people in the world suffer from moderate or severe food insecurity. Food and Agriculture Organization 2020j, p. 9. The Food Security Information Network (FSIN) reports that at least 100 million people have such high levels of food insecurity that they require urgent humanitarian action. Food Security Information Network 2020, p. 2. See also Pritchard et al. 2017 and International Food Policy Research Institute 2020 for broad surveys of food and nutritional insecurity in the developing world.
2. WFP is a subsidiary agency of the United Nations while FAO and IFAD are specialized agencies affiliated with the UN. Subsidiary funds and programs are established by the General Assembly and are directly administered by the UN. Specialized agencies are semi-autonomous international organizations that coordinate their work with the UN through negotiated agreements but have separate administrative structures, budgets, members, and rules.
3. Although the term *hunger* is commonly used, it is not a precise condition that can be easily measured. Hunger ranges in meaning from a short-term physical discomfort to a life-threatening condition.
4. MDER thresholds can vary among countries due to a range of social, cultural, climatic, and other factors.
5. See Food Security Information Network 2020, p. 14 for a distinction between acute and chronic malnutrition. Malnutrition can also occur due to the poor absorption or biological use of the micronutrients consumed as a result of illness or disease. Food and Agriculture Organization 2020j, p. 3. Micronutrient deficiencies may not be detected until the damage to a person's health becomes irreversible.
6. Obesity is also a form of malnutrition. Obesity is at least partially due to a dietary transition in which people consume nutrient-poor processed foods that are high in fat, sugar, and refined carbohydrates. These shifts in dietary patterns, along with less frequent physical activity, have contributed to a sharp increases in child, adolescent, and adult obesity in the developing world. Obesity increases the risk of non-communicable diseases, such as cardiovascular disease, diabetes, and various types of cancer.

7. The diseases that are most frequently contracted by individuals with compromised immune systems include malaria, measles, pneumonia, tuberculosis, and various coronavirus strains.
8. Food Security Information Network 2020, p. 11.
9. Food and Agriculture Organization 2020i, p. 6, Food and Agriculture Organization 2019b, p. 5.
10. Food and Agriculture Organization 2019a, p. 69, Food and Agriculture Organization 2019b, pp. 116–117.
11. Food and Agriculture Organization 2020j, p. 39. Iron Deficiency Anaemia occurs when a decline in healthy red blood cells compromises the delivery of oxygen to the body's tissues. Maternal Anaemia is associated with higher risks of mortality in expectant mothers, as well as prematurity, low birth weight, and infant physical and cognitive impairment. Food and Agriculture Organization 2019h, p. 18.
12. Anemia affects approximately a third of all women of reproductive age in the developing world and is highest among women in Sub-Saharan Africa. World Food Programme 2019a, p. 14.
13. As FAO notes, "… the nutritional status of the mother is decisive for the newborn because it determines their birthweight, their health, and their nutritional status…" Food and Agriculture Organization 2020j, p. 31.
14. Approximately a quarter of all infants in the developing world are born with low birth weights.
15. Illnesses due to malnutrition also prevent infants from absorbing nutrients from the food that they consume. Diarrhea, for example, quickly removes nutrients from the body before they can be fully utilized.
16. See Hassan 2016 (ed.) for a collection of studies on child malnutrition in the developing world.
17. Children are considered to have achieved minimum dietary diversity (MDD) if they consume food from at least five of eight food groups each day. Food and Agriculture Organization 2019h, p. 15.
18. Food and Agriculture Organization 2020j, p. 31. Approximately three million children die annually from malnutrition or malnutrition-related diseases. Human Rights Council 2019, p. 3. Limited access to safe water, sanitation, and hygiene (WASH) is a central reason for the spread of diseases among children.
19. Stunting is defined as height-for-age that is more than two standard deviations below the medium on the World Health Organization (WHO) Child Growth Standards while wasting is defined as weight-for-height that is more than two standards deviations below the medium on the Child Growth Standards.
20. World Food Programme 2019a, p. 14. Food and Agriculture Organization 2020i, p. 10. Africa and Asia account for thirty-six percent and

fifty-five percent respectively of all stunted children under five in the world. Food and Agriculture Organization 2020i, p. 10.

21. Briend, Khara, and Dolan 2015 offer detailed analysis of the causes and consequences of childhood wasting and stunting.
22. Unlike stunting, wasting can be remedied through improved nutritional intake and healthcare interventions.
23. Food and Agriculture Organization 2020i, p. 16, World Food Programme 2019a, p. 14.
24. Severe wasting is defined as weight-for-height that is more than three standard deviations below the medium on the WHO Child Growth Standards. Severe wasting is associated with a ninefold increased risk of mortality and requires urgent treatment for a child to survive.
25. Food and Agriculture Organization 2019b, pp. 4–7.
26. Food Insecurity Experience Scale, Food and Agriculture Organization 2019b, pp. 16–17. For detailed analysis of the relative utility of FIES see Ballard et al. 2013, Cafiero et al. 2018, and Smith et al. 2017.
27. The questions included in FIES are posed to a sample of individuals across 150 countries through the World Poll that is conducted annually by the Gallup Corporation. FIES is modeled after the United States Household Food Security Survey Module compiled by the Economic Research Service of the United States Department of Agriculture.
28. The Global Hunger Index is jointly published by Concern Worldwide and Welthungerhilfe.
29. World Food Programme 2018d offers an expansive analysis of the multiple factors that cause food insecurity and food crises.
30. Nobel Laureate economist Amartya Sen has long argued that hunger is more commonly due to limited access to food rather than actual food scarcities. See especially Sen 1981, which demonstrates that the majority of famine-related deaths have occurred in areas where sufficient food was available. The interrelationship between poverty and hunger is also examined by Rieff 2015 and Smith and Meade 2019.
31. It is also important to note that the economic impact of public health emergencies can rapidly undermine food security. When governments seek to contain the spread of a contagious virus by locking-down their economies, restricting movement, and mandating large-scale quarantines, the sudden loss of jobs, food production, and social protection programs will almost certainly produce sharp increases in food insecurity. The economic consequences of the current transmission of SARS-CoV-2, the virus that causes coronavirus disease 2019 (COVID-19), are causing dramatic increases in malnutrition in the developing world and thousands of additional child deaths each month.
32. Food and Agriculture Organization 2019g, pp. 39–41.
33. World Resources Institute 2018, p. 66.

34. The Land Matrix, an independent land monitoring initiative that is jointly sponsored by international organizations, research institutes, and civil society groups, documents large-scale land acquisitions in the developing world. See also Davis et al. 2014.
35. World Resources Institute 2018, p. 66.
36. The *International Convention on the Elimination of Racial Discrimination* provides a normative and legal framework for addressing all forms of racial discrimination.
37. The Human Rights Council of the United Nations estimates that women and girls constitute seventy percent of the world's hungry. Human Rights Council 2019, p. 4. See Carney 2015 for analysis of the link between gender and food insecurity.
38. Food and Agriculture Organization 2019b, pp. 98, 101.
39. Food and Agriculture Organization 2018d, p. 81.
40. World Resources Institute 2018, p. 14.
41. Debnath and Babu (eds.) 2019 explores the adverse impact of biofuel production on global food security. See also World Resources Institute 2018, p. 18.
42. Because the actual scale of corruption in a country is difficult to measure, researchers increasingly rely on the annual Corruption Perceptions Index (CPI) compiled by Transparency International (TI). The index ranks countries by their perceived levels of public sector corruption, as reflected in a survey of analysts, businesspeople, and experts in countries around the world.
43. The link between large natural resource endowments and adverse developmental outcomes, including corruption, has been extensively studied. See especially Williams and Le Billon 2017, Murshed 2018, van Nieuwland 2020, Hendrix and Noland 2014, Mosley 2017, Auty and Furlonge 2018, Humphreys et al. 2007, Haslam and Heidrich (eds.) 2016, Acar 2017, Papyrakis (ed.) 2019, and Papyrakis 2018.
44. See Adunbi 2015 and Le Billon 2013 for analysis of the extent to which competition over natural resources fuels civil conflicts in the developing world.
45. Food and Agriculture Organization/World Food Programme 2019 examines the impact of civil conflict on food security in the developing world. See also World Food Programme 2018c, pp. 14–15 and Food Security Information Network 2020, pp. 11–12.
46. Food Security Information Network 2020, pp. 26–29. There are currently 80 million people in the world who are refugees due to civil conflict.
47. WFP defines food systems as "… interlocking networks of relationships that encompass the entire range of functions and activities involved in the production, processing, marketing, consumption and disposal of

goods that originate from agriculture, forestry or fisheries" World Food Programme 2017c, p. 23. See also FAO 2019a, p. 5.

48. The Total Fertility Rate (TFR), which measures the average number of children born to women over their lifespan in a given country, has declined in all regions of the world. However, global population is still projected to rise from approximately 7.6 billion today to close to 10 billion by 2050. The global demand for food, which is expected to increase by fifty percent during this period, will place enormous pressures on land, water, forests, fisheries, and other natural resources.
49. In other words, environmental deterioration not only causes food insecurity but can also be the result of food insecurity. Food insecurity causes environmental decline when poor people engage in environmentally hazardous practices, such as slash and burn agriculture, cultivating marginal lands, and clearing forest areas, in order to meet their nutritional needs.
50. Land degradation is most evident in Africa where approximately two-thirds of the region's most productive agricultural land is either moderately or severely degraded.
51. Desertification refers to a type of land degradation in which arid, semi-arid, or dry subhumid areas becomes desert after losing their bodies of water, vegetation, and wildlife. Desertification, which is caused by both human activities and climatic variations, is evident in about a third of the world's land surface.
52. Clean water is essential for basic nutrition and an important component of the right to food. Over a billion people lack access to clean water and 2.7 billion people experience water scarcity at least partially each year. Contaminated water reduces the nutritional content of food and is a primary contributor to the spread of infectious disease.
53. World Resources Institute 2018, p. 10.
54. The highest rates of deforestation are presently occurring in Brazil, the Democratic Republic of the Congo, and Indonesia.
55. Deforestation is the second greatest cause of human-induced climate change—after the burning of fossil fuels—and accounts for almost twenty percent of all greenhouse gas emissions.
56. The projected impact of climate change on natural resources in the developing world is outlined in the multiple reports of the Intergovernmental Panel of Experts on Climate Change (IPCC). See also Christoplos (ed.) 2015, Niles and Salerno 2018, Palmer 2017, Pritchard et al. 2017, World Food Programme 2018c, and Food and Agriculture Organization 2018c.
57. The earth's surface temperature continues to rise, with twelve of the fourteen warmest years in recorded history having occurred since 2005. 2015–2019 have been the warmest years to date.

58. Food and Agriculture Organization 2018c, p. 53. See also Intergovernmental Panel of Experts on Climate Change 2019a. Soil is being lost many more times faster than it is forming.
59. The increased variety and number of insects that thrive under warmer conditions and erratic precipitation is also a major threat to human health. Some tropical vector-borne diseases, such as Chagas Disease, Chikungunya, Dengue Fever, Malaria, West Nile, and Zika, have emerged in new areas where local health systems are generally ill-prepared to effectively respond.
60. More than half of the world's wetlands have disappeared since 1900. Wetlands provide a range of essential ecosystem services, including water filtration, storm protection, flood control, and biodiversity preservation.
61. Food and Agriculture Organization 2018e, p. 32.
62. International Fund for Agricultural Development 2019a, p. 1, Food and Agriculture Organization 2018c, p. 67.
63. Food and Agriculture Organization 2019e, p. xiii.
64. The differential impact of trade on food security in the developing world is described by Fouilleux et al. 2017 and Wise 2019.
65. Here the concept of a "food supply chain," as defined by FAO, is important. A food supply chain refers to " ... the stages from food production to consumption. These stages are production, post-harvest, processing, storage, trade, (import and export) distribution, packaging, and wholesale and retail sale of food." FAO 2019g, p. 60. See also Food and Agriculture Organization 2019a, p. 5.
66. World Resources Institute 2018, p. 66. Kaag and Zoomers (eds.) 2014 and Wolford et al. (eds.) 2013 offer analyses of the impact of large-scale land acquisitions on farmers in the developing world.
67. The countries that have been most active in acquiring land abroad include China, Kuwait, Qatar, Saudi Arabia, Singapore, South Korea, and the United Arab Emirates. These countries lease land in the developing world either directly or through their sovereign wealth funds.
68. The link between foreign fishing fleets and food insecurity in the developing world is examined in FAO 2020d.
69. Exclusive Economic Zones refers to the area generally extending two hundred nautical miles (370 kilometers) from a country's coast. The 1982 *United Nations Convention on the Law of the Seas* (UNCLOS) established such areas to ensure countries would have special rights to the marine resources in these areas. Territorial waters are much smaller and extend just twelve nautical miles (22 kilometers) from the coast.
70. The world's fishing industry receives an estimated $35 billion in subsidies each year. World Resources Institute 2018, p. 40.
71. In 2001, FAO passed the *International Plan of Action to Prevent, Deter and Eliminate Illegal, Unreported and Unregulated Fishing* (IPOA-IUU).

This agreement calls for preventing ships that engage in IUU fishing from docking at port countries and outlines measures for reporting illegal fishing. The UN's 2015 document *Transforming Our World: 2030 Agenda for Sustainable Development* calls for ending fishing subsidies that contribute to overfishing or destructive fishing practices. UN 2015b.

72. At present, approximately forty countries in the developing world are dependent on external food aid.
73. World Food Programme 2017c, p. 8.
74. World Food Programme 2018d, p. 9.
75. Following the IFAD formulation, agriculture includes crop farming, livestock production, artisanal fishing, aquaculture, and forestry.
76. FAO defines rural transformation as "… a process in which rising agricultural productivity, increasing marketable surpluses, expanded off-farm employment opportunities, better access to services and infrastructure, and capacity to influence policy all lead to improved rural livelihoods and inclusive growth." Food and Agriculture Organization 2019d, p. 1.

CHAPTER 2

The Right to Food

Food insecurity threatens global stability. Hunger and malnutrition are not only debilitating for the millions of people directly impacted, but also cause a range of economic, political, social, and environmental crises that adversely impact everyone else. The global campaign to end hunger and malnutrition is based on the simple proposition that access to safe, sufficient, and nutritious food is a universal human right that must be guaranteed for all.

This chapter traces the evolution of the right to food regime, with focus placed on the work of the United Nations and its affiliated agencies. The UN played a lead role in establishing freedom from hunger as a fundamental human right and three UN agencies—the World Food Programme, Food and Agriculture Organization, and International Fund for Agricultural Development—have worked to make the right to food a reality for millions of desperate and displaced people around the world. The latter part of this chapter outlines the purpose, structure, and major programs of these agencies.

Regime Origins

While calls to feed the hungry are as old as recorded history, the contemporary right to food regime can be traced to the early post-war period.[1] The *Universal Declaration of Human Rights*—which was adopted by the United Nations General Assembly on December 10, 1948—was

F. Adams, *The Right to Food*,
https://doi.org/10.1007/978-3-030-60255-0_2

the first international attempt to identify the basic rights of all people. The declaration emerged in the wake of the abuses committed against civilian populations during the Second World War. Once the extraordinary magnitude and depravity of these abuses was exposed, nations were no longer willing to accept the notion that human rights are solely the domestic concern of sovereign states. The United Nations set out to identify basic human rights that must be guaranteed for all people at all times and in all places. Article 25 of the declaration identifies food as a fundamental human right. "Everyone has the right to a standard of living adequate for the health and well-being of himself and of his family, including food …"[2]

The *Universal Declaration of Human Rights* was an important statement of principle for the post-war world order. However, because the declaration was approved by a General Assembly resolution, it was not considered legally binding under international law. In 1966, the UN sought to codify the rights identified in the declaration by drafting the *International Covenant on Civil and Political Rights* (ICCPR) and the *International Covenant on Economic, Social and Cultural Rights* (ICESCR). The latter covenant, which entered into force in 1976, focused on meeting the basic needs of all people. State parties that sign and ratify the covenant are legally obligated to work toward the full realization of the rights identified.[3] A Committee on Economic, Social and Cultural Rights (CESCR) was later established to aid countries in meeting their obligations under the covenant.[4] Article 11 identifies a fundamental right to food. Section 11.1 states that everyone has the right " … to an adequate standard of living for himself and his family, including adequate food …"[5] Article 11.2 calls on state parties …

> [t]o improve methods of production, conservation and distribution of food by making full use of technical and scientific knowledge, by disseminating knowledge of the principles of nutrition and by developing or reforming agrarian systems in such a way as to achieve the most efficient development and utilization of natural resources.[6]

State parties are " … to ensure an equitable distribution of world food supplies in relation to need."[7]

Shortly after the covenant was drafted, a separate *Food Aid Convention* was negotiated within the context of the 1967 *International Grains Arrangement* (IGA) of the General Agreement on Tariffs and Trade

(GATT). The convention, which sought to strengthen global capacities to respond to food emergencies, required member countries to donate a minimum amount of surplus grains each year.[8] Although countries were free to decide how their donations would be distributed, they were encouraged to work through multilateral institutions whenever possible. A Food Aid Committee was established to oversee the implementation of the convention and monitor the amount of surplus grains donated each year.[9]

World Food Crisis

The early 1970s saw an alarming increase in the number of people who were food insecure. A series of natural disasters, including devastating droughts in Africa and Asia, had caused a precipitous decline in global food production. Cereal stocks dropped to their lowest levels in twenty years and prices for many basic food items skyrocketed. Nearly a quarter of all people in the developing world were unable to meet their daily nutritional needs and millions of people, especially in sub-Saharan Africa and South Asia, were at risk of famine.

As the severity of the global food crisis escalated, the United Nations convened a World Food Conference in November 1974.[10] Delegates to the conference drafted a series of measures to address the crisis and improve global food security. State participants agreed to provide at least ten million tons of in-kind food aid each year to countries in the developing world and to establish grain reserves that could be quickly disbursed during global emergencies. Delegates also adopted the *Universal Declaration on the Eradication of Hunger and Malnutrition*.[11] The declaration stated that "[e]very man, woman and child has the inalienable right to be free from hunger and malnutrition in order to develop fully and maintain their physical and mental faculties."[12] The declaration went on to affirm that "[i]t is a fundamental responsibility of Governments to work together for higher food production and a more equitable and efficient distribution of food between countries and within countries."[13] Because the world's poorest countries had both the most urgent needs and the most limited resources, the international community was called upon to " … ensure the availability at all times of adequate world supplies of basic food-stuffs by way of appropriate reserves, all countries should co-operate in the establishment of an effective system of world food security …"[14] Emphasis was placed on improving food production, land use, water quality, and storage facilities in the developing world.[15]

The conference established a World Food Council (WFC) to oversee implementation of the mandates and coordinate the work of all UN agencies involved in global food issues.[16] The council was later made a subsidiary body of the UN General Assembly. A separate Committee on World Food Security (CFS) was created to devise a strategic framework for achieving universal food security.[17] The United Nations Economic and Social Council (ECOSOC) established the UN System Standing Committee on Nutrition (UNSCN) in 1977 to advance interagency work on global nutrition. In 1983 the UN Subcommission on the Promotion and Protection of Human Rights appointed a Special Rapporteur on the Right to Food. The Special Rapporteur's initial report, *The Right to Adequate Food as a Human Right*, was approved by the Human Rights Commission in 1987.[18]

Regime Strengthening

A series of global agreements in the late 1980s and early 1990s helped strengthen the right to food regime. In 1987, ECOSOC Resolution 90 affirmed "... the right to food is a universal human right ..." that " ... should be guaranteed to all people..."[19] The resolution also stated that international cooperation on food and agricultural issues was necessary for universal food security.[20] The following year, the World Food Council identified access to food as a "... human right which must be defended by Governments, peoples and the international community."[21] WFC also adopted a *Program of Co-operative Action* that established four goals to be achieved before the end of the century: (1) the elimination of starvation and death caused by famine; (2) a substantial reduction in malnutrition and mortality among young children; (3) a tangible reduction in chronic hunger; (4) and the elimination of major nutritional-deficiency diseases.[22]

In 1990, the *Convention on the Rights of the Child*, which identifies the civil, political, economic, social, and cultural rights of the world's children, came into force under the auspices of the United Nations General Assembly. Article 24 calls on state parties to the convention to take all appropriate measures "[t]o combat disease and malnutrition ... through the provision of adequate nutritious foods and clean drinking-water ..."[23] A Committee on the Rights of the Child was established to receive annual reports on the wellbeing of children in the countries that sign and ratify the convention. The World Summit for Children, which was held in September 1990, called for a fifty percent reduction in child malnutrition by the end of the century.[24]

In December 1992, the First International Conference on Nutrition was convened in Rome. The conference, which was jointly sponsored by FAO and the World Health Organization (WHO), concluded with a pledge to substantially reduce chronic hunger, malnutrition, and micronutrient deficiencies. The conference's *World Declaration and Plan of Action for Nutrition* stated that "[h]unger and malnutrition are unacceptable in a world that has both the knowledge and the resources to end this human catastrophe."[25] A number of measures were advanced to achieve the objectives identified in the declaration.

General Comment Number 12

Food security continued to be identified as a basic human right throughout the 1990s. The *Rome Declaration on World Food Security*, adopted at the 1996 World Summit on Food Security, reaffirmed " ... the right of everyone to have access to safe and nutritious food, consistent with the right to adequate food and the fundamental right of everyone to be free from hunger."[26] Signatory countries pledged to " ... pursue participatory and sustainable food, agriculture, fisheries, forestry and rural development policies and practices ... which are essential to adequate and reliable food supplies at the household, national, regional and global levels."[27] A *World Food Summit Plan of Action* identified specific targets for governments, including a fifty percent reduction in the number of undernourished people in their country by 2015. Food security was deemed to exist "... when all people at all times have physical and economic access to sufficient, safe and nutritious food to meet their dietary needs and food preferences to lead a healthy and active life."[28] A Special Programme for Food Security (SPFS) was established with a mandate to improve agricultural productivity in low-income food-deficit countries (LIFDC).[29]

Delegates to the World Summit on Food Security also requested a more definitive statement on the rights identified in Article 11 of the *International Covenant on Economic, Social and Cultural Rights*.[30] This led to preparation of General Comment Number 12, entitled *The Right to Adequate Food*, by the Committee on Economic, Social and Cultural Rights. General Comment Number 12, which was adopted in 1999, is among the most authoritative legal interpretations of the right to food and the corresponding obligations of ICESCR signatory countries. The right to adequate food was defined as "[t]he availability of food in a quantity and quality sufficient to satisfy the dietary needs of individuals, free from adverse substances, and acceptable within a given culture."[31] It found this right to be " … indivisibly linked to the inherent dignity of the human person and … indispensable for the fulfillment of other human rights enshrined in the International Bill of Human Rights."[32] The right to adequate food would be realized when "… every man, woman and child, alone or in community with others, has physical and economic access at all times to adequate food or means for its procurement."[33]

General Comment Number 12 also identified the obligations of state parties to ICESCR. "Every state is obliged to ensure for everyone under its jurisdiction access to the minimum essential food which is sufficient, nutritionally adequate and safe, and to ensure their freedom from hunger."[34] This includes the obligation to *respect* (states should refrain from any measures that prevent people from having access to food), the obligation to *protect* (states should ensure that people are not deprived by others of access to food), and the obligation to *fulfill* (states must directly aid people gain access to food).[35] Although the rights identified by the covenant are to be achieved through progressive realization, governments must refrain from any actions that result in the deterioration of current food levels. States are required to "… recognize the essential role of international cooperation and to comply with their commitment to take joint and separate action to achieve the full realization of the right to adequate food."[36]

The *Food Aid Convention* was renegotiated in 1999 to strengthen the response of the international community to food emergencies.[37] Donor countries pledged to contribute specific amounts of food aid, agreed that food aid should be extended to the most vulnerable groups, and committed to increasing the proportion of food aid that is provided through local and regional purchases (LRP). Emphasis was placed on improving coordination among donor states and ensuring the transparency of all operations. The Committee on World Food Security was charged with overseeing implementation of the convention and ensuring the continued exchange of information among member countries.

In April 2000, the UN Human Rights Commission expanded the role of the Special Rapporteur on the Right to Food.[38] The Special Rapporteur was now charged with identifying emerging issues related to the right to food, monitoring the nutritional wellbeing of vulnerable groups, highlighting violations of the right to food, and working with UN agencies and other international organizations to promote food security. Annual reports on the overall state of global food security should be prepared as well as studies on specific issues related to food production, distribution, and consumption.[39] The right to food was defined by the Special Rapporteur as ".. the right to have regular, permanent and unrestricted access, either directly or by means of financial purchases, to quantitatively and qualitatively adequate and sufficient food corresponding to the cultural traditions of the people to which the consumer belongs, and which ensures a physical and mental, individual and collective, fulfilling and dignified life free of fear."[40]

Millennium Development Goals

In September 2000, world leaders gathered at the UN headquarters in New York for the Millennium Summit. The purpose of this meeting, which marked the opening of the fifty-fifth General Assembly, was to address the major challenges facing the global community at the turn of the twenty-first century. World leaders ratified the *United Nations Millennium Declaration* and identified eight Millennium Development Goals (MDG), along with eighteen specific targets and forty-eight indicators for measuring the progress achieved. All UN agencies and member governments were encouraged to formulate policy frameworks that incorporate the MDG and 2015 was designated the end date for meeting the eighteen targets.[41] The first goal called for eradicating extreme poverty and hunger.[42]

Although leaders across the developing world embraced the Millennium Development Goals, most countries did not have anywhere near the resources needed to achieve the specific targets. In an attempt to increase the resources available to developing countries, the UN sponsored a follow-up conference in March 2002. The International Conference on Financing for Development, which took place in Monterrey Mexico, focused on mobilizing the resources needed to achieve the MDG.[43] The concluding document of the conference—the *Monterrey Consensus*—called for increasing foreign economic assistance, promoting private investment, and lessening the burden of international debt.[44]

Another World Food Summit was convened in June 2002 at FAO headquarters in Rome.[45] The declaration adopted at this summit envisioned reducing the number of hungry people in the world to approximately 400 million by 2015. The declaration reaffirmed the "... right of everyone to have access to safe and nutritious food ..." and recognized the " ... important role of food assistance in situations of humanitarian crisis as well as an instrument for development."[46] The FAO's General Council was tasked with establishing an Intergovernmental Working Group (IGWG) to prepare specific guidelines on the right to food.[47]

Right to Food Guidelines

The *Voluntary Guidelines to Support the Progressive Realization of the Right to Adequate Food in the Context of National Food Security*, hereafter referred to as the *Right to Food Guidelines*, were completed and adopted unanimously by the FAO General Council in 2004.[48] The guidelines were presented to member countries as practical recommendations for achieving their national obligations under Article 11 of the International Covenant of Economic, Social and Cultural Rights. The guidelines called for incorporating the right to food into poverty reduction strategies, building enabling environments for people to meet their own food needs, and establishing safety nets for the most vulnerable populations. Countries were called upon to allocate sufficient resources to anti-hunger efforts, ensure the availability of food in domestic markets, and broaden access to land, water, forests, fisheries, livestock, genetic materials, and extension services. The *Right to Food Guidelines* recommended utilizing food insecurity and vulnerability maps to identify "... any form of discrimination that may manifest itself in greater food insecurity ... or in a higher prevalence of malnutrition among specific population groups, or both, with a view to removing and preventing such causes to food insecurity or malnutrition."[49] The guidelines are among the most comprehensive documents available for building national food and nutritional security. As noted by CFS, the *Right to Food Guidelines* were deliberately structured to affirm *rights and duties* rather than advocate *charity and benevolence*.[50] Soon after the guidelines were adopted, FAO sponsored an International Conference on Agrarian Reform and Rural Development (ICARRD) in Porto Alegre, Brazil that called for more equitable, transparent, and accountable access to land and natural resources for rural communities.

Another global food crisis occurred in 2007–2008. Rapidly increasing food prices, primarily due to drought and crop losses in major grain-producing countries, were jeopardizing global food security and causing civil unrest around the world.[51] The lives of millions of people were at risk. The United Nations established a High Level Task Force on Global Food Security (HLTF) that was composed of the heads of UN agencies, as well as representatives from the World Bank, International Monetary Fund (IMF), Organization for Economic Cooperation and Development (OECD), and World Trade Organization (WTO). The task force was charged with developing new strategies to achieve global food security. HLTF prepared a *Comprehensive Framework for Action* (CFA) that included specific measures to advance food and nutritional security.[52] The framework called for supporting the resilience of rural households and placing smallholder farmers and women at the center of all food assistance initiatives. A Global Partnership on Agriculture and Food Security was subsequently established by the Group of 8 (G8) countries to support implementation of CFA. In the same year, the Special Rapporteur on the Right to Food stated that the right to food is

> … the right to have access to the resources and to the means to ensure and produce one's own subsistence, including land, small-scale irrigation, seeds, credit, technology, and local and regional markets, especially in rural areas and for vulnerable and discriminated groups …[53]

A resolution adopted at the 2008 meeting of the Human Rights Council affirmed "… the right of everyone to have access to safe and nutritious food, consistent with the right to adequate food and the fundamental right of everyone to be free from hunger …"[54] The resolution also encouraged "… all States to take steps to achieving progressively the full realization of the right to food, including steps to promote the conditions for everyone to be free from hunger and, as soon as possible, to enjoy fully the right to food, and to create and adopt national plans to combat hunger …"[55]

Another World Summit on Food Security took place at FAO headquarters in Rome in November 2009. The declaration adopted at this summit committed all participating countries to "… collectively accelerate steps … to set the world on a path to achieving the progressive realization of the right to adequate food in the context of national food security."[56] The declaration included *Five Rome Principles for Sustainable Global Food*

Security. The international community was called upon to (1) invest in country-led strategies aimed at channeling resources to well-designed and results-based programs; (2) foster strategic coordination at national, regional, and global levels to improve governance, enhance the allocation of resources, avoid duplication of efforts, and identify response gaps; (3) implement a comprehensive twin-track approach to food security that consists of direct action to immediately tackle hunger for the most vulnerable and long-term sustainable agricultural, food security, nutrition, and rural development programs to address the root causes of hunger; (4) improve the efficiency, responsiveness, coordination, and effectiveness of multilateral institutions; (5) and ensure the sustained commitment of all partners to invest in agriculture, food security, and nutrition.[57]

The World Food Summit also called for reforming the Committee on World Food Security (CFS) to achieve greater policy convergence and coordination among all stakeholders.[58] This included UN agencies with a specific mandate in the area of food security and nutrition, international financial institutions, agricultural research institutes, private philanthropic foundations, and civil society organizations.[59] The reformed CFS would provide a platform to promote enhanced coordination, policy convergence, and the sharing of best practices at the global, regional, and national levels.[60] An independent High Level Panel of Experts on Food Security and Nutrition (HLPE) was created to analyze the current state of food insecurity and provide advice on specific policy-relevant issues. HLPE reports are requested by CFS and their findings serve as the basis for policy discussions. CFS subsequently developed a *Global Strategic Framework for Food Security and Nutrition* to provide an overarching reference document with core recommendations for food and nutritional security strategies and policies.[61] This framework is considered a living document and is updated annually by the CFS Plenary.[62]

The UN also launched a Zero Hunger Challenge (ZHC) initiative in 2012 to ensure work toward sustainable and inclusive food systems remains a central component of the global development agenda. Emphasis is placed on doubling small-scale producer incomes, reforming food systems to eliminate food loss, and ensuring adequate access to healthy diets. An annual report is prepared on the progress achieved toward reaching these goals in each region of the developing world.

Food Assistance Convention

The agreements reached during the first decade of the twenty-first century reflect an important transition in the global campaign against hunger and malnutrition. The international community gradually shifted focus and resources from the provision of emergency food aid to the broader objectives of food assistance.[63] This transition was reflected in the 2012 *Food Assistance Convention* (FAC).[64] As noted in the introductory chapter, rather than simply providing food to vulnerable communities, food assistance is structured to address the underlying causes of food insecurity. Poor communities should gain the knowledge, resources, and capabilities necessary to meet their nutritional needs on a continuing basis.[65] As stated in the convention, food assistance should be structured "... in a manner that protects livelihoods and strengthens the self-reliance and resilience of vulnerable populations and local communities ..."[66] Moreover, beneficiaries should be involved in the design, implementation, monitoring, and evaluation of all food assistance programs.[67] The convention also called on donor countries to "... monitor, evaluate and communicate, on a regular and transparent basis, on the outcomes and the impact of food assistance activities ..."[68] The Food Assistance Committee was again charged with overseeing implementation of the convention.

The Committee on World Food Security subsequently prepared *Voluntary Guidelines on the Responsible Governance of Tenure of Land, Fisheries and Forests in the Context of National Food Security* (VGGT).[69] These guidelines were designed to help establish legal frameworks for tenure and usage rights of natural resources. Governments were encouraged to draw upon these frameworks to prepare their own legislation, regulations, and policies. This effort was a response, at least in part, to the increasing threat that large-scale land acquisitions posed to farmers and rural communities in the developing world. VGGT called for more secure and equitable tenure and usage rights and affirmed customary tenure systems. CFS also endorsed the *Principles for Responsible Investment in Agriculture and Food Systems* in 2014 which applied to all types of agricultural investments, as well as investments in livestock, forests, and fisheries.[70]

A Second International Conference on Nutrition (ICN2) was held in November 2014 at FAO headquarters in Rome. The conference, which was co-sponsored with WHO, adopted the *Rome Declaration on Nutrition* and a corresponding *Framework for Action*.[71] The declaration, reaffirmed "... the right of everyone to have access to safe, sufficient, and nutritious food, consistent with the right to adequate food and the fundamental right of everyone to be free from hunger ..."[72] The declaration called upon the UN system to strengthen international collaboration and cooperation to achieve global food security and stated that "... the elimination of malnutrition in all its forms is an imperative for health, ethical, political, social and economic reasons ..."[73] The framework offered a set of strategies to achieve the goals enumerated in the declaration. Emphasis was placed on building sustainable food systems through strategic investments in small-scale agriculture, rural infrastructure, water systems, nutritional education, and school meal programs.[74] FAO also prepared a number of handbooks outlining legal and institutional strategies for incorporating the right to food into national constitutions and legislation.[75]

Sustainable Development Goals

With the *Millennium Development Goals* elapsing in 2015, the United Nations began work on a new set of goals to guide the global agenda for the next fifteen years. An Open Working Group of the General Assembly was established to draft these goals. In 2015, the UN presented *Transforming Our World: The 2030 Agenda for Sustainable Development* and the Sustainable Development Goals (SDG).[76] Seventeen core goals were identified to address a broad range of social, economic, and environmental challenges facing the global community and governments were encouraged to incorporate these goals into national planning, policies, and strategies.[77] 169 targets were developed to measure the progress achieved toward reaching the goals by 2030. Member states adopted both the agenda and SDG at a high-level plenary meeting of the General Assembly in September 2015.

Global food security is prioritized in the *2030 Agenda for Sustainable Development* and SDG. Both the preamble and the introduction of the agenda call for renewed efforts to abolish hunger and the second goal focuses on ending hunger, achieving food security, improving nutrition, and promoting sustainable agriculture. A number of targets were established to measure progress toward achieving these objectives. Target 2.1 focuses on ending hunger and ensuring access by all people to safe, nutritious, and sufficient food; target 2.2 calls for ending all forms of malnutrition, reducing stunting and wasting in children, and addressing the nutritional needs of adolescent girls, pregnant and lactating women, infants, and the elderly; target 2.3 prescribes doubling agricultural productivity and the incomes of small-scale food producers, especially women, indigenous peoples, family farmers, pastoralists, and fishers; and target 2.4 advocates agricultural practices that increase productivity, help maintain ecosystems, and strengthen resilience to climate change.[78]

In October 2015, CFS advanced a series of measures to address the food and nutritional needs of displaced and vulnerable populations within the context of crisis situations.[79] This created the impetus for establishing a Global Network Against Food Crises, which is jointly sponsored by WFP, FAO, and the European Union (EU).[80] The network, which includes numerous humanitarian and development actors, has three primary objectives: (1) to develop data-informed and evidence-based approaches to more effectively prevent, prepare for, and respond to food crises; (2) to leverage strategic investments to prevent and respond to food crises; and (3) to foster political coordination for integrated solutions to address food insecurity issues at the national, regional, and global levels. A Food Security Information Network (FSIN) was established by WFP, FAO, and the International Food Policy Research Institute (IFPRI) to provide reliable and accurate data to the Global Network Against Food Crises. FSIN serves as a technical platform for exchanging expertise, knowledge, and best practices related to food and nutrition security.

The General Assembly declared 2016–2025 the *United Nations Decade of Action on Nutrition*.[81] The UN pledged to redouble its efforts to improve global food security and nutrition and member countries were encouraged to set country-specific commitments for investments in nutritional programs. Additional mechanisms were proposed for sharing best practices and promoting improved coordination among all actors working to improve global nutrition.[82] Six areas were identified for immediate action: (1) building resilient food systems for healthy diets; (2) aligning health systems; (3) providing universal coverage of essential nutrition actions, social protections, and nutrition education; (4) structuring trade and investment relations for improved nutrition; (5) ensuring safe and supportive environments for nutrition at all ages; and (6) strengthening governance and accountability for nutrition. FAO and WHO are the lead agencies responsible for implementing this initiative.

The years 2019–2028 were declared the UN Decade of Family Farming (UNDFF). Family farms were identified as essential for ensuring food security, improving livelihoods, managing scarce resources, protecting natural environments, and achieving sustainable development. Enabling and supporting family farmers, it was argued, will increase the availability of nutritious, sustainably produced, and culturally appropriate food in rural communities. UN member countries were called upon to develop public policies that support family farming and rural poverty reduction. A *Global Action Plan* was prepared to provide guidance to all countries on how best to support family farmers, with FAO and IFAD designated the implementing agencies.

Lastly, the Human Rights Council adopted a resolution in March 2019 that reaffirmed " ... the right of everyone to have access to safe, sufficient and nutritious food ..." and the " ... fundamental right of everyone to be free from hunger."[83] Hunger was deemed an "outrage" and a "violation of human dignity" which must be eliminated.[84] The resolution called upon states, individually and through international cooperation, to take all measures necessary to ensure the realization of the right to food as an "essential" human rights objective.[85] The international community was urged to provide the assistance needed to ensure universal access to food.[86]

Food Assistance Agencies

The United Nations and its affiliated agencies played a lead role in establishing the right to food regime. While freedom from hunger has become a universally recognized human right, ensuring that the right to food becomes a reality for all people requires mobilization and effective use of the world's resources. Since countries with the highest levels of food insecurity are also the countries with the fewest resources, guaranteeing the right to food requires a collective response by the global community. Food aid is required at times of humanitarian emergency and food assistance is needed for sustainable food security. The importance of food aid and assistance was continually stressed through the various conventions, declarations, and action plans that were adopted over the course of the past half century. Much of the food aid and assistance that is currently provided is under the auspices of the World Food Programme, Food and Agriculture Organization, and International Fund for Agricultural Development. The remainder of this chapter outlines the purpose, structure, and major programs of these Rome-based agencies.

World Food Programme

The World Food Programme of today would have been difficult to imagine when it first began operations in 1963. The programme was initially created on an experimental basis within FAO and did not become an independent agency of the UN until 1966. Today, WFP is the world's largest humanitarian agency and was awarded the 2020 Nobel Peace Prize. WFP has a thirty-six member Executive Council, with eighteen members elected by the ECOSOC and eighteen members elected by FAO for renewable three-year terms. The Executive Council, which includes representatives from both donor and recipient countries, coordinates food aid policies, approves project proposals, and oversees six regional bureaus, eighty-two country offices, and a worldwide staff of approximately 17,000.[87] An Executive Director, who is appointed for a five-year term, is responsible for overall administration of the institution and implementation of its various programs and projects. A Strategic Plan, which is renewed every four years, sets general policy and programmatic objectives.[88] The WFP's annual budget is mostly funded by voluntary contributions from UN member countries rather than assessed contributions. Although over sixty governments make voluntary contributions to WFP each year, most resources are contributed by just fifteen major donors. Additional support is provided by multilateral institutions, private corporations, charitable foundations, and nongovernmental organizations.

The provision of food aid is the primary purpose of WFP. In times of humanitarian crisis, WFP extends in-kind food aid directly to people in need. WFP also provides cash-based transfers (CBT) and commodity vouchers for the purchase of food from specially contracted retailers. This is done in those cases where food is available in local markets but is beyond the reach of large numbers of people.[89] WFP's digital beneficiary and transfer management platform SCOPE is used to identify and register people who are eligible for food aid. Once beneficiary information, including biometric data, is entered into the platform, individuals and households can receive food aid. SCOPE-CODA (conditional on-demand assistance) is used for specialized malnutrition treatments.[90]

WFP plays a key role at times of emergency. In the aftermath of a natural disaster, an Emergency Food Security Assessment (EFSA) is undertaken to determine the immediate needs of affected communities. WFP stockpiles rapid response equipment, organizes emergency shipments of food and other humanitarian supplies, and administers the

UN Humanitarian Response Depots (UNHRD). WFP also manages the United Nations Humanitarian Air Service (UNHAS) which transports aid workers and emergency supplies to areas which cannot be reached by ground. WFP's Fast IT and Telecommunications Emergency and Support Team (FITTEST) works to restore information and communications technology services where local infrastructure has been damaged or destroyed. This enables relief organizations and governments to coordinate their response and interact with affected populations.

WFP also helps countries recover from natural disaster or civil conflict. Under Food-for-Assets (FFA) and Food-for-Work (FFW) initiatives people receive cash-based transfers or commodity vouchers to meet their immediate nutritional needs in return for helping rehabilitate their communities.[91] This might include restoring agricultural lands, digging wells, repairing irrigation canals, constructing roads, building bridges, terracing hillsides, or planting trees. WFP also has a Food-for-Training (FFT) program that focuses on improving the knowledge, skills, and capabilities of people in rural areas, and a Purchase-for-Progress (P4P) program that aids low-income farmers connect to markets.[92]

WFP also supports disaster preparation efforts at the national and local levels. Much of this work involves developing early warning systems.[93] The Early Warning Early Action (EWEA) initiative focuses on consolidating available forecasting information and reducing the impact of a range of different hazards, including climate extremes.[94] The Seasonal Monitor uses satellite imagery of weather patterns and vegetation to track changes in growing seasons and issue early warnings of potential threats. The Food Insecurity and Climate Change Vulnerability Map provides local governments with data and analysis regarding the potential impact of climate change on food availability and general nutrition. This information is then used to improve climate change mitigation and adaptation strategies. The Food Security Climate Resilience Facility helps strengthen public sector capacity to lessen the negative impacts of climate change. Because WFP is accredited with the Green Climate Fund (GCF), it can draw upon additional resources to invest in low-emission and climate-resilient agriculture.[95]

WFP is the largest provider of school meals in developing countries.[96] Such meals, which typically include enriched cereal-based drinks, fortified porridge or biscuits, and fresh fruits and vegetables, contribute toward the intake of calories, proteins, and micronutrients by children in poor communities. Each year WFP provides daily meals to more than seventeen million children worldwide. A third of these children live in areas that are either in a state of emergency or recovering from a crisis. WFP also provides take-home rations to parents if their children regularly attend school. Under the Home-Grown School Feeding Program, WFP purchases local products exclusively from smallholder farmers. WFP also provides technical assistance to governments to enhance their capacities to manage school meal programs.

Food and Agriculture Organization

The Food and Agriculture Organization was founded in 1945 as a specialized agency of the United Nations to improve all aspects of food security and nutrition, including developing agricultural, fishery, and forestry sectors and sustainably managing natural resources. Much of its work involves providing advice and technical assistance to government officials, community leaders, and farmers in the developing world. The Conference of Member Nations, which meets biennially, oversees the work of the organization, approves its budget, and elects a governing body of forty-nine countries that serve three-year rotating terms. The Conference also elects a Director-General for a four-year term, which can be renewed once. The organization is composed of six departments, five regional offices, ten sub-regional offices, eighty-five country offices, and a staff of approximately 11,500.[97] The FAO's budget is funded by assessed and voluntary contributions. The assessed contributions, which cover approximately forty percent of the total budget, are made by its 194 member countries while the voluntary contributions are provided by member countries, international organizations, and private foundations.[98]

Building productive, efficient, and sustainable agricultural systems is central to the work of FAO. Technical assistance is provided to small-scale farmers to ensure they have the knowledge and skills needed to increase overall output. New practices and technologies are introduced by extension agents who organize Farmer Field Schools (FFS) in rural communities. The FAO's Monitoring and Analyzing Food and Agricultural Policies (MAFAP) program helps build country-owned systems that enhance agricultural development and productivity.

FAO also supports fishing sectors in poor countries. The Fisheries and Aquaculture Department works to strengthen the managerial and technical capacities of local governments to improve the conservation and sustainable use of aquatic resources. The department also provides scientific advice, strategic planning, and training materials to strengthen national policies on fisheries and aquaculture. The department supports a network of regional fishery commissions and works to implement the *Code of Conduct for Responsible Fisheries*.

Building sustainable forestry is also prioritized. The Forestry Department works to balance social and environmental imperatives with the economic needs of people living in rural areas. Technical assistance is provided to develop national forest programs that enhance the conservation, management, and use of forest resources. FAO shares information on forest resources with governments in developing countries and helps build local public sector capacities to generate forest data.[99]

Building resilience to natural disasters and environmental hazards is central to the work of FAO. The organization supports the sustainable management of land, water, forests, fisheries, and biodiversity.[100] Technical assistance is also provided to countries to address the threats posed by climate change. FAO supports Climate Smart Agriculture (CSA) which is defined as "... an integrated approach to managing cropland, livestock, forests, and fisheries that addresses the interlinked challenges of food security and climate change."[101] CSA is based on three key principles: (1) sustainably increasing agricultural output and incomes; (2) adapting and building resilience to climate change; and (3) reducing GHG emissions.[102] CSA provides a framework for climate adaptation and mitigation planning.[103] FAO also promotes Conservation Agriculture to improve soil quality, conserve water, reduce fuel costs, and improve yields. Conservation Agriculture is built on three principles—minimum soil disturbance, permanent soil cover, and crop rotation. Farmers are encouraged to dig individual holes to plant seeds, maintain soil cover to guard against erosion, and alternate crops in order to improve soil fertility.

International Fund for Agricultural Development

The International Fund for Agricultural Development is dedicated to combating poverty and food insecurity in rural areas of developing countries.[104] Established in 1977 as a specialized agency of the United Nations, IFAD provides grants and concessional loans to finance agricultural and rural development projects, as well as improve natural resource management.[105] IFAD's mandate calls for "... investing in rural people and enabling inclusive and sustainable transformation of rural areas, notably through smallholder agricultural-led growth ..."[106] IFAD has three strategic objectives: (1) increase the productive capacity of poor rural people, (2) increase poor rural people's benefits from market participation, and (3) strengthen the environmental sustainability and climate resilience of poor rural people's economic activities.[107] Since its founding, IFAD has provided over twenty billion dollars in grants and low-interest loans to support projects that have reached approximately 500 million people in the developing world.

IFAD's organizational structure mirrors that of other UN agencies. A Governing Council is the highest decision-making authority and meets annually. Each member state is represented on the council by a governor and an alternate governor. The Governing Council sets the Strategic Framework which outlines the overarching goals, principles of engagement, and programmatic objectives that guide all activities.[108] An Executive Board, which is responsible for overseeing operations and approving grants and loans, is composed of eighteen members and eighteen alternates who serve three year terms. The President, who serves for a four year term (renewable once) is the chief executive officer and chair of the Executive Board. IFAD's budget is funded through the contributions of 176 member countries, multilateral institutions, project participants, and various other donors. IFAD has five regional bureaus and more than forty country offices.[109]

IFAD supports programs that aid people in rural areas obtain the tools, technology, and services needed to improve nutrition, increase agricultural productivity, and strengthen resilience. Projects are designed to increase yields through the introduction of new equipment, technologies, quality seeds, and irrigation systems.[110] IFAD also works to protect animal health and boost the productivity of livestock. Fishing communities are supported through the development of small-scale aquaculture production in coastal and inland waters. This typically involves improving fishery management, developing fish value chains, and promoting the sale of commodities produced by fishing communities.

Broader rural development is also prioritized. IFAD works with national and local governments to improve country level capacity for rural policy and program development, implementation, and evaluation.[111] Developing the knowledge, skills, and organizational capacity of community leaders is a core objective. IFAD also partners with banks, microfinance institutions, and credit unions to provide financial services and insurance products to rural communities for both farm and off-farm activities. Ensuring farmers obtain legal rights to land is supported through initiatives to register and record land ownership. IFAD also supports greater market access for the rural poor. Projects are designed to connect rural people to functioning markets so they can sell their products more easily and at higher prices.

Natural resource management and environmental conservation is also central to the mission of IFAD. Emphasis is placed on devising agricultural and rural development programs that are environmentally sustainable and help preserve local ecosystems. IFAD is an executing agency of the Global Environmental Facility (GEF) and accredited with the Green Climate Fund (GCF). Both of these funds promote sustainable ecosystem management and climate change adaptation.[112] IFAD's Adaptation for Smallholder Agriculture Program (ASAP) aids farmers cope with the impact of climate change and build more resilient livelihoods. IFAD's Weather Risk Management Facility provides small-scale farmers with insurance against weather related losses.[113]

Conclusion

The United Nations has played a lead role in the global campaign to end hunger and malnutrition in the world's poorest countries. This chapter traced the evolution of the right to food regime. A series of international conventions, declarations, and resolutions have established freedom from hunger as a fundamental human right. The latter part of this chapter outlined the purpose, structure, and major programs of the three United Nations food agencies—the World Food Programme, Food and Agriculture Organization, and International Fund for Agricultural Development—that have worked to make the right to food a reality for millions of people around the world.

The right to food regime can be traced to the broad principles first enumerated in the *Universal Declaration of Human Rights* and later codified in the *International Covenant of Economic, Social and Cultural Rights*. The *Food Aid Convention* recognized the collective responsibility of countries with food surpluses to support the needs of low-income food-deficit countries. The convention was renewed a number of times over the years and ultimately replaced by the *Food Assistance Convention*. A universal right to food was also identified in statements adopted by the global community, including the *Universal Declaration on the*

Eradication of Hunger and Malnutrition (1974), *ECOSOC Resolution 90* (1988), *World Declaration on Nutrition* (1992), *Rome Declaration on Food Security* (1996), *General Comment Number 12* (1999), *Right to Food Guidelines* (2004), *Rome Declaration on Nutrition* (2014), and the *Right to Food* resolution of the Human Rights Council (2019). A number of permanent bodies were established to promote compliance with these statements. The World Food Council, Committee on World Food Security, Special Programme for Food Security, High Level Panel of Experts on Food Security and Nutrition, and Global Network Against Food Crises, are especially important in this respect.

The work of the United Nations and its affiliated agencies over the course of the past half century was critical to establishing access to safe, sufficient, and nutritious food as a universally recognized human right. Of course, the right to food regime could be dismissed as little more than a self-congratulatory gesture advanced by a global elite with no real impact on the lives of those directly suffering from hunger and malnutrition. It is important to recognize, however, that regime creation can have a powerful impact on local and national policy-making. When the global community identifies a universal human right, normative expectations are established that influence and condition policy choice at the domestic level. Political leaders who ignore or reject global standards jeopardize their moral standing within the community of nations. Although sanctioning human rights violations can be difficult, it has been done in a number of cases. More importantly, normative expectations reduce the likelihood of such violations occurring in the first place. Once global standards are created, international institutions are in a stronger position to pressure governments to conform with these standards. International regimes also strengthen the position of societal groups working to hold governments accountable for their actions. By empowering both international institutions and global civil society, the right to food regime represents an important step toward achieving the goal of universal food security. The following four chapters describe how this goal has been advanced in each region of the developing world.

Notes

1. There is an extended literature on different aspects of the right to food regime. See especially Kent 2005, Kent (ed.) 2008, de Schutter and Cordes (eds.) 2011, Mazumdar 2015, Claeys 2015, Zeigler et al. 2011,

Schanbacher 2019, Cresswell Riol 2017, Friedmann 2005, Knuth and Vidar 2011, Margulis 2013, and McMichael 2009a.

2. United Nations, 1948, Article 25, Paragraph 1.
3. *The International Covenant of Economic, Social, and Cultural Rights* is phrased in aspirational terms, with governments expected to fulfill these rights to the maximum extent possible given available resources. United Nations 1966, Articles 2 (1), 11 (1), and 23.
4. The Committee on Economic, Social and Cultural Rights was established in 1985. By signing the Optional Protocol to the *International Covenant of Economic, Social, and Cultural Rights*, which came into force in 2013, states recognize the competence of the Committee on Economic, Social and Cultural Rights to consider complaints from individuals or groups who believe their rights under the covenant have been violated and they have been denied access to justice in their home countries.
5. United Nations 1966, Article 11.1.
6. United Nations 1966, Article 11.2 (a).
7. United Nations 1966, Article 11.2 (b).
8. The *Food Aid Convention* included a pledge by member countries to provide annual food aid totaling 4.6 million tons of grain to developing countries. Numerical requirements were set for each donor country.
9. The *Food Aid Convention* was renewed and modified in 1971, 1980, 1986, 1995, and 1999 and then replaced by the *Food Assistance Convention* in 2012.
10. The 1974 World Food Conference was sponsored by FAO and took place in Rome. Food and Agriculture Organization 1974.
11. *The Universal Declaration on the Eradication of Hunger and Malnutrition* was endorsed by the United Nations General Assembly through Resolution 3348 of December 17, 1974. United Nations 1974.
12. United Nations 1974, Paragraph 1.
13. United Nations 1974, Paragraph 2.
14. United Nations 1974, Paragraph 12.
15. The *Universal Declaration on the Eradication of Hunger and Malnutrition* was not intended to establish binding obligations for countries, but rather to serve as a framework to guide policy development.
16. The World Food Council was dissolved in 1993 and its functions were absorbed by FAO and WFP.
17. The Committee on World Food Security was established as an inter-agency committee within FAO.
18. Human Rights Commission 1987.
19. United Nations 1987, p. 1.
20. United Nations 1987, p. 1.
21. World Food Council 1988, p. 1.
22. World Food Council, 1989.

23. United Nations 1989, Article 24.2 (c).
24. United Nations, 1990.
25. Food and Agriculture Organization and World Health Organization 1992, Paragraph 1.
26. Food and Agriculture Organization 1996a, Paragraph 1.
27. Food and Agriculture Organization 1996a, Paragraph 10.
28. Food and Agriculture Organization 1996b, Paragraph 1.
29. The Committee on World Food Security was charged with implementing the Special Programme for Food Security.
30. This request was included in objective 7.4 of the *Plan of Action* of the World Food Summit, Food and Agriculture Organization 1996b.
31. United Nations Committee on Economic, Social, and Cultural Rights, 1999, Paragraph 8.
32. United Nations Committee on Economic, Social, and Cultural Rights, 1999, Paragraph 4.
33. United Nations Committee on Economic, Social, and Cultural Rights, 1999, Paragraph 6.
34. United Nations Committee on Economic, Social, and Cultural Rights, 1999, Paragraph 14.
35. United Nations Committee on Economic, Social, and Cultural Rights, 1999, Paragraph 15.
36. United Nations Committee on Economic, Social, and Cultural Rights, 1999, Paragraph 36.
37. Food Aid Committee, 1999.
38. The appointment of the Special Rapporteur on the Right to Food was made by the UN Human Rights Commission through Resolution 2000/10 in April 2000. When the Human Rights Commission was replaced by the Human Rights Council (HRC) in June 2006, the mandate of the Special Rapporteur was endorsed and extended through Resolution 6/2 of September 27, 2007.
39. The Special Rapporteur was charged with examining a range of specific issues related to food security, including international trade, agrarian reform, access to water, and the nutritional status of women and indigenous people.
40. Human Rights Commission, 2002, paragraph 17.
41. The United Nations Development Programme (UNDP) was assigned primary responsibility for overseeing the progress of each nation toward achieving the Millennium Development Goals.
42. Member countries were called upon to achieve a fifty percent reduction in the proportion of people suffering from extreme hunger. The Prevalence of Undernourishment measurement is used to monitor progress toward achieving the nutritional objectives included in the Millennium Development Goals. The primary measurements for extreme hunger

included the prevalence of underweight children under five years of age and the proportion of the population below the minimum level of dietary energy consumption.

43. Follow-up conferences on financing for development were held in Doha in 2008 and Addis Ababa in 2015.
44. United Nations, 2003. ECOSOC was assigned responsibility for overseeing implementation of the *Monterrey Consensus*. A Financing for Development Office was established within the Department of Economic and Social Affairs to monitor the progress of member countries toward meeting their commitments under the agreement.
45. This summit was officially entitled the World Food Summit: Five Years Later and was convened to assess the progress achieved since the 1996 World Food Summit.
46. Food and Agriculture Organization 2002, p. 1.
47. FAO provided the secretariat for the Intergovernmental Working Group.
48. Food and Agriculture Organization 2005a.
49. Food and Agriculture Organization 2005a, Guideline 13.2.
50. Committee on World Food Security, 2017, p. 13.
51. A number of additional factors contributed to the 2007–2008 global food crisis, including the diversion of land for the cultivation of biofuel crops, rising price of energy, and declining public investments in agriculture.
52. In 2008, the *Comprehensive Framework for Action* (High Level Task Force on Food and Nutrition Security 2008) was revised and became the *Updated Comprehensive Framework of Action*. (High Level Task Force on Food and Nutrition Security 2010).
53. Human Rights Council, 2008b, Paragraph 17, p. 9.
54. Human Rights Council, 2008a, Paragraph 2, p. 3.
55. Human Rights Council, 2008a, Paragraph 8, p. 4.
56. Food and Agriculture Organization 2009, Paragraph 2, p. 1.
57. Food and Agriculture Organization 2009, Paragraphs 9–41, pp. 3–7.
58. Committee on World Food Security, 2009. See also de Schutter 2013b for a description of the steps leading up to reform of the Committee on World Food Security.
59. An International Food Security and Nutrition Civil Society Mechanism was later established to ensure civil society organizations would be able to monitor CFS policies and procedures.
60. The Committee on World Food Security was reaffirmed as a committee based in FAO, with a secretariat jointly sponsored by FAO, IFAD, and WFP.
61. Committee on World Food Security, 2012.
62. The framework underwent substantial revision in 2014 and 2017. Committee on World Food Security, 2017, p. 4.

63. The transition from food aid to food assistance is more fully examined in von Oppeln-Bronikowski, 2011.
64. United Nations 2012. The *Food Assistance Convention* was opened for signature on June 11, 2012 and entered into force on January 1, 2013.
65. The *Food Assistance Convention* effectively replaced the *Food Aid Convention* that had been in place since 1967 and revised multiple times, most recently in 1999.
66. United Nations, 2012, Article 2.a.iii. The convention advocated the use of local and regional purchases (LRP) to obtain emergency food aid whenever possible. Annual food aid contributions for each donor country were no longer specified in the convention.
67. United Nations, 2012, Article 2.c.ii.
68. United Nations, 2012, Article 2.d.ii.
69. Food and Agriculture Organization 2012. The VGGT were endorsed at the 38th Special Session of CFS in May 2012.
70. Food and Agriculture Organization 2014d. *The Principles for Responsible Investment in Agriculture and Food Systems* were endorsed at the 41st session of CFS in October 2014.
71. Both the *Rome Declaration on Nutrition* (FAO and World Health Organization 2014a) and the *Framework for Action* (FAO and World Health Organization 2014b) were endorsed by General Assembly Resolution A/RES/70/259.
72. Food and Agriculture Organization and World Health Organization 2014a, Paragraph 3, p. 1.
73. Food and Agriculture Organization and World Health Organization 2014a, Section 13.a, p. 3.
74. Food and Agriculture Organization and World Health Organization 2014b.
75. Food and Agriculture Organization 2014c. In 2015, FAO developed *Voluntary Guidelines for Protecting the Rights and Improving the Livelihoods of Marine and Inland Small-Scale Fisheries and Fish Workers within the Context of Sustainable Fish Management*. Food and Agriculture Organization 2015a.
76. United Nations 2015b. The Sustainable Development Goals were based on the principles agreed upon in General Assembly Resolution A/RES/66/288.
77. The central challenges identified in SDG involved poverty, hunger, healthcare, education, climate change, gender equality, water, sanitation, energy, and the environment.
78. To measure progress toward achieving Targets 2.1 and 2.2, data is collected from a representative sample of the population in all countries. Moderate and severe food insecurity are then assessed using the Food Insecurity Experience Scale.

79. Food and Agriculture Organization 2015b. The *Framework for Action for Food Security and Nutrition in Protracted Crises* was endorsed at the 42nd session of CFS in October 2015.
80. Food Security Information Network 2020, p. 10.
81. General Assembly Resolution A/RES/70/259. Establishing the UN Decade of Action on Nutrition was first proposed at the Second International Conference on Nutrition in November 2014.
82. Food and Agriculture Organization 2018c, p. 18. The first report on the Nutrition Decade was presented by the UN Secretary-General to the General Assembly during its 72nd session.
83. Human Rights Council, 2019, p. 3.
84. Human Rights Council, 2019, p. 3.
85. Human Rights Council, 2019, p. 5.
86. Human Rights Council, 2019, pp. 4–5.
87. WFP has regional bureaus for Latin America and the Caribbean (Panama), West Africa (Dakar), East Africa (Nairobi), Central and Southern Africa (Johannesburg), the Middle East and North Africa (Cairo), and Asia (Bangkok).
88. The WFP's five strategic objectives include ending hunger by protecting access to food, improving nutrition, achieving food security, supporting implementation of the Sustainable Development Goals, and partnering with other agencies to advance the SDG. World Food Programme 2020b, p. 26.
89. WFP currently provides emergency food aid to approximately fifty million people each year.
90. World Food Programme 2019a, p. 55.
91. World Food Programme 2019a, p. 56.
92. World Food Programme 2018c, p. 46; World Food Programme 2019a, p. 60.
93. World Food Programme 2018c, pp. 42–43.
94. Food and Agriculture Organization 2018c, p. 105.
95. World Food Programme 2018c, p. 48.
96. World Food Programme 2019a, pp. 51–54.
97. The six departments of FAO are Agriculture and Consumer Protection; Economic and Social Development; Fisheries and Aquaculture; Forestry; Corporate Services and Technical Cooperation; and Program Management. The five regional offices are Latin America and the Caribbean (Santiago), Africa (Accra), the Near East and North Africa (Cairo), Asia and the Pacific (Bangkok), and Europe and Central Asia (Budapest).
98. The assessed contributions required of member states are set by the biennial FAO Conference.
99. FAO carries out periodic assessments of forest resources in the world. The *Global Forest Resources Assessment* offers a comprehensive report

on forests worldwide every five years. Food and Agriculture Organization 2020b. Every two years FAO publishes the *State of the World's Forests* which covers current and emerging challenges facing the forestry sector. FAO 2020c. The *FAO Yearbook of Forest Products* provides data on the volume, value, and direction of trade in forest products. Food and Agriculture Organization 2017.

100. FAO also works at the international level to promote agricultural development. This typically involves the establishment of international agreements, codes of conduct, and technical standards related to agriculture. FAO also mobilizes resources for agricultural and rural development from multilateral institutions and regional development banks.
101. Food and Agriculture Organization 2019e, p. 55.
102. Food and Agriculture Organization 2019e, p. 55.
103. Climate Smart Agriculture was initially proposed by FAO in 2010 at the Hague Conference on Agriculture, Food Security, and Climate Change.
104. International Fund for Agricultural Development 2016, p. 5.
105. The establishment of IFAD was one of the major outcomes of the 1974 World Food Conference.
106. International Fund for Agricultural Development 2016, p. 5.
107. International Fund for Agricultural Development 2016, p. 5.
108. International Fund for Agricultural Development 2016, p. 5.
109. International Fund for Agricultural Development 2018d, p. 3. IFAD's regional bureaus are Latin America and the Caribbean; East and Southern Africa; West and Central Africa; the Near East, North Africa, Europe, and Central Asia; and Asia and the Pacific. Twelve of the country offices also serve as regional hubs and three of these offices are Knowledge Centers that are designed to ensure successful innovations are shared, replicated, and scaled-up.
110. IFAD's Technical Assistance for Project Start-Up Facility (TAPS) provides grants to lower-income countries with the most fragile economies. International Fund for Agricultural Development 2019a, p. 2.
111. International Fund for Agricultural Development 2016, p. 6. IFAD's Agri-Business Capital Fund works to increase private sector investments in rural enterprises. International Fund for Agricultural Development 2019a, p. 2.
112. International Fund for Agricultural Development 2019a, p. 2.
113. International Fund for Agricultural Development 2019a, p. 43.

CHAPTER 3

Latin America

Latin American countries have made progress in reducing hunger and malnutrition. Robust economic growth since the turn of the century pulled millions of people out of poverty and improved overall living conditions throughout the region. Most countries are now classified as middle income.[1] Despite this economic and social progress, a significant portion of the population continues to be food insecure. Almost 200 million people struggle to meet their daily food needs and in some parts of the region, especially in the Andean highlands, rural Central America, and select Caribbean islands, nearly a quarter of the population is chronically malnourished.

This chapter describes and explains food insecurity in Latin America. A range of economic and political factors limit the access of poor communities to safe, sufficient, and nutritious food. The increasing scarcity of natural resources, especially land, water, forests, and fisheries, also undermines food security in the region. The chapter then turns to multilateral efforts to combat hunger and malnutrition in Latin America. Although emergency food aid continues to be provided in those cases where nutritional needs are urgent, especially in the immediate aftermath of natural disasters, most international assistance is extended to build sustainable food systems in the region. This includes a diverse range of initiatives to raise agricultural productivity, promote rural development, and preserve natural environments.

F. Adams, *The Right to Food*,
https://doi.org/10.1007/978-3-030-60255-0_3

Regional Context

The thirty-three countries of Latin America are spread across three distinct subregions. *South America*, which extends from the Gulf of Darién to Tierra del Fuego, has the greatest geographic expanse and is home to two-thirds of the region's people. It includes Brazil, by far the largest and most populous country in Latin America, the Andean countries of the north and west (Bolivia, Colombia, Ecuador, Peru, and Venezuela), and the southern cone countries of Argentina, Chile, Paraguay, and Uruguay.[2] *Mesoamerica*, which occupies the land expanse between the Caribbean Sea and the Pacific Ocean, includes Mexico and the countries of the Central American isthmus.[3] The *Caribbean,* which includes the Greater and Lesser Antilles, is also considered part of Latin America, although many of these island nations have distinct histories, institutions, cultures, and languages.[4]

As noted above, Latin American countries have made progress in meeting overall nutritional needs. Malnutrition rates are considerably lower for the 650 million people of the region than comparable rates in other regions of the developing world. The percentage of people who are malnourished has been cut in half since 2000.[5] Child malnutrition has also declined by fifty percent during this same time period. Latin America not only produces sufficient food to easily meet the needs of its population but has emerged as a major supplier of grains, fruits, vegetables, meat, and other food products to world markets.[6] Agricultural exports are an engine of growth for many countries in the region.[7]

At the same time, food insecurity remains a daily reality for millions of Latin Americans.[8] Nearly 200 million people are food insecure.[9] In some of the poorest countries—Bolivia, Ecuador, El Salvador, Guatemala, Haiti, Honduras, Nicaragua, Paraguay, Peru, and Venezuela—a quarter of the population is chronically malnourished. Micronutrient deficiencies, especially with respect to Vitamins A and B, Iodine, and Zinc, are common within the poorest communities and fifty-five million people suffer from Iron Deficiency Anaemia.[10]

Food insecurity is disproportionately high for children.[11] Ten percent of children are born at a low birth weight, fifteen percent of children are malnourished, and more than a third of children suffer from vitamin and mineral deficiencies. Nine percent of all children under five years of age—almost five million children—are stunted.[12] The rates of stunting among indigenous children are twice as high as for non-indigenous children and come close to the highest rates in the world. An additional 700,000 children under five years of age are wasted.[13]

Causes of Food Insecurity

A number of factors contribute to food insecurity in Latin America. Although food production is more than enough to meet the nutritional needs of all people, the poorest members of society are often unable to access sufficient food for themselves and their families.[14] At present, nearly 200 million people, almost a third of the region's total population, live in poverty and 63 million people live in extreme poverty.[15] Poverty is largely a consequence of extreme inequalities in the distribution of income and wealth. Latin America has long held the dubious distinction of being the world's most unequal region. The richest ten percent of the population earns approximately forty percent of total income while the poorest ten percent of the population earns just over one percent of total income.[16] Eight of the twenty-five most unequal countries in the world are in Latin America.[17]

Poverty is three times higher in the countryside than in cities.[18] Nearly half of the rural population is poor and one-third of these people are extremely poor.[19] People in rural areas have considerably less access to safe drinking water, health care, education, and other basic services.[20] Although Latin America continues to have a sizable number of family farms, the most fertile lands are increasingly concentrated in the hands of large landholders and commercial agribusinesses.[21] *Half of all agricultural land is owned by one percent of the population.*[22] Because large landowners have monopsony power in local labor markets, wage rates are lower than rates in more competitive labor markets. The concentration of land holdings, which has its origins in the era of Spanish and Portuguese colonization, has intensified through the increasing common practice of acquiring lands—often illegally —from small-scale farmers and local communities.[23]

Indigenous and African-descendant communities are especially impoverished.[24] There are approximately forty-five million indigenous people in Latin America, with the highest concentrations in southern Mexico, Central America, the Amazonian rainforest, and the Andean highlands.[25] These communities have long endured poverty, overt discrimination, and social exclusion. Living conditions are markedly lower than national averages in almost all respects and malnutrition rates are considerably higher.[26] People of African descent also suffer from higher levels of malnutrition. There are approximately 105 million Afro-Latinos in the region and fifteen countries have African origin populations that constitute at least forty percent of their total populations.[27] African-descendant populations are highest in the Caribbean, the Atlantic coast of Central America, and the South America countries of Brazil, Colombia, French Guiana, Guyana, Suriname, and Venezuela. As with indigenous communities, people of African descent have long endured overt discrimination, structural racism, economic exploitation, and social exclusion.[28]

Food insecurity is also higher for women than men in Latin America.[29] Clearly gender inequalities have declined in some respects and women now represent almost half of the region's formal labor force. However, women are often relegated to lower paid jobs with little security and few benefits. Women also do the majority of work in the informal sector where they earn even lower pay, have even less security and do not receive any benefits. In rural areas, women hold less than ten percent of land titles and receive just fifteen percent of credit and extension services. Although there is considerable variation by age, ethnicity, economic status, and geographic location, the region continues to reflect entrenched cultural traditions that favor men over women.

Governments also contribute to food insecurity in Latin America. This is true despite repeated commitments by political leaders to combat hunger and malnutrition. Latin America was the first region to call for the complete abolition of hunger. The *Hunger-Free Latin America and Caribbean 2025 Initiative* (HFLACI), which was endorsed by all governments in the region in 2005, envisioned eradicating hunger by 2025.[30] The *Food Security, Nutrition and Hunger Eradication Plan*, adopted by the Community of Latin American and Caribbean States (CELAC) in 2015, also called for ending hunger by 2025.[31] National legislatures formed the Parliamentary Front Against Hunger in Latin America and the Caribbean to advance a common strategy to achieve universal food security.[32]

Despite these public declarations, governments have done little to effectively address the problem of food insecurity. The region has a poor record of allocating public resources for social protection programs and the limited resources that are expended typically flow to urban areas.[33] While large-scale farms have adopted advanced technologies and raised overall output, little public investment is channeled toward improving the productivity of small-scale farmers. Just six percent of smallholder farmers have access to any form of irrigation and the poor quality of storage and processing facilities result in high levels of post-harvest loss. Although Latin America has less than one-tenth of global population, the region accounts for nearly one-fifth of the world's annual post-harvest loss.

Latin American governments typically favor the production of cash crops for export over the production of staples to meet domestic food needs. As noted above, large-scale, export-oriented production is increasingly replacing traditional farming in virtually all countries. Agricultural exports to the United States, Europe, and Asia have rapidly expanded since 2000 and political leaders have encouraged this trend as a means of generating scarce foreign exchange.[34] Latin American governments have entered into free trade accords with North American and European countries with the goal of expanding exports. Because these accords have led to dramatic increases of foreign grains entering the region, small-scale farmers have been seriously harmed. The fifteen million Mexican farmers who were displaced after implementation of the *North American Free Trade Accord* (NAFTA) is the most dramatic example of the negative consequences that can result from free trade accords.

Public sector corruption also contributes to food insecurity in Latin America.[35] Government officials routinely solicit bribes for the delivery of basic services, receive kick-backs on the award of public sector contracts, and embezzle state resources.[36] Officials have even been implicated in the trafficking of illegal narcotics, especially in the drug-producing countries of the Andes and the transit countries of Mesoamerica and the Caribbean.[37] The limited transparency and accountability of political institutions at least partially explains high levels of corruption in the region. Judicial systems that might curtail corrupt behavior are exceedingly weak and highly dependent on the executive branch. Public sector corruption engenders a broader culture of contempt for political institutions and the rule of law. The region is plagued by high levels of tax evasion which results in billions of dollars of revenues not being collected each year. Because public funds are diverted to private accounts, fewer resources are available for nutrition, agricultural, and rural development programs.

Although Latin America experienced multiple armed conflicts in the latter half of the twentieth century, especially in Central America and the Andean region, civil conflict is no longer a major cause of food insecurity in the region. At the same time, political instability and social unrest continue to plague some countries. Colombia is a prominent example in this respect. Despite a 2016 peace accord between the government and opposition groups that officially ended fifty years of armed conflict, sporadic violence continues, especially in the eastern regions of the country. Violence is perpetrated by a range of armed groups, including security forces, paramilitary militias, criminal gangs, rebel armies, and drug cartels. Access to food is limited for hundreds of thousands of people living in these areas, many of whom have been forced to abandon their homes and primary sources of income.

Venezuela is also crippled by economic collapse and social discord. Falling petroleum production at home and declining prices on global markets have dramatically reduced public sector revenues. Petroleum exports account for virtually all of the country's foreign exchange earnings. At the same time, a fifty percent decline in agricultural production since 2000 has limited the availability of basic foods in local markets and caused prices to spike.[38] Food shortages, economic crisis, and the collapse of basic services have caused a mass exodus of people from the country. Approximately 4.3 million Venezuelans have fled to neighboring countries, especially Colombia, as well as Brazil, Ecuador, and Peru. This has become the largest migration crisis in Latin American history.[39] Those who remain in Venezuela face an ever-increasing humanitarian emergency.

Food insecurity can also be linked to changes in natural resources and environments. To be sure, Latin America is endowed with an abundance of natural wealth, including significant deposits of minerals and precious metals and the largest petroleum and natural gas reserves outside of the Middle East.[40] Land, water, and forest resources are also extensive. With just nine percent of global population, the region has twenty-three percent of the world's arable land and a third of the world's freshwater.[41] Latin America contains four of the world's twenty-five largest rivers—the Amazon, Magdalena, Orinoco, and Paraná—and the total runoff from these rivers nearly equals the runoff from the other twenty-one rivers combined. Some of the world's largest lakes are also in Latin America, including Lake Argentino in Argentina, Lake Buenos Aires in Argentina and Chile, Lake Maracaibo in Venezuela, Lake Nicaragua in Nicaragua, and Lake Titicaca in Peru and Bolivia. Together, these water resources provide Latin Americans with the highest per capita supply of freshwater in the world. Latin America is also home to the largest expanse of tropical and dry forests anywhere on Earth.[42] The Amazon alone constitutes twenty-two percent of global forest coverage and is home to the greatest concentration of plant and animal life in the world.[43]

Despite Latin America's abundance of natural resources, food insecurity can be linked, at least in part, to a growing imbalance between population size and the availability of natural resources. The region's total population has nearly tripled since 1960, from 220 million to 650 million people.[44] Population growth is placing enormous stress on natural environments.[45] The increased exploitation of land has caused rapid soil loss, with approximately 250 million hectares of lands now moderately or severely degraded.[46] When small-scale farmers are no longer able to farm in certain areas, they often move to semi-arid regions, steep hillsides, or other marginal areas. Farmers also clear forest areas for cultivation. Without a protective canopy of dense vegetation, fragile topsoils in these areas eventually become unfit for farming.[47]

Water resources are also diminishing. Latin America has one of the fastest rates of aquifer depletion in the world and the declining availability of freshwater jeopardizes continued agricultural output. The contamination of lakes, rivers, and coastal estuaries, due to inadequate wastewater treatment, excessive application of fertilizers, herbicides, and pesticides, and runoff from energy, industrial, and mining operations, further reduces the availability of water for agricultural use.[48]

Forest areas are also under extreme stress. Latin America has the fastest rate of deforestation in the world with millions of hectares cleared each year.[49] At least eighty million hectares of forest have been lost since 1990.[50] The Amazon River Basin alone, which constitutes one-third of the world's rainforests, has lost, on average, two million hectares of trees annually since 2005.[51] Central America and the Caribbean are also marked by unsustainable rates of deforestation. Half of the rainforests in these areas have been cleared or severely degraded since 1950.[52] Deforestation is mostly driven by the ever-expanding needs of agribusinesses, cattle ranchers, and mining operations.[53] Because deforestation increases surface temperatures, it is a major cause of land degradation and soil erosion. The destruction of tropical forests also contributes to water scarcity by reducing water cycling, precipitation, and runoff.[54]

Climate change is intensifying the loss of natural resources in Latin America.[55] This is especially evident with respect to the supply of freshwater. A number of Andean cities rely on snow melt from mountain glaciers for seasonal renewal of water supplies. However, warmer temperatures at higher elevations are contributing to glacier loss. Some glaciers have receded to levels not seen in thousands of years and many have disappeared altogether.[56] The decreased runoff from glacier snowmelt is reducing water supplies in towns and villages throughout western Argentina, Bolivia, southern Chile, central Peru, and parts of Colombia and Ecuador. Glacier loss is also reducing the availability of water to irrigate farmlands and maintain livestock.[57]

Climate change is also causing more frequent and severe weather events.[58] Warmer temperatures in the Pacific Ocean have fueled the El Niño Southern Oscillation (ENSO) and corresponding changes in the hydrological cycle.[59] This has altered precipitation patterns and reduced rainfall in large parts of the region. Droughts have been especially severe in western Argentina, the Bolivian-Peruvian Altiplano, northeastern Brazil, and central Chile. The Dry Corridor of Central America, (which runs along the Pacific coast from Guatemala to Panama), and parts of Mexico, have also experienced severe drought in recent years. This has led to the shortening of crop cycles and reduced food production, especially the cultivation of barley, maize, wheat, and rice.[60] Dry weather conditions have also contributed to lower water levels in inland water bodies. Lake Poopó in the Bolivian Altiplano, is an extreme example of this phenomenon. Although once the second largest lake in the country, it is now completely dried up without any chance of recovery.

Warmer ocean temperatures and elevated humidity have also fueled more frequent tropical storms in Central America and the Caribbean. The Caribbean Basin is directly located in the path of many hurricanes that form out of tropical depressions that initially emerge off the coast of West Africa. These storms are pushed by the trade winds west, often reaching the peak of their power in the Caribbean Basin. Hurricanes, which can also develop in the Gulf of Mexico, Caribbean Sea, and western North Atlantic, destroy crops, damage rural infrastructure, and displace tens of thousands of people throughout this region. In other parts of Latin America, especially southern Brazil, Colombia, Ecuador, and northwest Peru, ENSO has caused torrential rains and catastrophic floods.[61]

Climate change induced sea level rise is causing greater flooding in low-lying coastal areas. Latin America is particularly vulnerable to rising sea levels because of its numerous islands and long coastlines. Flooding in these areas is contributing to coastal soil erosion and salinization of groundwater aquifers.[62] The bleaching of coral reefs and acidification of seawater due to warming ocean temperatures has reduced fish populations in coastal waters, especially on the Pacific coast of Central and South America.

Emergency Food Aid

Although the need for food aid is not nearly as great in Latin America as other regions of the developing world, such aid remains imperative at times of natural disaster. As noted above, such disasters are common in the region and have struck with greater frequency and intensity in recent years. Food aid is distributed in the immediate aftermath of these disasters, with WFP often coordinating the emergency response. WFP pre-positions food stocks in strategically located areas to be able to meet the immediate needs of displaced populations. Protracted Relief and Recovery Operations (PRRO) provide longer-term support for the rehabilitation of agricultural lands and rural infrastructure.

Food aid has been especially critical during times of drought. The 2014–2017 drought that struck Central America destroyed more than half of the annual harvest in the most severely impacted countries, especially Guatemala and Honduras, and left nearly four million people in need of humanitarian aid. WFP distributed food aid to communities that suffered the greatest losses. Identity cards to purchase vegetables, fruits, and poultry in locally-contracted shops were issued to tens of thousands of people in rural areas. Similar support is provided to people living in drought impacted regions of South America.

Emergency relief is also provided in the immediate aftermath of hurricanes. Hurricane Matthew, which struck Cuba and Haiti in October 2016, caused extensive flooding and severely damaged roads, buildings, electrical power plants, and water supplies in both countries. Significant loses to crops and livestock also occurred. WFP partnered with FAO to undertake emergency assessments of immediate nutritional needs. WFP then provided in-kind food aid, including high energy biscuits, to the communities most severely impacted. Particular focus was placed on meeting the nutritional needs of pregnant and nursing women, children under three, and the elderly. FAO aided local governments in both countries to assess the extent of the damage to their agricultural sectors and draft reconstruction plans. Food-for-Work programs supported the repair of infrastructure, including stone terraces that help prevent the loss of topsoil and stabilize hillsides.

In September 2017, two powerful Category 5 hurricanes ravaged the Caribbean. Hurricanes Irma and Maria caused massive damage to crops and rural infrastructure, especially in Barbuda, Central Cuba, Dominica, and Puerto Rico. Despite enormous difficulties reaching communities that were largely cut-off from the outside world, WFP distributed high-energy biscuits within the first week of the disasters and continued to provide rice, beans, and fortified vegetable oil to displaced families for the next two months. WFP also assisted local governments in the distribution of other relief materials. Once markets were functioning, WFP provided emergency cash transfers that allowed people to purchase food from participating shops. WFP later worked with government officials in each country to rebuild port, warehouse, and market operations.

In September 2019, Hurricane Dorian struck the Bahamas as a category 5 hurricane. Because the hurricane stalled over the country for two days, the destruction was near total on a number of islands. WFP distributed eighty-five metric tons of ready-to-eat meals to the worst-affected communities within the first week of the disaster. An airlift of storage units, generators, and satellite equipment to support the government's emergency operations was also organized. Once the initial rescue operation was completed, WFP and FAO worked with the Ministry of Agriculture to implement a number of agricultural rehabilitation initiatives.

WFP has also mobilized emergency food aid in the immediate aftermath of floods. In March 2017, heavy rainfalls associated with the El Niño weather pattern caused severe flooding and landslides in Colombia, Ecuador, and Peru. The rains damaged agriculture, rural infrastructure, water supplies, and sanitation services. WFP provided commodity vouchers and cash-transfers to those communities displaced by the flooding and worked with local authorities to prepare emergency response plans should similar flooding reoccur in the future.

Latin America is also highly susceptible to earthquakes and volcanoes. A large subduction zone and a series of complex fault lines lie beneath the Pacific coast of South America. Central America is also located where several tectonic plates, including the North America, Caribbean, Cocos, and Nazca plates, continuously assert pressure against each other. The tectonics in the Caribbean are similarly unstable, with a number of subduction zones and active crustal faults that interact offshore. The numerous volcanoes in Central America are due to the active subduction zone that runs along the western boundary of the Caribbean Plate while volcanoes in the Caribbean are formed by the North American Plate sliding under the Caribbean Plate.[63]

On January 12, 2010, a 7.0 earthquake centered 17 kilometers southwest of Port-au-Prince caused massive devastation to the western part of the island of Hispaniola. Approximately, 200,000 people in Haiti were killed and over a million people lost their homes. Port-au-Prince suffered severe damage to critical infrastructure, including buildings, roads, electricity, water supply, and communications networks. WFP was named the lead agency to coordinate the emergency response to the earthquake. Despite damage to infrastructure and warehouses, a food distribution system was established to provide immediate nutritional support for up to four million people. Much of food was delivered through hospitals, orphanages, and community kitchens. Once the emergency phase of the operation transitioned to a recovery phase, food aid continued to be provided to people living in temporary camps. In partnership with CARE, WFP provided a flour mixed with vitamins and minerals as well as beans, bulger, wheat, and fortified cooking oil. Mobile field kitchens were established to provide hot meals. Under a Purchase-for-Progress (P4P) initiative food was obtained directly from local farmers. WFP also employed thousands of people in Food-for-Assets and Food-for-Work programs to rebuild key infrastructure and rehabilitate the agricultural sector.

The eruption of the Fuego Volcano in Guatemala on June 3, 2018 was the most severe volcanic eruption in more than a century. An eight kilometer stream of hot lava flowed into nearby villages while ash, mud, and rocks descended over homes, roads, and rivers. The eruption killed hundreds of people and forced thousands of others to evacuate. The annual maize crop was completely destroyed within a twelve-mile radius. WFP coordinated delivery of humanitarian aid to affected communities. Although extensive damage to rural infrastructure made it especially difficult to reach isolated villages, in-kind food aid and cash-based transfers were distributed to ten thousand people in the departments of Chimaltenango, Escuintla, and Sacatepéquez. WFP and FAO collaborated with the Guatemalan government and civil society groups to develop rehabilitation plans for the most adversely impacted communities and the agricultural sector.

WFP also provides food aid in response to ongoing political crises in Colombia and Venezuela.[64] The 2016 peace accord in Colombia expanded access for humanitarian organizations to remote parts of the country. WFP has since deployed advanced technologies, including drones, to improve the delivery of food aid to displaced populations. Food aid is also provided to Venezuelan refugees who are living in temporary shelters in neighboring countries. Venezuelans living in Colombia, for example, receive monthly e-cards valued at thirty-five dollars per person that can be redeemed for food at local shops.

WFP also supports school meal programs in a number of Latin American countries. Although most countries have assumed primary responsibility for their meal programs, WFP continues to manage the programs in some of the poorest countries, including Haiti, Honduras, and Nicaragua. WFP also provides implementation support for school meals in some of the most destitute regions of Bolivia, Colombia, and Ecuador. In most cases, children in food-insecure communities are given an enriched dairy drink and a micronutrient-fortified biscuit. In areas where childhood malnutrition levels are severe, primary school students receive two hot meals each day.[65]

WFP typically purchases food for school meals from local suppliers. The Home-Grown School Feeding program allows farmers to have a predictable outlet to sell their products. In Haiti, WFP worked with the Ministry of Agriculture to train smallholder farmers producing fresh vegetables, pulses, tubers, and milk to meet the procurement standards of the school lunch program. In Ecuador, produce from home gardens is included in school meals. Community members who contribute to the school meals receive a voucher equivalent to the value of the produce donated. The voucher can be exchanged for food at specially contracted shops. In some regions of Guatemala and Nicaragua, the parents of primary students are largely responsible for preparing and transporting school meals. WFP supported the *Multiactiva Paz para Colombia*, an agricultural cooperative composed of smallholder farmers who grow fruits, vegetables, and tubers. Produce from this cooperative is purchased for inclusion in local school meals.

FAO also supports school meal programs in Latin America. Its Strengthening School Feeding Programs in the Framework of the Hunger Free Latin American and Caribbean 2025 initiative focuses on fourteen countries where child nutritional needs are greatest. The initiative includes direct purchases for school meals from local families as a way of stimulating rural economies. FAO has also worked with governments to reform and strengthen school meal programs. In Guatemala, FAO helped initiate reforms that ensure at least fifty percent of the food used for school meals is purchased from smallholder farmers. FAO helped restructure school meals in the Bahamas to ensure children learn healthy eating habits. In Ecuador, FAO helped match school meals with the nutritional requirements of children in each age group and geographical location of the country. FAO regularly trains school staff in food preparation, nutrition, hygiene, and sanitation. School cooks in Guatemala, Haiti, and Honduras were trained in water purification, food preparation, and nutritional health. Programs in Bolivia, Ecuador, and Peru targeted indigenous communities for training in nutrition and food preparation.

Agricultural Productivity

Raising agricultural productivity is also a central objective of food assistance programs. IFAD has helped develop and disseminate high-yield, nutritionally-fortified seeds that are more resistant to changing weather patterns, pests, and disease. In Nicaragua, IFAD worked with the Institute of Agricultural Technology to develop two varieties of bio-enriched bean seeds that contain sixty percent more Iron and Zinc than traditional varieties. Similar work was done to develop nutritionally fortified varieties of maize and sweet potatoes. In Ecuador, FAO supported a sustainable seed initiative that improved the availability, access, and use of improved seeds. FAO also distributed high-quality potato and cassava seeds to thousands of Haitian farmers.

UN food agencies have also worked to ensure small-scale farmers have access to extension services. Farmers Field Schools in Haiti provide training in sustainable agricultural practices, including Conservation Agriculture, to small-scale farmers and seasonal agricultural workers. In the Mixteca region of Mexico, an IFAD project introduced a number of innovations to raise productivity. The primary beneficiaries were subsistence farmers who cultivate communal lands, small-scale livestock producers, and indigenous women. In northern Brazil, IFAD provided financing to improve agricultural production, develop agro-processing businesses, and more effectively manage natural resources. An FAO-sponsored project in the highlands of Peru helped promote the use of bioabonos as an alternative to traditional fertilizers. FAO also worked with the Caribbean Agricultural Research and Development Institute (CARDI) to organize a series of training workshops for farmers in sustainable agricultural practices.

Extension services have also been structured to support fishery sectors in Latin America. FAO introduced an "ecosystem approach" in a number of countries that is designed to strengthen the resilience of coastal fishing communities. In Haiti, aquaculture farmers were trained in the marketing of produce directly to local restaurants and hotels. FAO worked with the Ministry of Fishing and Aquaculture in Brazil to support sustainable small-scale aquaculture, with emphasis placed on increasing output, strengthening production chains, and enhancing social inclusion. Workshops in Suriname focused on aquatic animal health and regeneration. FAO has also aided countries combat illegal fishing in their territorial waters through the provision of advanced detection and surveillance equipment.

Protecting the land rights of poor communities has also been a component of multilateral aid to Latin America. Formal titles are critical for ensuring small-scale farmers have continued access to land and are able to retain the proceeds of their work. IFAD has worked with local communities in a number of countries to resolve land tenure disputes and facilitate the registration of land titles. In Honduras, IFAD provided legal services to indigenous communities that clarified their rights to the lands that they have worked for generations. Mapping technologies were used to clearly delineate the boundaries of these lands. The Dom Helder Câmara Project in Brazil supported land registration and agrarian reform in some of the poorest regions of the country. In Colombia, FAO supported land restitution efforts immediately following completion of the 2016 peace accords.[66]

UN food agencies have helped to strengthen farmers associations in Latin America. This work is designed to ensure small-scale farmers retain more of the benefits of their labor and are included in the formulation of rural development policies. The FAO's Family Farming and Inclusive Food Systems for Sustainable Rural Development initiative expands participation in the policy-making process. FAO also supported the Caribbean Farmers Network (CaFAN) to ensure their members were represented in the construction of agricultural and rural development policies. Farmers' organizations are now participating more regularly in food and nutrition planning meetings throughout the region. FAO worked with members of the Eastern Caribbean Trading and Agricultural Development Organization (ECTAD) to enhance production technologies and post-harvest marketing. IFAD has also been engaged in this area.

In Argentina, Cuba, Haiti, and Paraguay, IFAD provided technical assistance to smallholder cooperatives with the goal of increasing agricultural productivity. IFAD-sponsored projects also helped build the institutional and managerial capabilities of farmers' cooperatives in Bolivia, Ecuador, and Honduras. In Nicaragua, technical assistance helped strengthen the production capacities of farmers' cooperatives. This allowed collective farmers to obtain more favorable contractual arrangements for their produce.[67]

Rural Development

Food assistance has also supported broader initiatives to improve the overall well-being in rural communities. Much of this work, which is largely spearheaded by IFAD, focuses on increasing income and employment opportunities for the poor. IFAD has worked with government officials throughout the region to strengthen public sector engagement with smallholder producers, rural cooperatives, and indigenous communities.[68] In Uruguay, IFAD helped establish a nationwide dialogue on rural development that included representatives from both public sector agencies and civil society organizations. The policies that emerged from this dialogue enhanced support for family farmers and non-farm workers in rural areas. In Colombia, IFAD partnered with FAO to undertake many of the rural rehabilitation measures that were included in the country's peace accords.[69] IFAD also helped reform and improve public sector programs in Mexico that support smallholder farmers.

The expansion of rural enterprises has also been aided in a number of Latin American countries. An IFAD project in semi-arid regions of Brazil, for example, strengthened the capacities of community organizations to develop agro-processing businesses. In the high plateau region of Bolivia, where camelid production has traditionally been hampered by low productivity, limited water availability, and the lack of extension services, an IFAD project strengthened camelid value chains and improved the marketing of such by-products as wool and meat. IFAD also aided people in this region develop enterprises outside of agriculture, including the production of bread, cheese, dried fruits, and handicrafts.[70] Similar training helped establish rural small businesses in Peru.[71] In semi-arid regions of Mexico, IFAD expanded non-farm employment opportunities for the rural poor and indigenous households. Emphasis was placed on developing the managerial capacities of micro-enterprises and facilitating access to wider markets. In Paraguay, an IFAD project strengthened the capacity of grassroots organizations to identify and undertake business activities. Similar projects were supported in the Dominican Republic, Ecuador, and Guatemala.

As noted above, the advancement of rural communities is often limited by poor access to financial services. IFAD has played a lead role in expanding financial services in Latin America. In Bolivia and Paraguay, indigenous communities were among the primary beneficiaries of an IFAD initiative to help smallholder farmers gain access to savings, credit, and insurance. IFAD also worked to establish rural savings and loan associations in Colombia, Guyana, Mexico, Nicaragua, and Peru. In the Dry Corridor of Central America, financial risk mechanisms were developed for family farmers. IFAD supported projects in Brazil's semi-arid northeast provided financial services to smallholder farmers and landless people. Micro-credit and training programs have also been developed to expand entrepreneurial opportunities for women in a number of Central American and Caribbean countries.

External assistance has been structured to help farmers secure reliable access to agricultural markets for their products. In Argentina, Bolivia, the Dominican Republic, and Paraguay, IFAD supported the development of inclusive value chains that focused on partnerships between rural organizations and private-sector actors. Much of this work involved brand creation, public procurement, and investments in market infrastructure. A project in Honduras helped integrate small-scale producers into agriculture and forestry value chains. In Nicaragua, market access for coffee and cocoa cooperatives in indigenous and Afro-descendent communities was expanded. IFAD helped negotiate partnerships between these cooperatives and private companies to ensure stable markets for their products.[72]

Environmental Preservation

Multilateral aid has also been structured to support the sustainable management of natural resources. Much of this work involves aiding Latin American governments in the design of environmental preservation programs and policies. FAO recently supported diagnostic studies of agro-environmental policies throughout the region and proposed a number of recommendations to strengthen these policies.[73]

The preservation of arable land is a central component of FAO's environmental work in Latin America. The Action Against Desertification initiative, which focuses on Central America and the Caribbean, draws on mapping and satellite technologies to improve land use practices and restore degraded lands. In Ecuador, FAO worked with the Environment Ministry to improve land management in degraded areas. Emphasis was placed on preserving local environmental services and supporting improved regulation of hydrological cycles. FAO also encouraged the use of trickle irrigation, windbreaks, organic fertilizers, and crop rotation techniques as a means of reducing soil erosion and restoring degraded lands.

UN agencies have also worked to preserve water resources in Latin America. FAO provided technical assistance to officials from Bolivia's Environment Ministry on the effective management of water harvesting, micro-irrigation, and storage systems. Community leaders were trained in the construction and use of sustainable water systems. In Haiti, FAO helped rehabilitate the country's irrigation infrastructure and improve watershed management. IFAD has also supported water preservation projects in Latin America. This includes aiding the recovery of mangrove swamps in Ecuador and supporting efficient water management practices in Colombia. In Brazil, IFAD built thousands of cisterns to store rainwater and provide safe drinking water to rural communities. IFAD also built waste treatment units that convert surface water from lagoons into drinking water.[74] External assistance has supported water conservation projects in the Dry Corridor of Central America

Forest preservation has also been a central component of these environmental efforts. FAO has worked with national park directors throughout the region to enhance forest protection measures. Much of this work focuses on those areas of the Amazon Rainforest that are at greatest risk. FAO worked with Brazilian authorities to establish new protected zones in these areas. Support for Ecuador's first national forest inventory enhanced the forest management capacities of local governments and community groups. In Chile, FAO drew on financing from the Global Environmental Facility (GEF) to support a national forest monitoring system. WFP has also been engaged in reforestation efforts, especially in Mesoamerica, with much of this work carried out through Food for Assets (FFA) programs. In Mexico, WFP partnered with IFAD to support agroforestry projects and the sustainable use of non-timber forest resources that directly aid indigenous communities.[75]

Lastly, international assistance has addressed the threats posed by climate change. This includes a series of initiatives to lessen greenhouse gas emissions. Under the Reduce Emissions from Deforestation and Forest Degradation (REDD+) program, Latin American governments are granted financial incentives to expand forest preservation. FAO has partnered with UNEP and UNDP to advance this initiative. In Brazil, FAO aided the Ministry of Agriculture's efforts to reduce the loss of native forests. This included support for sustainable agriculture and livestock farming in the Amazon. An IFAD project in Colombia aided the post-conflict recovery and rehabilitation of forest resources.[76] Drone technology was used to identify areas in both rainforests and watersheds that were at the greatest risk. In Guatemala and Peru, wood-saving stoves were provided to rural households to reduce reliance on forest products for cooking.[77]

Strengthening the resilience of rural communities to the negative impacts of climate change is also included in region-wide initiatives. FAO helped improve national capacities for risk management and emergency response.[78] Much of this work has been carried out in the Dry Corridor of Central America where early warning systems for drought have been instituted. Similar work was undertaken in the Caribbean. In Barbados, FAO helped strengthen disaster risk management systems, including implementation of an early warning system to detect potential threats to food security. An early warning system was established in the Dominican Republic to identify the onset of food crises.

WFP and IFAD have also supported climate change adaptation initiatives. A WFP project promoted disaster risk reduction activities throughout Central America, including training in soil and water conservation, weather-resistant agricultural practices, and natural disaster response planning.[79] The initiative also strengthened monitoring systems for food and nutritional security. An IFAD project in Nicaragua helped introduce water efficiency and crop diversification measures, such as coffee-cocoa intercropping, to buffer the effects of rising temperatures. In Mexico, IFAD enhanced the sustainable use of forest resources in order to strengthen resilience to drought and other climate shocks. Information services were established in Paraguay that enabled smallholder farmers to receive climate alerts. IFAD aided Bolivian municipalities in the highlands to incorporate risk management and climate adaptation into their land use planning programs.[80] In Haiti, IFAD promoted Climate-Smart Agriculture to build resilience to adverse climatic conditions. A similar project in the Dominican Republic improved farmers' access to technologies that strengthen resilience to the threats posed by climate change.

Conclusion

Although food insecurity is lower in Latin America than other regions of the developing world, almost 200 million people find it difficult to meet their daily nutritional needs. In some of the poorest countries, nearly a quarter of the population is chronically malnourished. Poverty is the primary causes of food insecurity. Almost a third of Latin America's total population are poor and unable to afford sufficient food for themselves and their families. Poverty is largely a consequence of extreme inequalities in the distribution of income and wealth, with indigenous and African-descendant communities especially disadvantaged. The majority of public resources flow to urban areas while agricultural and rural development are neglected. Public resources are also lost to unproductive investments or corruption. Governments favor the production of cash crops for export over the production of staples to meet domestic needs while population growth and climate change are placing enormous stress on the natural resources required for sustainable food production.

The United Nations provides both food aid and food assistance to Latin American countries. Although the need for emergency food aid is not as urgent in Latin America as other regions of the developing world, it remains imperative at times of natural disaster. Relief and reconstruction aid is provided in response to droughts, hurricanes, earthquakes, and volcanic eruptions. Aid is also provided in response to ongoing political crises in Colombia and Venezuela. Support for agricultural development includes the provision of quality seeds, newer technologies, and extension services to small-scale farmers. UN food agencies also help strengthen farmers associations and protect the land rights of poor communities. Broader rural development efforts increase income and employment opportunities for the rural poor. The expansion of non-farm rural enterprises and provision of rural financial services are considered especially critical. Multilateral assistance is also structured to preserve the natural resources needed for sustainable food production.

Despite setbacks in recent years and a number of new challenges that have recently emerged, the prospects for continued progress toward universal food security in Latin America are relatively strong. Food assistance can play an important role in supporting and accelerating this progress. Assistance to family farmers, who account for a significant share of food production in the region, will be critical. These farmers will need access to quality inputs, newer technologies, and enhanced irrigation in order to increase their productivity and reduce post-harvest loss. Special focus should be accorded the needs of indigenous and Afro-Latino communities. Food assistance can also play a vital role in addressing the many environmental challenges that confront the region, especially in the Dry Corridor of Central America and the Amazonian rainforest. By increasing support for land, water, forest, and fishery preservation, as well as building resilience to the adverse impacts of climate change, UN food agencies can help establish sustainable food systems that meet the needs of all Latin Americans.

Notes

1. Economic growth in Latin America was especially strong from 2000 to 2014 due to surging global prices for many of the region's raw material exports. Although the benefits of the "commodity boom" were by no means equitably distributed, it did help reduce poverty and expand the middle class in a number of countries in the region. Because global commodity prices have since declined, economic growth has slowed throughout much of the region.
2. Although French Guiana, Guyana, and Suriname are located on the South American continent, they are often grouped with the Caribbean subregion due to their historical, cultural, and linguistic similarities with other Caribbean countries.
3. Central America, which ranges from the Mexican border in the north to the Colombian border in the south, includes Belize, Costa Rica, El Salvador, Guatemala, Honduras, Nicaragua, and Panama.
4. The Greater Antilles includes Cuba, the Dominican Republic, Haiti, and Jamaica, while the Lesser Antilles includes Antigua and Barbuda, Barbados, Dominica, Grenada, Guadeloupe, Martinique, St. Kitts and Nevis, and St. Lucia.
5. The prevalence of undernourishment in Latin America fell from 11.9% in 2000 to 6.5% in 2018. Food and Agriculture Organization 2020j, p. 5. Latin America was the only world region to achieve the goal of halving the percentage of people suffering from hunger by 2015. This was one of the benchmarks included in the Millennium Development Goals. United Nations 2000b.
6. Argentina, Bolivia, Brazil, Colombia, and Mexico are the largest exporters of agricultural goods in Latin America.
7. It is important to note that not all Latin American countries enjoy food surpluses. A number of Caribbean countries in particular have food

deficits and imports are essential to meet domestic food needs. Food and Agriculture Organization 2020j, p. 44.

8. For analysis of the nature and causes of food insecurity in Latin America see Galicia et al. 2016, and Smith, Kassa, and Winters 2017.
9. FAO reports that 187 million people in Latin America are food insecure, with 53.7 million people being severely food insecure. Food and Agriculture Organization 2020j, p. 9.
10. Roughly 120 million Latin Americans lack access to safe drinking water. This includes about seven percent of the urban population and one-third of the rural population. The poor quality of water systems is a major cause of gastrointestinal diseases and childhood mortality.
11. See United Nations Economic Commission for Latin America and the Caribbean 2018a.
12. Food and Agriculture Organization 2020j, p. 17.
13. Food and Agriculture Organization 2020j, p. 17.
14. See Rossi et al. 2017 and Vakis et al. 2016 for analysis of the socio-economic determinants of food insecurity in Latin America.
15. Food and Agriculture Organization 2020j, pp. 62–63. Poverty rates vary considerably throughout Latin America. While countries in the southern cone have chronic poverty rates of just ten percent, nearly half of all people in Central America are impoverished.
16. Food and Agriculture Organization 2019g, p. 41.
17. The countries with the greatest inequality in Latin America include Bolivia, Brazil, Colombia, Guatemala, Haiti, Honduras, Panama, and Paraguay while countries with the least inequality are Argentina, Costa Rica, and Uruguay.
18. Food and Agriculture Organization 2019g, pp. 79–81. It is important to note that Latin America is a highly urbanized region, with seventy-five percent of all inhabitants living in cities with at least 100,000 people. Urbanization levels are lower than the regional average in Central America.
19. Food and Agriculture Organization 2020j, p. 64. This compares to approximately a quarter of people living in urban areas being impoverished.
20. Food and Agriculture Organization 2020j, p. 64. These figures for rural poverty are even higher in southern Mexico, Central America, and the Andes.
21. Family farming is the primary source of rural employment in Latin America and accounts for approximately sixty-five percent of all agricultural employment.
22. Latin America has the most unequal distribution of land in the world. The Gini coefficient for land concentration in Latin America is 0.79, far exceeding Africa (0.56) and Asia (0.55).

23. von Bennewitz 2017 reviews changes in land tenure arrangements in Latin America over time.
24. Food and Agriculture Organization 2019g, pp. 81–85. See Telles 2014 for a discussion of racial and ethnic inequalities in Latin America.
25. Food and Agriculture Organization 2019g, pp. 81–85. Indigenous communities constitute the majority of people in Bolivia and Guatemala and are significant minorities in Ecuador, Mexico, Panama, and Peru.
26. Half of all indigenous households in Latin America are poor and one-fifth are extremely poor. These rates are twice as high as non-indigenous households. Food and Agriculture Organization 2020j, p. 64.
27. Food and Agriculture Organization 2019g, pp. 81–85.
28. Although the marginalization of indigenous and African-descendant communities can be traced to the colonial and immediate post-colonial eras, it continues today through overt discrimination and prejudice, language barriers, geographic isolation, insecure and limited land ownership, and inadequate access to primary and secondary education.
29. Food and Agriculture Organization 2020j, pp. 11–13, 64; Food and Agriculture Organization 2019g, p. 74. Almost twenty percent of Latin American women are food insecure and nearly thirty percent of all pregnant women suffer from Iron Deficiency Anaemia. Food and Agriculture Organization 2020j, p. 39.
30. Food and Agriculture Organization 2005b.
31. Community of Latin American and Caribbean States 2014. The goal of eradicating hunger in Latin America by 2025 is five years ahead of the global target under the Sustainable Development Goals. United Nations 2015b.
32. Food and Agriculture Organization 2020j, p. 43. Since its formation in 2009, the Parliamentary Front Against Hunger in Latin America and the Caribbean has promoted laws on family farming, food labeling, food loss, and school meals, among others.
33. Notable exceptions include the PROGRESSA program in Mexico, the Familias en Acción initiative in Colombia, the Bolsa Familia program in Brazil, and the JUNTOS program in Peru which were designed to address food insecurity in poor communities.
34. The export of soybeans, for example, has grown 140% during this time period. Brazil has become the world's largest exporter of soybeans, accounting for more than forty percent of total global exports.
35. Arellano-Gault 2019 and Rotberg (ed.) 2019 offer detailed analyses of corruption in Latin America.
36. For example, the Brazilian construction firm Odebrecht is currently under investigation for allegedly paying bribes to high ranking government officials for construction contracts in a number of Latin American countries. It is estimated that $800 million dollars in bribes were paid for contracts

worth more than $3 billion. Similar kickbacks have been exposed in the awarding of mining, petroleum, and natural gas contracts.

37. Most Latin American countries score relatively low on the Corruption Perceptions Index, with the Dominican Republic, Guatemala, Haiti, Honduras, Mexico, Nicaragua, Paraguay, and Venezuela perceived as having the most extensive corruption. Only Bahamas, Barbados, Chile, Costa Rica, and Uruguay have above average scores in the CPI. Transparency International, 2019.
38. It is important to note that the humanitarian crisis in Venezuela has been deepened due to economic sanctions imposed by the United States. These sanctions have made it more difficult for Venezuela to export petroleum and import needed food and medicines.
39. Food and Agriculture Organization 2019g, pp. 54–55.
40. Latin America has especially large deposits of Bauxite, Copper, Gold, Iron Ore, Nickel, Silver, and Zinc.
41. The Amazon River Basin alone has an area of almost seven million square kilometers, making it the largest watershed in the world. Twenty percent of global run-off flows from the Amazon Basin.
42. Latin America has the greatest proportion of land area covered by forests of all world regions. The Amazon Rainforest alone covers forty percent of the South American continent and includes parts of Bolivia, Brazil, Colombia, Ecuador, Guyana, Peru, Suriname, and Venezuela. The most extensive dry forests are in northern Argentina, southeastern Bolivia, northeastern Brazil, and in parts of Central America and Mexico.
43. The Amazon Rainforest is estimated to hold half of the world's terrestrial species of animals, plants, and insects.
44. It is important to note that Latin America's population growth rate has declined from three percent to under one percent during this same time period. Population density, which is thirty-two people per square kilometer of land area, is considerably lower than other regions of the developing world.
45. Analysis of environmental threats in Latin America can be found in Delgado and Marín 2019, Lorenzo (ed.) 2020, Pinto et al. 2017, Rodríguez Goyes et al. (eds.) 2017, and Robins and Fraser 2020.
46. Latin America accounts for fourteen percent of global land degradation. Twenty-six percent of the land in Central America is degraded.
47. Soil erosion and desertification are most extensive in Argentina, Bolivia, Chile, Ecuador, Mexico, Paraguay, and Peru.
48. Water scarcity also threatens consumption in urban areas. Sixteen of Latin America's twenty largest cities are currently experiencing household water shortages.
49. Approximately 4.3 million hectares of forests in Latin America are cleared annually and deforestation rates have increased by seventeen percent since

2000. See Armenteras et al. 2017, Manners and Varela-Ortega 2017, and Pendrill and Persson 2017 for empirical documentation of forest loss in Latin America.

50. Forty percent of the world's loss of natural forests in the last thirty years has occurred in Latin America.
51. One-fifth of the Amazonian rainforest has now been destroyed.
52. In Central America, deforestation is most evident in Guatemala where sixty-five percent of original forest cover has been destroyed in the last three decades. At the current rate, the remainder of this country's forests would disappear within twenty-five years. Haiti, where forest cover has fallen from fifty percent a century ago to just two percent today, constitutes an even more extreme case of deforestation.
53. Cattle ranching is responsible for sixty percent of Brazil's deforestation. Degraded and current grazing lands now exceed almost a quarter of Brazil's entire territory.
54. Half of Latin America's total annual rainfall originates as water recycled from the Amazon rainforest.
55. For analysis of the impact of climate change on food security in Latin America see Barker et al. 2017, Filho and Esteves de Freitas (eds.) 2018, Reyer et al. 2017.
56. Glaciers in Bolivia, Chile, Colombia, Ecuador, and Peru have lost between twenty and fifty percent of their surface area. The three major ice fields in the Patagonian Andes have also declined by one-third.
57. Lindsay 2018 explores how climate change is impacting water resources in Latin America.
58. Food and Agriculture Organization 2019g, pp. 50–53.
59. Grove and Adamson 2017 consider the most significant impacts of the El Niño weather phenomenon. See also Food and Agriculture Organization 2018c, p. 41.
60. The northern triangle of Central America—El Salvador, Guatemala, and Honduras—experienced its worst drought on record during the 2015–2016 ENSO. Honduran farmers, who were most severely impacted, lost eighty percent of their maize and bean crops because of the drought. See especially Food Security Information Network 2020, p. 49; Food and Agriculture Organization 2018c, p. 67; Food and Agriculture Organization 2020j, p. 17.
61. Warming temperatures have caused changes in disease vector populations and the incidence of water-borne diseases. Mosquito-based Chikungunya, Dengue, Malaria, and Zika are spreading into new areas and seafood is increasingly contaminated with aquatic pathogens.
62. Coastal flooding and saline intrusion are most evident in northeast Argentina, southern Brazil, Ecuador, northwest Mexico, Paraguay, northwest Peru, and Uruguay.

63. The Central American Volcanic Arc is a chain of volcanoes that parallels the Pacific coastline of this subregion.
64. World Food Programme 2019a, p. 42.
65. School meals are also provided to Colombian children who have been displaced by civil conflict.
66. Food and Agriculture Organization 2018d, p. 110.
67. International Fund for Agricultural Development 2019c, p. 38.
68. FAO and IFAD established a joint Alliance for the Elimination of Rural Poverty in Latin America.
69. Food and Agriculture Organization 2018d, p. 110.
70. International Fund for Agricultural Development 2018d, p. 11.
71. International Fund for Agricultural Development 2019a, p. 14.
72. International Fund for Agricultural Development 2018d, p. 12. WFP's Purchase-for-Progress initiative also links smallholder farmers to local markets in a number of Latin American countries.
73. FAO recently developed guidelines for Latin American and Caribbean countries with respect to agro-environmental policies. See Food and Agriculture Organization 2016.
74. International Fund for Agricultural Development 2019a, p. 14.
75. International Fund for Agricultural Development 2019a, p. 15.
76. International Fund for Agricultural Development 2018d, p. 11.
77. International Fund for Agricultural Development 2019a, p. 14.
78. Much of this work has focused on Belize, Bolivia, Colombia, the Dominican Republic, El Salvador, Grenada, Guatemala, Guyana, Haiti, Honduras, Jamaica, Nicaragua, Paraguay, Saint Vincent and the Grenadines, and Suriname.
79. This project was entitled "Building Resilient Communities and Municipalities in the Dry Corridor of Central America".
80. International Fund for Agricultural Development 2018d, p. 11.

CHAPTER 4

Africa

The African continent is endowed with a third of the world's primary commodities, including large deposits of highly valuable metals, minerals, and hydrocarbons.[1] Unfortunately, the proceeds from this natural wealth have not been used to meet the basic needs of the region's people or establish sustainable food systems. Malnutrition is either "serious" or "alarming" in most countries and the threat of famine is ever-present.[2] Half of all people in the region are either moderately or severely food insecure and malnutrition rates have actually risen during the first two decades of the twenty-first century.

This chapter outlines the size and scope of food insecurity in Africa before turning to the central causes of hunger and malnutrition. A range of economic, political, and environmental factors contribute to food insecurity in the region. Endemic poverty, civil conflict, and environmental deterioration are among the leading causes of malnutrition. The last section reviews multilateral efforts to meet the nutritional needs of poor communities across the continent. Emergency food aid is provided to people whose lives have been disrupted by natural hazards or civil conflict. More people are dependent on emergency food aid in Africa than any other world region. Food assistance is also structured to raise agricultural productivity, promote rural development, and preserve natural environments.

F. Adams, *The Right to Food*,
https://doi.org/10.1007/978-3-030-60255-0_4

Regional Context

The African continent includes fifty-four countries and hundreds of different ethnic, cultural, and linguistic groups. The Sahara Desert separates the countries of North Africa—which share many cultural characteristics with the Middle East—from the other countries of the continent. The sub-Saharan region is further divided into four subregions. *West Africa* includes most of the Sahelian countries (the semi-arid transitional zone between the Sahara Desert to the north and the savannah to the south), and the low-lying plains states to the south and west. This is the most populated subregion of the continent. *East Africa* includes countries in both the Horn of Africa and the Great Lakes region. *Central Africa*, which is the least populated subregion, includes countries in the Congo Basin—the second largest river basin in the world—and in the surrounding equatorial area. *Southern Africa*, which is dominated by the Republic of South Africa, includes the low-lying countries south of the Cunene and Zambezi rivers.

The African continent—which is home to over 1.3 billion people—has the highest malnutrition rates in the world. Approximately 277 million people are severely food insecure.[3] This constitutes more than a fifth of the continent's entire population. An additional 400 million people are moderately food insecure, without regular access to sufficient and nutritious food.[4] Forty-three of the eighty-six food-deficit countries in the world are in Africa. In the last thirty years, there has been almost no improvement in meeting the nutritional needs of poor communities throughout the continent. The region's per capita food production is lower today than it was in 1990.

African children also have the highest rates of malnutrition in the world.[5] Seventy percent of children do not have a minimally acceptable diet and forty percent of children do not eat regular meals each day. Vitamin deficiencies are twice as high as global averages and thirty percent of African children suffer growth disorders due to malnutrition. Nearly sixty million children under five years of age are stunted and fourteen million children are wasted.[6] Africa is the only world region where the percentage of stunted and wasted children has risen since 2000. *Nearly 2 million children die each year from malnutrition or malnutrition-related diseases.*

Causes of Food Insecurity

Food insecurity in Africa stems from a confluence of forces.[7] Per capita incomes are three times lower than other regions of the developing world and have declined over the course of the past three decades. Forty percent of all people earn less than two dollars a day. Eighty percent of impoverished people live in rural areas and rely on small-scale farming and livestock for the little money that they earn.[8] Those who are landless are dependent on the highly variable seasonal demand for agricultural labor.[9] Because rural areas generate few non-farm jobs, large numbers of people migrate to towns or cities on either a rotational or long-term basis.[10] A large segment of the population is simply unable to purchase food of sufficient quantity and quality to meet the nutritional needs of themselves and their families.

Ethnic inequalities also contribute to food insecurity.[11] Most countries are marked by intense rivalries between different ethnic groups over access to land and other natural resources. While these rivalries can be traced back multiple centuries, they were intensified during the colonial period when European powers imposed arbitrary boundaries and privileged some groups over others. Political entities were created with little regard for ethnic, linguistic, and cultural differences among the people who lived in these areas. Many countries continue to reflect the permanence of lineage, clan, and tribal identities rather than function as unitary nation-states. Political parties are often organized around ethnic identities and the party in power generally favors members of its own ethnic group when distributing public sector jobs and resources.

Women endure higher levels of food insecurity than men.[12] Although the position of women varies by country, region, age, ethnicity, and social status, overall legal and customary norms typically favor men over women. Educational advantages for boys begin in primary school and expand at the secondary and post-secondary levels. Women are less likely to be employed in the formal sector and the jobs that they do obtain generally require longer hours for lower pay.[13] The distribution of property also reflects gender inequalities. In rural areas, women constitute just fifteen percent of all landholders and the lands that they do own are typically smaller and less fertile than those of men. Women also have less access to the seeds, livestock, tools, technology, credit, and extension services needed to be successful in the agrarian economy.[14] Because men often leave rural areas to seek employment in cities, women are expected to do the majority of agricultural work while simultaneously caring for their children.

Governments also contribute to food insecurity. This is true despite numerous public commitments to combat hunger and malnutrition. The continent's *New Partnership for Africa's Development (NEPAD)*, which was adopted by the African Union in 2001, advanced a range of initiatives to improve agricultural productivity.[15] The *Maputo Declaration on Agriculture and Food Security* of the same year supported allocating ten percent of public sector resources to agricultural development.[16] In 2003, the African Union (AU) endorsed the *Comprehensive Africa Agriculture Development Program (CAADP)* that also called for major investments in agricultural development and food security.[17] The *Malabo Declaration*, adopted by African Heads of State in June 2014, envisioned completely ending hunger by 2025.[18] The *African Regional Nutrition Strategy for 2016–2025* (ARNS) proposed major investments in nutritional support programs.[19] Lastly, *Agenda 2063: The Africa We Want*, which was adopted by the AU in 2015, set 2025 as the end date for abolishing hunger across the continent.[20]

Despite these public commitments, African governments have allocated few resources toward combatting food insecurity. Although two-thirds of all people in the region are employed in agriculture, average per capita investment in this sector is the lowest in the developing world. Most governments do not come anywhere close to allocating ten percent of public expenditures for agrarian development.[21] Underinvestment in agriculture explains, at least in part, low levels of productivity. African farmers have the lowest food output per hectare of any world region. Just five percent of agricultural land is irrigated and farmers rarely have access to quality seeds, equipment, and extension services. Post-harvest loss due to inadequate processing and storage facilities is about a third of all agricultural output. African governments generally favor the cultivation of cash crops for export over staples for domestic consumption. The demand for agricultural goods—especially from Europe, the Persian Gulf, and Asia—is fueling this transition. Export crops, cultivated on lands that were previously used to grow basic staples, have emerged as valuable sources of foreign exchange for governments throughout the continent.

African governments have even leased fertile agricultural lands to foreign governments and global agribusinesses.[22] In what is sometimes referred to as the *new scramble for Africa*, large-scale land acquisitions by foreign interests have grown substantially in both number and scale during the past two decades.[23] Many of these acquisitions, which typically have twenty-five to fifty year contracts, are undertaken by Asian and Persian Gulf countries that are dependent on food imports. China has been especially active in this area. Chinese interests have leased large tracks of land in Cameroon, the Democratic Republic of the Congo, Mozambique, Tanzania, and Zambia. The crops grown on these lands are then used to meet rapidly expanding food and fodder needs at home. Saudi Arabian interests have also leased arable land in Egypt, Ethiopia, Sudan, and Tanzania, and similar investments have been made by Kuwait, Qatar, and the United Arab Emirates. Land has also been leased to foreign agribusinesses seeking to profit from the global demand for crops that can be used for human consumption, animal feed, or biofuel production.

Transnational land acquisitions adversely impact food security in sub-Saharan Africa. The most fertile lands are used to produce crops for export rather than for local consumption. Many of these lands were previously worked collectively by small-scale farmers under customary arrangements that did not include formal ownership. Because less than ten percent of land in Africa is tenured, most farmers do not have legal standing to challenge the land transfers. Such acquisitions are typically negotiated between African governments and foreign entities with little transparency, regulation, or inclusion of those people most directly impacted.

Public sector corruption can also be linked to food insecurity.[24] The annual Corruption Perceptions Index consistently ranks African governments among those perceived to have the highest levels of corruption.[25] Many of the conditions that engender corrupt behavior—low levels of public sector transparency, accountability, and judicial independence—are evident throughout much of the continent. Institutions that are ostensibly responsible for monitoring and punishing corrupt behavior are invariably underfunded and unable to enforce anti-corruption laws. As noted in the introductory chapter, natural resource wealth tends to increase the likelihood of public sector corruption.[26] Government officials routinely solicit kickbacks for the award of mining concessions and construction contracts. Family members of top officials often benefit financially from access to public sector resources. These resources are then transferred to offshore accounts to avoid detection. Resources that could have been invested in social protection programs, agricultural productivity, or rural development are diverted for the personal benefit of political elites. The annual cost of corruption in Africa is estimated to be greater than the total amount of foreign aid that is provided by all multilateral and bilateral donors each year.

Food insecurity can also be linked to civil conflicts in Africa. Such conflicts have tripled in the past three decades.[27] Although the immediate causes of these conflicts are complex, many have their origin in the colonial boundaries that were drawn with little regard for the cultural, linguistic, and ethnic make-up of local populations. The intense competition that is evident today over arable land, water, minerals, and other natural resources is one of the most destructive legacies of the colonial period. These conflicts cause massive damage to food production, as crops, livestock, and rural infrastructure are routinely destroyed. Civil conflicts have also caused approximately thirty million people to abandon their homes and move to other parts of their country or flee to neighboring countries.

Population pressures also contribute to food insecurity. The region's population has increased from 177 million in 1950 to over 1.3 billion today. While fertility rates have begun to decline, women give birth on average to five children during their lifetimes. This is compared to a global average of 2.5 children.[28] Although population density is not especially high for the continent as a whole, most people are clustered in overcrowded urban areas, near coastlines, or on the limited arable land that is available.[29] Population growth, which is the highest of all world regions, is placing enormous stress on the natural resources needed for sustainable food production.[30]

Population growth is clearly contributing to land degradation. Two-thirds of the continent is either savanna, desert, or steppe and not suitable for agriculture. The arable land that does exist is being exploited at unsustainable rates. At present, sixty-five percent of agricultural land and thirty percent of pasture are either partially or fully degraded.[31] Land degradation is often a consequence of destructive agricultural practices.[32] Because farmers typically remove large quantities of nutrients from the soil and leave very little crop residues, the organic matter and water-holding capacity of soils decline. The cultivation of export crops, which typically involves extensive application of chemical inputs, also contributes to land degradation.

Water resources are also declining. The African continent has the largest number of water-stressed countries in the world. Agricultural practices tend to be highly inefficient in their use of freshwater and aquifers are falling throughout the region. Almost all crops are rainfed rather than irrigated. This poses significant problems for rural communities, since rainfall is highly variable and often inadequate in many parts of the continent. The annual dry season typically lasts six to seven months. Because most rural families produce the majority of their own food, water scarcity is a leading cause of food insecurity.

Forest resources are also in decline.[33] The countries of West Africa have lost almost all of their original forest cover and the Congo Basin—the world's second largest tropical rainforest—is being destroyed at twice the world rate. Deforestation is principally due to the conversion of forest land for agriculture, logging, and mining operations. Reliance on wood for cooking and heating by the rural poor is also a major cause of forest loss. The common practice of clear cutting, which indiscriminately strips large areas of trees and vegetation, greatly diminishes the potential for natural regeneration and wastes nearly half of the trees that are removed. As noted previously, the loss of forests disrupts ecological functions that are essential to preserve soil and water resources. Run-off from hills that have been deforested washes away both crops and topsoil.

A decline in coastal and inland fish populations is also jeopardizing food security in Africa. Fishing is an important source of employment and income for more than twelve million people across the continent. Much of the decline in fish populations, especially in West Africa, is due to overfishing by foreign vessels from Asia and Europe. This has jeopardized the well-being of millions of people who depend on fishing for their livelihood and significantly reduced per capita fish consumption in the region.

Climate change is intensifying many of these environmental problems.[34] Higher surface temperatures, heat waves, and reduced precipitation have accelerated soil erosion and desertification in many parts of Africa.[35] Rising sea levels, which are about fifteen centimeters higher than a century ago, are causing extensive inland flooding. In some parts of both the western and eastern coastal regions saline intrusion is damaging soils and reducing food production. Higher sea levels in the Mediterranean are causing saline intrusion into the fragile agricultural lands of North Africa.

Climate change is also placing added stress on scarce water resources.[36] A number of countries, especially in eastern and southern Africa, have experienced irregular rainfall patterns and less precipitation in recent years. Reduced rainfall has lowered the flow of rivers that feed lakes and watersheds. Water levels in the Niger River have decreased by nearly half and Lake Chad has shrunk by ninety percent since the 1960s. Lower water levels in the Nile River have reduced the silt needed to replenish soils in the delta region. Declining precipitation is shortening the length of growing seasons and reducing agricultural output in many parts of the continent while changes in seasonal rainfall patterns are reducing the availability of pasture for livestock.[37] The 2015–2016 drought in North Africa significantly reduced grain production in Algeria, Morocco, and Tunisia. Droughts have also disrupted food production in Somalia, southeastern Ethiopia, eastern Kenya, and the Sahelian countries of Burkina Faso, Chad, Mali, Mauritania, and Niger. Prolonged drought has caused consecutive poor harvests in a number of southern African countries already facing high levels of food insecurity.[38] Because droughts have damaged animal health, the production of meat, milk, and eggs has substantially declined.

African countries have also experienced more frequent tropical storms and cyclones. Despite an overall decline in average annual rainfall, warmer air temperatures are causing more rain to be stored and then rapidly released. These heavier rains cause extensive flooding, soil erosion, crop loss, and the destruction of rural infrastructure.[39] Tropical storms have become increasingly frequent in eastern and southern Africa. The cyclones that ravaged Malawi, Mozambique, Tanzania, and Zimbabwe in the Spring of 2019 were among the strongest on record. Changes in temperature and moisture conditions also allow crop diseases and insect infestations to emerge in new areas.[40] East African countries are currently coping with the largest locust infestation on record.[41] The locusts, which rapidly reproduce after unusually heavy rains, are causing massive damage to food crops and rangelands. Locust swarms can travel 150 kilometers and consume as much as 400 million pounds of vegetation in a single day.[42] The increased incidence of Rift Valley Fever, a mosquito-borne viral disease that causes the loss of livestock, is also attributed to climate change.[43] Fall Armyworms, an invasive caterpillar that devastates maize fields, also has an expanded presence on the continent. Fisheries and aquaculture in Africa have been adversely impacted by changes induced by a warming climate, including reduced oxygen levels, acidification, and the spread of aquatic pathogens.[44]

Emergency Food Aid

Given the scope and severity of malnutrition throughout Africa, this region is prioritized in the allocation of international food aid. Nearly sixty percent of the WFP's annual budget is allocated to African countries. Much of this aid has been in the form of emergency disbursements to desperate communities across the continent. The distribution of food aid is frequently carried out under extremely hazardous conditions, with humanitarian workers placing their own lives in danger as they attempt to reach remote communities with the most urgent needs. Aid workers have been subjected to forced abductions, extortion, unauthorized roadblocks, harassment, and the seizure of goods. Some areas are completely inaccessible to humanitarian actors.

WFP has primary responsibility for coordinating the delivery of food aid among all UN agencies. The program manages the UN Humanitarian Air Service (UNHAS) which transports both humanitarian workers and food supplies. Food stocks are pre-positioned in strategic locations throughout the continent in order to quickly respond to emergencies. A logistics hub near the Port of Djibouti has four cargo silos with each silo capable of holding 10,000 metric tons of grain. These storage units allow WFP to dispatch humanitarian assistance to countries in the Horn of Africa and more broadly in the region. A quarter of all people that WFP assists worldwide live in countries supported by the Djibouti hub.[45] WFP also maintains storage and warehouse facilities in Tanzania.

Food aid is frequently provided in response to natural disasters. Recent droughts in the Sahel region have caused massive damage to agricultural production and left millions of people with little access to food and water. WFP's Sahel Shock Response program provides in-kind and cash-based transfers to drought-stricken communities in Burkina Faso, Chad, Mali, Mauritania, and Niger.[46] Children in these countries are regularly screened for signs of malnutrition and those children who fall below the average weight for their age are enrolled in supplemental feeding programs. Food distributions typically include daily portions of Plumpy' Sup, a fortified ready-to-use porridge that is specially designed for children showing signs of moderate acute malnutrition.

Countries in the Horn of Africa have also endured extended periods of drought in recent years. WFP is providing food aid to affected communities in parts of Djibouti, Ethiopia, Kenya, and Somalia.[47] Many of these communities are extremely hard to reach due to poor transportation infrastructure and high levels of insecurity. Because ground transportation is cut off to many of the worst-affected areas, WFP relies increasingly on air drops to deliver food aid. Drought has also endangered the food security of millions of people in Southern Africa. In-kind food aid and cash transfers have been distributed to at-risk communities in Botswana, Eswatini, Lesotho, Madagascar, Malawi, Namibia, and Zimbabwe.

As noted above, cyclones have occurred with greater frequency and intensity in recent years, especially in Eastern and Southern Africa. In March 2019, Tropical Cyclone Idai brought torrential rains and severe flooding to Madagascar, Malawi, Mozambique, and Zimbabwe. Just five weeks later Tropical Cyclone Kenneth battered the very same region. This was the first time on record that two cyclones had struck this region in a single season. The extent of destruction was catastrophic. Thousands of acres of farmland were ruined, along with roads, bridges, and other rural infrastructure, and millions of people were left without food, water, or shelter.

WFP coordinated the emergency response in the immediate aftermath of the cyclones. Drones were deployed to assess which areas had suffered the greatest damage. Food stocks, including beans, maize, peas, and fortified vegetable oil, had already been pre-positioned in mobile storage units, twenty tons of fortified biscuits were delivered by air from a WFP-managed depot in Dubai, and food was trucked in from neighboring countries. In-kind food aid was quickly disbursed to the most severely impacted areas. Because many of the roads and bridges in the region had been damaged, freight planes and specialized helicopters were used to deliver food, along with medicines, tents, and other humanitarian supplies. Two amphibious vehicles were also deployed to pass through flooded terrains. WFP delivered Supercereal Plus, a fortified porridge mix, to those people most at risk of malnutrition, including women who were pregnant or nursing and children under the age of five. When the emergency phase of the operation was completed, WFP continued to support affected populations in all four countries. Temporary medical centers were constructed to aid people who had contracted infectious diseases and food aid was provided to patients at treatment centers operated by Doctors without Borders.

WFP also delivers emergency food aid in response to multiple civil conflicts occurring throughout the region. Sudan has been the site of conflicts over water, forests, and rangelands between settled farmers and pastoralists for decades. Since declaring independence in 2011, South

Sudan has been in a state of continued conflict and sixty percent of all people are in need of emergency food aid. In Mali, a secessionist conflict that began in the northern regions of the country in 2012 and later spread to the central region, has caused large-scale population displacement. Three decades of clan-based warfare in Somalia, especially in southern and central parts of country, coupled with severe drought, has left nearly three million people food insecure. In northeast Nigeria, violence that began in 2009 in the states of Borno, Adamawa, and Yobe has now spread to Cameroon's far north, western Chad, and Southeast Niger. 2.5 million people in the Lake Chad region have been displaced and an estimated ten million people are in need of humanitarian assistance. Protracted armed conflict in the eastern and southern regions of the Central African Republic since 2014 has left nearly half of all people in the country food insecure. Despite a 2019 peace accord, militias operate in two-thirds of the country and sporadic violence continues. Three million people are in need of urgent humanitarian assistance. In the Democratic Republic of the Congo, armed conflict in eastern parts of the country, especially in northeast Ituri, North Kivu, South Kivu, and Tanganyika provinces, have raged for more than two decades. Much of the fighting is over access to arable land, water, and valuable raw materials. This is by far the largest humanitarian crisis in Africa, with sixteen million people severely food insecure and facing famine. Five million children are acutely malnourished.[48]

WFP provides emergency food to displaced and beleaguered populations in response to each of these conflicts.[49] The majority of the food and other urgently needed items are air-dropped to remote locations. UNHAS planes and helicopters transport emergency food supplies and humanitarian workers.[50] Portable survival kits, which include water containers, water purification tablets, oral rehydration salts, mosquito nets, and vegetable seeds are also distributed to the most critical regions of each country.[51] WFP also provides specialized nutritional products and supplemental feeding programs for women who are pregnant or nursing and for children who show signs of malnutrition.

Civil conflicts have caused millions of people to flee to neighboring countries.[52] Because people living in refugee camps are generally restricted from farming or earning income outside of the camps, they are almost completely dependent on food aid.[53] Refugee families typically receive a package that includes Supercereal Plus, maize, beans, pulses, fortified vegetable oil, and Iodized salt. Pregnant and nursing women, as well as children under five years of age, receive additional nutritional support, including micronutrient powders that are rich in vitamins and minerals.[54] Commodity vouchers, which are based on the size of each household, can be used to purchase pre-approved items in local shops, including sorghum, wheat flour, maize, rice, lentils, beans, and milk. Biometric registration ensures food aid reaches people with the most urgent needs.

Food aid is also distributed more generally to address the nutritional needs of children. This typically involves the distribution of specially prepared blends that are fortified with a combination of vitamins and proteins. In Malawi, children receive a nutritious porridge.[55] When the porridge is combined with fruit it ensures children consume all six food groups on a daily basis. In Somalia and Uganda, a porridge fortified with Iron and Vitamin C is provided to children showing signs of malnutrition. In Sudan, where more than eighty percent of children under five suffer from micronutrient deficiencies, WFP worked with a local company to create Vitamino, a micronutrient powder that contains fifteen essential vitamins and minerals. The powder, which is designed for children between six months and five years of age, can be sprinkled on food. In Ghana, children are provided GrowNut—a locally produced nutritional product. WFP also trains parents, guardians, and extension workers in a number of countries on the use of local ingredients to cook diversified and nutrient-dense meals.[56] In Niger, IFAD established nutritional improvement and recovery centers that offer practical sessions on care for malnourished children.[57] In Burundi, IFAD trained women in nutrition, health, and hygiene.[58]

WFP also supports school meal programs in most African countries.[59] The meals typically include cereals, such as maize or rice, as well as pulses and vegetables. Fortified flour and enriched vegetable oil are used in food preparation to address chronic needs, especially Vitamin A and Iron deficiencies. Food for school meals is purchased from local farmers whenever possible. Home Grown School Feeding (HGSF) programs have been established in Benin, Chad, the Democratic Republic of the Congo, Liberia, Nigeria and Zambia. In Burkina Faso, WFP supported Projet Lait which purchases a locally produced yogurt for the meals. Milk for the yogurt is supplied by small-scale cattle breeders. In Tunisia, WFP worked with the Ministry of Education to ensure smallholder farmers and rural food cooperatives were the primary suppliers for school meals. In

Madagascar, school gardens produce the vegetables and cassava that are included in the meals.

Technical assistance is also provided to local governments to strengthen their school meal programs. WFP worked with governments in Namibia, Rwanda, and Zambia to enhance public sector capacity to manage school meal programs. Initiatives in Benin and Tunisia raised the consistency, efficiency, and accountability of school meal programs. After managing school meals in Kenya for three decades, WFP recently transferred authority to the central government. WFP continues to provide technical assistance regarding safety and quality control standards. Training in nutrition, hygiene, and sanitation is provided to school cooks and teachers are encouraged to include information about healthy eating habits in their lesson plans.[60]

Agricultural Productivity

UN food agencies also provide broader assistance to countries throughout Africa, with much of this work focused on raising the productivity of small-scale farmers. This includes expanding access to equipment and quality seeds. Electronic voucher systems have been established in a number of countries that allow farmers to purchase agricultural inputs, including seeds and fertilizer, directly from designated agro-dealers.[61] In Niger, IFAD provided seeds and other inputs directly to farmers.[62] IFAD also partnered with the Africa Rice Center to develop New Rice for Africa (NERICA), a cross between drought-tolerant African and high-yielding Asian rice varieties. NERICA, which requires less water and is more resistant to insects, has substantially increased the yields of small and medium size farms. In Kenya and Tanzania, IFAD distributed new varieties of sorghum that were developed by the International Crops Research Institute for the Semi-Arid Tropics. These seeds are more tolerate of heat and drought.

FAO has also provided high yield and nutritionally fortified seeds to African farmers. A program in Zimbabwe worked with local extension officers to promote the cultivation of maize fortified with Vitamin A and Iron and sugar beans fortified with Iron and Zinc. FAO also ensured small-scale farmers had access to high-yield sorghum, cowpea, and millet seeds. Community-based seed production and distribution centers were established in a number of districts throughout the country. FAO also provided drought resistant seeds to farmers in Madagascar, Somalia, and

Sudan. In the Central African Republic, Nigeria, and Rwanda, improved seeds were distributed for maize, beans, soya, and potatoes. Farmer Field Schools throughout the continent include instruction on the use of nutritionally fortified seeds. FAO also works with African governments to ensure local ownership and control of new seed varieties. This included helping to certify the seeds of smallholder farmers in Angola and establishing regulatory frameworks for bio-fortified food crops in the Democratic Republic of the Congo and Sudan. In Nigeria, FAO worked with the National Agricultural Seeds Council to strengthen community-based seed production and ownership. Seed processing and certification centers are supported in a number of additional countries in the region.

Reducing post-harvest losses has also been a core objective of international assistance programs. In Rwanda, Sudan, Tanzania, and Zambia, WFP provides farmers associations with hermetically sealed Polyethylene bags that better preserve harvested grains. Farmers are also given access to Polyvinyl Chloride storage silos. Because the silos are water resistant, pest proof, and highly durable, grains are preserved without a need to add chemicals. In Mozambique, FAO supported smallholder farmers construct silos with locally available materials and technology. Humidity-controlled warehouses were built in Liberia to store cocoa beans during the wet season when roads are often impassable. In the Republic of the Congo, new technologies were introduced to improve food processing and storage.

Food assistance has also supported the expansion of irrigation systems. As noted above, rainfall in many parts of Africa is extremely variable in amount, intensity, and distribution. Only five percent of arable land on the continent has some form of water management. IFAD has played a lead role in supporting the introduction of small-scale irrigation systems.[63] In Cote d'Ivoire, Eritrea, Ethiopia, Eswatini, Madagascar, Mali, Niger, Rwanda, and Zimbabwe, IFAD implemented irrigation schemes that are more resilient to climate variation. IFAD has also funded spate irrigation systems in a number of countries. Because spate irrigation stores water in different layers of soil and in shallow aquifers, it is more economical than storing water in surface reservoirs. In Mauritania and Morocco, IFAD introduced solar-powered water pumps that are more efficient in their use of water. Water points and reservoirs were rehabilitated in the Gambia and Tunisia.[64] FAO has also been engaged in this area, especially in North Africa. In Egypt, FAO worked with the Ministry of Agriculture to develop solar-powered water-lifting technologies that could be used in the Nile Delta. FAO also helped introduce irrigation systems in Morocco that improve water storage and recharge.

The provision of extension services has been a central component of international assistance. FAO plays a lead role in disseminating information on agricultural methods and technologies. Farmers Field Schools introduce improved agricultural practices such as the consociation of maize and pulses, the use of organic compounds, enhanced pest management, and disease control. In Madagascar, training in crop diversification allows farmers to undertake two harvests per year, increasing both food availability and rural incomes. IFAD trained Egyptian farmers in agricultural practices and technologies to increase the production of beans, onions, and garlic.[65] FAO also worked to develop urban and peri-urban gardens in the Democratic Republic of the Congo.

Fish production is also supported. In the Democratic Republic of the Congo, an IFAD program that provided training in fish culture and pond maintenance helped double the production of tilapia. IFAD also introduced improved techniques for aquaculture and fish processing in Mozambique, the Republic of the Congo, and Sudan. Fishers were trained in the use of more efficient ovens for drying and smoking. In Burundi and Cote d'Ivoire, fishing communities were provided with elevated driers to speed fish processing. Because fish products can now be transported more easily both inland and across borders, the nutritional well-being of communities that are located far from any source of fresh fish has improved. In the Gambia, FAO helped improve fish processing and waste management.

Strengthening the land rights of poor farmers, forest dwellers, fishing communities, pastoralists, and indigenous peoples is also a core objective. Much of this work involves land use mapping to document group rights to agricultural lands, rangelands, forests, and artisanal fishing waters. In Madagascar, IFAD helped establish local land offices that issue the identity cards needed to register land ownership. Work was also undertaken to secure secondary land rights for landless farmers.[66] IFAD also aided farmers in Ethiopia, Sudan, and Tanzania secure their rights to communal lands.[67] In Burundi, IFAD's Transitional Program of Post-Conflict Reconstruction informed small-scale farmers of the laws governing land ownership and provided legal support for making land claims. In neighboring Rwanda, IFAD strengthened the capacity of community groups to negotiate and resolve land disputes.[68] A program in Mozambique taught functional literacy to peasant farmers so they could read and negotiate land contracts.[69] FAO has also worked to strengthen the land rights of poor communities. In Coit d'Ivoire and Tanzania, FAO promoted the peaceful management of land disputes through land demarcation processes and the issuance of property titles. FAO helped people in the Democratic Republic of the Congo gain legal access to land for the cultivation of urban gardens. FAO also aided the development of national policies in Sierra Leone that help secure tenure rights for small-scale farmers. This included preparation of the National Land Policy that mandated recognizing communal tenure rights.

UN food agencies have also supported farmers associations and cooperatives in a number of African countries. These organizations are viewed as essential for defending the legal rights of the rural poor and increasing access to public services. IFAD has played the lead role in strengthening the institutional capacities of farmers organizations, improving their services to members, and increasing their influence in the construction of agricultural policies.[70] In Benin, Madagascar, Mali, Mauritania, and Niger, IFAD provided training and equipment to strengthen the institutional capacities of farmers associations, in Gambia, Guinea, and the Republic of Congo, IFAD helped increase the participation of rural organizations in local and national planning processes, and in Rwanda, IFAD trained members of coffee cooperatives to more effectively advance their rights with public sector actors. IFAD trained members of Tanzanian cooperatives in record keeping, group governance, and product quality.[71]

Rural Development

Rural development initiatives have emphasized the expansion of non-agriculture enterprises. The Purchase-for-Progress (P4P) initiative, which is co-sponsored by WFP and FAO, provides training in a number of African countries on the process for initiating small handicrafts and other income-generating activities. Women have been the primary beneficiaries of this initiative. The profits generated from these enterprises are often reinvested to expand operations. IFAD has also provided technical and financial support for the development of agropastoral products.

Expanding access to financial services is integral to rural development initiatives. Because financial services are limited in rural areas, agricultural or small business investments often require borrowing from local lenders at excessive interest rates. When rural people have access to low cost credit, they are in a stronger position to invest in their farms and enterprises. IFAD has worked to expand financial services in a number of African countries.[72] Its Rural Finance Institution Building Program (RUFIN) supports community-based financial services that are designed to meet the needs of rural communities. IFAD helped strengthen microfinance institutions and financial cooperatives in Benin, Burundi, Egypt, Morocco, Nigeria, and Sudan. In Ethiopia, IFAD provided capacity building training for members of rural savings and credit cooperatives.[73] IFAD also worked with Kenyan banks to provide financial services to smallholder farmers, herders, fishers, and rural cooperatives. A range of new financial products were introduced, including savings and remittance services, community infrastructures loans, and value-chain financing.[74] IFAD supported the Women Finance Trust, a microfinance institution that extends loans to low-income women seeking to establish small enterprises. In Zambia, IFAD provided technical assistance to help reform the institutional and regulatory environment for rural finance. These reforms enabled small-scale enterprises to access credit without needing land as collateral.[75] Smallholder farmers and fishers in Mozambique were aided in the organization of self-managed financial associations. In Ethiopia, Lesotho, and Togo, IFAD assisted grassroots institutions tailor their financial products to the needs of small and medium size enterprises. IFAD supported development of a cashless credit model in Ghana that enables farmers to purchase seeds, fertilizers, and other agricultural inputs directly from service providers. In Chad, a joint IFAD-FAO project provided finance to women for the purchase of agricultural land.

The expansion of insurance products in rural areas has also been prioritized. WFP supported a program in Zimbabwe where farmers received weather index insurance that provides protection from drought. Farmers are reimbursed when rainfall drops to levels that correspond with drought conditions. In Ethiopia, Malawi, Senegal, and Zambia, WFP partnered with Oxfam to provide climate risk insurance to small-scale farmers. Recipients are required to engage in risk reduction activities in their communities that lessen the likelihood of weather-related losses.[76]

International assistance also aids small-scale farmers sell their commodities on broader markets. The WFP's Market Access Initiative and Farm to Market Alliance (FtMA) are designed to help African farmers receive fair contracts before planting and access commercial markets for their crops. WFP also finances the building of warehouses to store grain that allows farmers to bargain for better prices in commercial markets. In Mauritania, for example, cereal banks were established so farmers can store produce until prices are higher.[77] In Burundi, IFAD financed the construction of warehouses and rice storage hangers equipped with hulling and whiting machines. Warehouses in Sierra Leone were weather-proofed to improve product drying and storage capacity. IFAD supported farmers associations in the Central African Republic, Cote d'Ivoire, and the Democratic Republic of the Congo in the marketing of their agricultural products.[78] The Purchase-for-Progress initiative in Madagascar established a system for linking farmers to wholesale markets in larger towns. IFAD's Commodity Value Chain Development Support Project in Cameroon aided farmers in the marketing of rice and onions. IFAD also helped build agricultural value chains in Morocco and Nigeria that enabled small-scale farmers to connect with markets.[79] Road building projects that linked farms to markets were financed in Liberia, the Gambia, Guinea, Morocco, Niger, and Rwanda.[80]

Environmental Preservation

External assistance is also allocated to promote the sustainable use of natural resources. The Conservation Agriculture in Africa initiative, which is jointly sponsored by FAO and IFAD, preserves the soil resource base of countries throughout the continent.[81] Emphasis is placed on minimal soil disturbance, permanent soil cover, inter-cropping, crop rotation, and agroforestry.[82] FAO has also supported a soil fertility initiative in twenty eastern and southern African countries where technical specialists provide training in land management practices that restore soil functions and maintain land productivity. The FAO's Action Against Desertification initiative assists local communities in a number of countries in the management and restoration of croplands.[83] Farmer Field Schools (FFS) have also incorporated instruction on the prevention of land degradation and soil erosion into their workshops.[84] Food-for-Assets projects in Ethiopia, Kenya, and Niger supported community improvement projects aimed at restoring degraded land. In Lesotho, FAO supported brush control, stone-line construction, and the re-seeding of rangelands while in Burkina Faso, Burundi, Morocco, and Namibia techniques were introduced to reduce water evaporation and improve soil health. The FAO's Integrated Production and Pest Management Program aids farmers transition from the use of synthetic pesticides and fertilizers to organic methods that are less harmful to soils.[85] A project in Mali provided biodigesters that produce organic fertilizers.[86] FAO also works with regional governments to increase the capacity of local officials in soil preservation and sustainable land management.[87]

The UN food agencies also support water preservation projects in Africa. The FAO's Water Use Efficiency (WUE) instrument, which measures the ratio between effective water use and actual water withdrawal, identifies areas where water loss is due to drainage, seepage, and non-productive evaporation. Smallholder farmers in West Africa and the Sahel were trained in the use of this instrument.[88] FAO also aided development of a Master Plan for Water Resources Management on the Senegal River.[89] Technical assistance to the Egyptian government aided the formulation of a national policy on the sustainable use of wastewater in agriculture. Marine resources management projects have also been introduced in Cabo Verde, Cote d'Ivoire, and Senegal. IFAD has also supported sustainable water preservation and management projects. An IFAD project in Eritrea aided the building water points, diversion of rivers, and water harvesting for supplemental irrigation. In Rwanda, IFAD helped protect watershed areas and install rooftop rain collectors. A project in Niger that restored degraded landscapes and watersheds helped improve soil fertility, water filtration, and replenishment of underground water supplies.[90] Women in Eswatini were trained in the construction of water harvesting tanks. Water from the tanks is now used to grow vegetables for home consumption and sale in local markets. In Chad, IFAD promoted drainage and rainwater collection methods to increase the availability of water for pastoral communities.[91] An IFAD project in Djibouti built or repaired fifty community water tanks, expanding the water storage capacity of pastoral families. A similar project in Senegal contributed to the enhanced management and conservation of water resources. IFAD projects to rehabilitate marshlands, watersheds, and mangroves in Burundi, the Democratic Republic of the Congo, and the Gambia aided nutrient and sediment retention and water recharge.

Forest preservation is also a core objective of multilateral assistance. Much of this work focuses on increasing public sector capacity for sustainable forest management. FAO worked with public officials in a number of countries to design and implement national monitoring, reporting, and verification (MRV) systems that improve forest management. FAO also aided the Economic Community of West African States (ECOWAS) in the development of a Convergence Plan for the Sustainable Management and Utilization for Forest Ecosystems in West Africa. Participating countries are now in a stronger position to coordinate and harmonize management of the region's forest resources. A transfrontier conservation area for forest reserves was established between Cote d'Ivoire and Ghana. Technical assistance in mapping the forest of Tanzania helped local officials develop sustainable forest management plans and Farmer Field Schools in Burundi and Kenya trained farmers on viable ways to engage in income-generating activities while simultaneously protecting forest resources.

Lastly, UN food agencies have addressed the threats posed by climate change. Farmer Field Schools introduce Climate Smart Agricultural practices to reduce the production of greenhouse gas emissions. FAO is also working to raise organic matter in soil and other forms of biomass as a means of increasing carbon sequestration. Resources have been allocated for renewable energy projects, such as the development of biogas systems and photovoltaic cells, to reduce the use of fossil fuels. Fuel-efficient stoves have also been distributed to lessen the need for firewood.[92] A joint FAO—World Bank study identified areas in Africa's coastal zones that are vulnerable to climate change and proposed adaptation measures to protect fisheries. FAO also worked with the Rwanda government to better manage the Yantze River. Because increased flooding routinely washes away valuable soil in areas near the river, bamboo trees were planted to help stabilize the riverbanks and reduce soil loss.

International assistance has strengthened public sector capacities to manage climate fluctuations and extreme weather events. FAO works with governments to integrate climate change adaptation strategies into agricultural and fisheries development initiatives. This includes building food security monitoring systems, early warning systems, and emergency response capabilities. The FAO's Early Warning Early Action (EWEA) program, which draws upon a range of climate and seasonality data, helps establish early warning thresholds. Once these thresholds are reached, FAO works with local governments to implement Early Action Plans. In Madagascar and Sudan, early warning systems were developed in areas that are especially vulnerable to natural disasters. A comprehensive monitoring system was established in Egypt to forecast the impact of sea level rise on soil and groundwater in the Nile Delta. In Ethiopia, FAO uses drones to assess climate conditions in remote parts of the country. The FAO's regional initiatives in the Sahel and the Horn of Africa have strengthened regulatory frameworks for disaster risk reduction and crisis management. A Special Fund for Emergency and Rehabilitation Activities was established to aid countries in these areas. In the Gambia and Sudan, climate-based information provided by IFAD was incorporated into the early response systems that help farmers protect their harvests. WFP partnered with Oxfam to support the R4 Rural Resilience Initiative. This initiative, which has been implemented in Ethiopia, Malawi, Senegal, and Zambia, enables vulnerable rural families to increase their food and income security by managing climate-related risks.[93] WFP also worked with farmers in Egypt to develop early warning alerts for extreme weather events. The alerts reduced crop losses of wheat, sorghum, and maize.[94]

Conclusion

Africa has the highest rates of hunger and malnutrition of all world regions. Food insecurity, which impacts half of all people in the region, is due to multiple factors. Per capita incomes are three times lower than other regions of the developing world. Underinvestment in agriculture contributes to African farmers having the lowest food output per hectare of any world region. Large-scale land acquisitions have displaced smallholder farmers and these lands are now used to produce crops for export rather than for local consumption. Resources that could have been invested in social protection programs, agricultural productivity, or rural development are diverted for the personal benefit of political elites. Civil conflicts cause massive damage to crops, livestock, and rural infrastructure and millions of people have been forced to flee to other parts of their country or to neighboring countries. Population growth and climatic changes are placing enormous stress on the resources needed for sustainable food production.

African countries are major recipients of emergency food aid, with more than half of the World Food Programme's annual budget allocated to this region. Much of this aid supports communities adversely impacted by drought and other natural hazards, especially in the Sahel and Horn of Africa as well as countries in southeastern and southern Africa. Emergency food aid is also distributed to millions of people displaced by conflict and living in refugee camps. Broader food assistance is provided to support agricultural development and rural transformation. The provision of tools, quality seeds, storage equipment, irrigation systems, financial services, and improved infrastructure helps increase agricultural productivity and household incomes in rural areas. External assistance is also allocated to promote the sustainable use of natural resources and address the adverse consequences of climate change.

Given the tragically high levels of hunger and malnutrition in Africa, continued food aid will be essential for the foreseeable future. The millions of people who have lost their homes, land, and productive assets as a result of natural hazards or civil conflicts are almost entirely dependent on humanitarian aid. These needs will not subside until communal violence declines and the region's natural resources are rehabilitated. Food assistance can contribute to both of these objectives. Greater resources must be allocated to improve the productivity of small-scale farmers and foster rural development. Pressure can be asserted on public officials to match these resource allocations and recommit to the food security promises made in regional declarations. Food assistance is also needed to rehabilitate degraded lands, preserve freshwater resources, protect forest areas, and rebuild inland and coastal fisheries.

Notes

1. The African continent contains 54% of the world's Cobalt reserves, 32% of Bauxite, 64% of Platinum, 90% of Copper, 80% of Coltan, 55% of Diamonds, 34% of Manganese, 81% of Chromium, and 25% of Gold, as well as significant deposits of Titanium, Uranium, Silver, Chromite, Phosphates, Vanadium, Iron Ore, and Nickel.
2. The Global Hunger Index 2019 lists thirty-three African countries with GHI scores that are either "serious" or "alarming." The GHI score for the Central African Republic is considered "extremely alarming." Concern Worldwide and Welthungerhilfe 2019.
3. Food and Agriculture Organization 2020i, p. 6.
4. Food and Agriculture Organization 2020i, p. 6.
5. Akombi et al. 2017 draw on demographic and health surveys to outline child malnutrition in Sub-Saharan Africa.
6. Food and Agriculture Organization 2020i, pp. 10, 16.
7. Conceicão et al. 2016 and Wambogo et al. 2018 offer analyses of the broad parameters of food insecurity in Africa.
8. Poverty rates are three times higher for people living in the countryside than for people living in cities. Deininger et al. 2017 examine the plight of small-scale farmers in Africa, especially regarding access to land.
9. Food and Agriculture Organization 2019b, p. 98.

10. Migration is also common within rural areas. In the vast Sahel region, for example, large numbers of people migrate from one area to the next in search of land and pasturage.
11. The causes and consequences of ethnic conflict in Africa have been extensively studied. See especially Nasong'o (ed.) 2016, Sangmpan 2017, Roessler 2016, du Toit (ed.) 2019, McCauley 2017, Chuku (ed.) 2015, and Udogu 2018.
12. Approximately 110 million women of reproductive age in Africa suffer from Iron-Deficient Aneamia. This constitutes more than a third of all women of reproductive age in the region. FAO 2020i, p. 32. Analysis of gender inequality in Africa can be found in Achebe and Robertson (eds.) 2019, Wane 2019, Okech (ed.) 2020, Konte and Tirivayi (eds.) 2020, Dzanku 2019, and Quisumbing et al. (eds.) 2019.
13. Food and Agriculture Organization 2020i, p. 49.
14. Food and Agriculture Organization 2020i, p. 49.
15. African Union 2001a.
16. African Union 2001b.
17. African Union 2003.
18. This declaration is officially the *2014 Malabo Declaration on Accelerated Agricultural Growth and Transformation for Shared Prosperity and Improved Livelihoods*. African Union 2014. The declaration was endorsed at the 2014 African Union Summit in Malabo, Equatorial Guinea. A biennial Agricultural Review Process was established to monitor progress toward achieving the goals of the Malabo Declaration.
19. African Union 2015b.
20. African Union 2015a.
21. It is important to recognize that some African countries, including Burkina Faso, Ethiopia, Malawi, Mozambique, and Niger, have made substantial public investments in their agricultural sectors.
22. African countries that have entered into transnational land agreements with foreign governments and agribusinesses include Angola, Cameroon, the Democratic Republic of the Congo, Ethiopia, Kenya, Madagascar, Malawi, Mali, Mozambique, Somalia, Sudan, Tanzania, and Zambia.
23. For further review of the impact of large-scale land acquisitions on food insecurity in Africa see Allan et al. (eds.) 2013, Cotula 2013, and Nhamo and Chekwoti (eds.) 2014.
24. A number of scholars have examined the problem of corruption in Africa. Among the most recent works include Okonjo-Iweala 2018, Amundsen (ed.) 2019, Munyai 2020, Tobias 2019, Hope 2017, Fombad and Steytler 2020, Agang et al. 2019, and Yacob-Haliso et al. (eds.) 2018.
25. The 2019 Corruption Perceptions Index lists twenty-two African countries among the forty countries with the lowest CPI scores. The following five countries are among the ten countries with the lowest CPI scores:

Equatorial Guinea, Libya, Somalia, South Sudan, and Sudan. Transparency International 2019.

26. Schubert et al. (eds.) 2018, Besada ed. 2016, and Mailey 2017 consider the adverse impacts of natural resource wealth on development outcomes in Sub-Saharan Africa.
27. The relationship between civil conflict and food insecurity in Africa is explored by Uchendu 2018. See also Food Security Information Network 2020, p. 3.
28. More than half of global population growth between 2020 and 2050 is expected to take place in Africa.
29. Africa has twenty percent of the world's land area and accounts for approximately seventeen percent of global population.
30. See Darkoh and Rwomire (eds.) 2018 and Paquet 2017 for analyses of the relationship between demographic pressures and environmental decline in Africa.
31. The drylands of Africa, which cover much of the continent, exhibit the most extensive degradation. World Resources Institute, 2018, p. 25. The United Nations University (UNU) Institute for Natural Resources of Africa estimates that, if current trends of soil degradation continue, the continent will only be able to feed twenty-five percent of its population by 2025.
32. Much of the land degradation taking place in Africa is in the vast Sahel belt which stretches from Mauritania to Sudan.
33. See Aleman et al. 2018, Djenontin et al. 2018 and Ordway et al. 2017 for documentation of forest loss in Sub-Saharan Africa.
34. As FAO notes, the African continent is particularly vulnerable to the effects of climate change due to a heavy reliance on climate-sensitive activities and high levels of food insecurity. Food and Agriculture Organization 2019e, p. 52. The impact of climate change on social and economic conditions in Africa has been extensively studied. See especially Zinyengere et al. (eds.) 2017, Matondo et al. (eds.) 2017, Filho (ed.) 2017, Kuwornu (ed.) 2018, Perkins (ed.) 2015, Hope (ed.) 2016, Berck et al. (eds.) 2018 and Tumushabe 2018.
35. Food and Agriculture Organization 2019e, p. 52.
36. Food and Agriculture Organization 2019e, p. 52.
37. Food and Agriculture Organization 2018c, p. 65. In some East African countries, most notably Ethiopia, Kenya, Burundi, and Tanzania, annual rainfall has dropped approximately fifteen percent since 2000.
38. Drought has been especially destructive in Eswatini, Lesotho, Madagascar, Malawi, Mozambique, Namibia, South Africa, Uganda, and Zimbabwe.
39. Food and Agriculture Organization 2018c, p. 65.
40. Food and Agriculture Organization 2019e, p. 54.

41. The countries most severely impacted by the current locust infestation include Djibouti, Eritrea, Ethiopia, Kenya, Somalia, South Sudan, Sudan, Tanzania, and Uganda.
42. The Nairobi-based Climate Prediction and Application Center views climate change as at least partially responsible for the locust outbreak in East Africa. The increased spread of vector-borne diseases such as Dengue, Malaria, and Schistosomiasis is also attributed to climatic changes. Food and Agriculture Organization 2018c, p. 77.
43. Food and Agriculture Organization 2018c, p. 72.
44. Food and Agriculture Organization 2019e, p. 53.
45. The Djibouti port is especially critical for emergency operations to Ethiopia, Somalia, and South Sudan.
46. World Food Programme 2019a, p. 42.
47. World Food Programme 2019a, p. 42.
48. The spread of disease has further jeopardized food security in the Democratic Republic of the Congo. The country has recently experienced the worst Ebola outbreak in its history. World Food Programme 2019a, p. 43.
49. World Food Programme 2019a, pp. 46–49.
50. World Food Programme 2018c, p. 52.
51. Development of the survival kits was supported by FAO, the International Organization for Migration (IOM), UNICEF, and the International Rescue Committee (IRC).
52. At present, an extraordinary number of people in Africa have fled to neighboring countries. This includes, but is not limited to, Nigerian refugees in Cameroon, Chad and Niger; South Sudanese refugees in the Democratic Republic of the Congo, Uganda, Kenya, Sudan, Ethiopia, and the Central African Republic; Somali refugees in Kenya and Ethiopia; Eritrean refugees in Djibouti and Kenya; Central African Republic refugees in the Republic of the Congo, the Democratic Republic of the Congo, and Cameroon; Malian refugees in Burkina Faso; Congolese refugees in Angola, Rwanda, Burundi, Malawi, Tanzania, and Zimbabwe; and Burundian refugees in the Democratic Republic of the Congo, Rwanda, Tanzania, Uganda, and Zimbabwe.
53. WFP coordinates its support for refugees with the United Nations High Commission for Refugees.
54. Food aid is also provided more generally to pregnant and nursing women in Africa. The WFP's Mother and Child Health Nutrition Program is active in a number of countries where the risk of malnutrition is high. WFP frequently partners with United Nations Children's Fund (UNICEF) to provide nutritional support for new mothers.
55. The porridge includes a starchy food such as potatoes, cassava, or maize flour, a high protein food such as beans, groundnut flour, fish powder, or

goatmilk, a vegetable such as pumpkin or squash, and a fat such as oil or avocado.

56. The largest nutritional training programs provided by WFP have been in Eritrea, Madagascar, Mozambique, and Zambia. WFP also distributes circumference tapes to community groups in order to monitor the nutritional well-being of children.
57. International Fund for Agricultural Development 2019a, p. 20.
58. International Fund for Agricultural Development 2019a, p. 11.
59. The largest school meal programs sponsored by WFP have been in Benin, Burkina Faso, Cote d'Ivoire, Madagascar, Nigeria, Rwanda, Sudan, and Togo.
60. In Kenya, Senegal, and Zambia, WFP provided training in food preparation, storage, and quality control to school cooks and canteen managers.
61. International Fund for Agricultural Development 2018d, p. 9.
62. International Fund for Agricultural Development 2018d, p. 17.
63. International Fund for Agricultural Development 2018d, p. 17.
64. International Fund for Agricultural Development 2019a, pp. 17, 21.
65. International Fund for Agricultural Development 2018d, p. 51.
66. International Fund for Agricultural Development 2019c, p. 43. Secondary land rights allow farmers to cultivate lands that they do not own for part of the year and retain the proceeds of their labor.
67. International Fund for Agricultural Development 2019a, p. 17.
68. International Fund for Agricultural Development 2019c, p. 43.
69. International Fund for Agricultural Development 2018d, p. 8.
70. International Fund for Agricultural Development 2019a, p. 38.
71. International Fund for Agricultural Development 2019a, p. 12.
72. IFAD has been most active in developing financial services for rural communities in Benin, Burundi, Djibouti, Eswatini, Guinea, Mozambique, and Zambia.
73. International Fund for Agricultural Development 2019a, p. 11.
74. International Fund for Agricultural Development 2018d, p. 8.
75. International Fund for Agricultural Development 2018d, p. 8.
76. Food and Agriculture Organization 2018c, p. 109.
77. International Fund for Agricultural Development 2018d, p. 17.
78. Similar IFAD programs assisted small-scale farmers in the processing and marketing of their products in Burundi, Chad, the Democratic Republic of Congo, Gambia, Ghana, Kenya, Mozambique, and the Republic of Congo.
79. International Fund for Agricultural Development 2018d, p. 14.
80. See International Fund for Agricultural Development 2019c, p. 43; International Fund for Agricultural Development 2019a, p. 21; and International Fund for Agricultural Development 2018d, p. 17 for description of IFAD's efforts to expand market access for small-scale farmers in Africa.

81. Tambo and Mockshell 2018.
82. Conservation Agriculture has been most extensively introduced in Eritrea, Eswatini, Ethiopia, Kenya, Lesotho, Malawi, Rwanda, Sudan, Uganda, Zambia, and Zimbabwe. Because Conservation Agriculture is more labor-intensive than conventional methods, FAO frequently provides mechanical planters to increase incentives for farmers to adopt these practices.
83. The Action Against Desertification initiative has sponsored activities in Burkina Faso, Ethiopia, Gambia, Mali, Niger, Nigeria, and Senegal. FAO is also supporting the Great Green Wall for the Sahara and the Sahel Initiative, which is designed to combat land degradation and desertification in these areas.
84. The FAO's sustainable land management programs in Africa often draw upon resources from the Global Environmental Fund (GEF).
85. The Integrated Production and Pest Management Program has been implemented in Benin, Burkina Faso, Guinea, Mali, Mauritania, Niger, Rwanda, Senegal, Tanzania, and Zambia.
86. Biodigesters also convert organic waste into biogas, a fuel that can be used to power stoves and other household appliances.
87. IFAD has financed efforts to restore degraded lands in East Africa and the Sahel.
88. This project focused on aiding farmers in Cote d'Ivoire, Gambia, Mali, and Niger.
89. FAO supported similar water management projects in Ethiopia, Madagascar, and Rwanda.
90. International Fund for Agricultural Development 2018d, p. 17.
91. International Fund for Agricultural Development 2019c, p. 60.
92. Because fuel-efficient stoves produce less smoke than traditional fires, their introduction helps reduce respiratory illnesses.
93. Food and Agriculture Organization 2019e, p. 57.
94. Food and Agriculture Organization 2018c, p. 102.

CHAPTER 5

The Middle East

Near the end of the twentieth century, most Middle Eastern countries were close to achieving universal food security. Malnutrition rates had fallen throughout much of the region and extreme hunger was rare. Unfortunately, this progress was not sustained over the course of the past three decades and food insecurity has risen dramatically in many of these countries. Much of this reversal is due to protracted civil conflicts that have caused widespread damage to agricultural production, disrupted food distribution systems, destroyed rural infrastructure, and displaced millions of people. 120 million people in the region are now either moderately or severely food insecure.

This chapter begins with a broad outline of food insecurity in the Middle East and then turns to the central causes of hunger and malnutrition. Although it would be difficult to overstate the catastrophic impact of civil conflict, a number of other factors contribute to food insecurity in the region. The latter part of the chapter reviews multilateral efforts to meet the nutritional needs of poor communities. While the provision of emergency food aid to besieged populations in conflict zones and refugee camps currently constitutes the largest part of these efforts, UN agencies have also worked to promote agricultural and rural development, as well as preserve the land, water, and other natural resources needed for sustainable food production.

F. Adams, *The Right to Food*,
https://doi.org/10.1007/978-3-030-60255-0_5

Regional Context

There is little consensus regarding the precise boundaries of the Middle East. In fact, the term "Middle East" only came into common usage in the early twentieth century and remains a contested term for the region today.[1] Many of the countries in this region, which stretches from the eastern boundary of Europe to the western boundary of Asia, were established as British and French mandates following the collapse of the Ottoman Empire at the end of the First World War. For the purposes of this volume, the Middle East will include the countries bounded by the Mediterranean and Red Seas to the west, the Black and Caspian Seas to the north, and the Arabian Sea to the south and east. The region thus includes the countries of the Levant (Israel, Jordan, Lebanon, the Palestinian Territories, and Syria), the Arabian Peninsula (Kuwait, Oman, Saudi Arabia, and Yemen), the Persian Gulf (Bahrain, Qatar, and the United Arab Emirates), Asia Minor (Turkey), Mesopotamia (Iraq), and Persia (Iran).

Economic conditions vary tremendously across the Middle East. The petroleum exporting countries of the Arabian Peninsula and Persian Gulf have some of the highest per capita incomes in the world.[2] The enormous revenues generated from hydrocarbons place these countries in a strong position to meet the basic needs of their citizens and food security is virtually guaranteed. It is important to note, however, that these countries constitute just fifteen percent of the total population of the Middle East. Residents of other countries in the region are not nearly as fortunate. Approximately thirty percent of all people outside of the Arabian Peninsula and Persian Gulf are food insecure and malnutrition rates have doubled in the past twenty years.[3] Iran, Jordan, Lebanon, the Palestinian Territories, and Turkey have serious levels of food insecurity while Syria, Yemen, and large parts of Iraq are experiencing dire humanitarian emergencies.[4] Approximately sixteen million children under five in the Middle East suffer from acute malnutrition and childhood micronutrient deficiencies are common. Nearly a quarter of all children under five (ten million children) are stunted and eight percent of children under five (3.5 million children) are wasted.[5]

Causes of Food Insecurity

Food insecurity in the Middle East is the product of multiple forces. Outside of the petroleum exporting countries, forty percent of the region's people are impoverished and struggle to meet their nutritional needs. Middle Eastern countries are highly dependent on food imports, with at least half of all food consumed being produced outside of the region.[6] Poor communities are thus highly vulnerable to disruptions in world grain supplies and price fluctuations.[7] Rising demand for food products from other regions of the world (especially maize, soybeans, wheat, and meat) have caused significant price increases in the Middle East. The distribution of income and wealth is highly unequal with most countries characterized by a wealthy elite, relatively small middle class, and large underclass. About sixty percent of total income accrues to the top ten percent of the population. Minority ethnic and religious groups generally endure higher levels of poverty and food insecurity.[8] The region is comprised of a diverse range of group identities that reflect different languages, religions, and shared histories.

Gender inequalities also contribute to food insecurity in the Middle East.[9] Despite entrenched and systematic patriarchy throughout the region, it is important to recognize that women have made some advances in recent years and their overall physical wellbeing compares favorably to women in other regions of the developing world. Access to health care and education, for example, is largely equal to that of men in most countries. However, strict cultural and religious traditions discourage women from working outside of the home or having male colleagues. Middle Eastern countries have the lowest rates of female labor force participation in the world. Moreover, because "guardianship" rules in a number of countries relegate women to being the legal dependents of male relatives, most wealth is in the hands of men. With less access to income or property, women endure higher levels of food insecurity than men.

The petroleum exporting countries of the Arabian Peninsula and Persian Gulf attract millions of laborers from poorer countries in the Middle East and from outside of the region, especially from countries in South and Southeast Asia. Foreign workers constitute a significant percentage of the total population of host countries and even outnumber national citizens in some cases.[10] These migrant workers, who are largely excluded from social protection programs, are regulated by the *kafala* system. Under this system, workers receive entry visas, residence permits, and work permits through sponsorship by citizens, organizations, or corporations. The ability to change jobs or move elsewhere in the country is highly restricted. With limited income and no real mobility, migrant workers endure difficult living conditions and chronic food insecurity.

Resource allocations generally favor urban and coastal centers, with little public sector investment directed toward agrarian or rural development.[11] Although just forty percent of the region's people live in rural areas, they constitute seventy percent of all impoverished people. Rural areas have less access to health care, education, and other public services.[12] Agricultural productivity is far below global averages and food production does not meet rising demand. As noted above, a number of countries, especially in the Persian Gulf, are highly dependent on food imports to meet their nutritional needs. Some countries have purchased or leased land abroad to grow food that is returned for domestic consumption.[13]

Food insecurity can also be linked to public sector corruption.[14] The petroleum exporting countries of the Arabian Peninsula and Persian Gulf exhibit many of the characteristics associated with the resource curse.[15] Petroleum wealth has led to the development of rentier states, with governments relying almost exclusively on the revenues generated from extractive industries. The Middle East has two-thirds of the world's known petroleum reserves. Ruling families control much of the petroleum revenues with few limitations on the accumulation of personal wealth. Public access to information regarding government revenues, budgets, and expenditures is highly restricted. Resources that could be used for social protection programs or productive investments are often diverted to overseas bank accounts or used to fund the extravagant lifestyles of a privileged elite. Even countries that do not have large export earnings are plagued by high levels of public sector corruption. Because democratic institutions and individual rights are generally weak, government officials exercise considerable discretion over the use of public resources. Military budgets are almost completely exempted from public scrutiny. The oversight agencies and judicial institutions that do exist are largely ineffective in combatting corruption and public sector institutions have broken down almost completely in countries experiencing civil conflict.

Conflict is a major cause of hunger and malnutrition in the Middle East. While the region has been at the crossroads of foreign invasion and political violence for centuries, the wars, insurrections, and separatist movements that have emerged over the course of the past three decades have caused human suffering at levels rarely seen in the past. Military intervention by outside powers has greatly escalated violence, destruction, and displacement in the region. Conflicts have caused extensive damage to farms, crops, livestock, productive assets, irrigation systems, dams, and other rural infrastructure. Food production and distribution systems have been disrupted, local economies have contracted, and massive numbers of people have lost their primary sources of income. The prices of many basic food items, including rice and wheat, have increased by as much as a five hundred percent since 2000. The vast majority of the people who are food insecure live in countries that are experiencing or recovering from civil conflict. Malnutrition rates in these countries are, on average, six times higher than in non-conflict countries.

Civil conflict has caused incalculable suffering for people in Syria, Yemen, and Iraq. At present, 13.5 million Syrians, over half of the country's pre-war population, are acutely food insecure.[16] The Syrian conflict has damaged or destroyed agricultural lands, irrigation systems, public utilities, and rural infrastructure. Nearly seventy percent of the population is impoverished and 6.5 million people have been internally displaced. A breakdown in water and sanitation services has caused infectious diseases epidemics and the mortality rate of children has tripled since the conflict began.

Food insecurity has also reached catastrophic proportions in Yemen. After six years of civil war and foreign intervention, the country's economy is barely functioning and more than half of all households have lost their primary source of income. Fifteen million people face severe food shortages and child malnutrition rates are among the highest in the world.[17] Two million children are severely malnourished and half of all children under five years of age are stunted. Failing water and sanitation systems have caused virulent outbreaks of cholera, dengue, and diarrhea.

Three decades of successive wars, invasions, and externally imposed economic sanctions have dramatically reduced agricultural production in many parts of Iraq. From 2014 to 2018 large parts of the country were occupied by a separatist militia that brutalized local populations and displaced six million people from their homes. Farmers faced shortages of seeds, equipment, and other essential inputs and many were forced to abandon their farms altogether. Agricultural production declined by forty percent. Although the government has regained control over most of these areas, intermittent violence continues and much of the country's infrastructure has been damaged or destroyed, including water systems and irrigation facilities. Those farmers who attempt to cultivate crops risk being killed or injured by unexploded ordnance. A lack of animal health services and high feed prices has forced herders to sell or abandon their livestock. Thirty-five percent of Iraq's population is now impoverished and ten million people are food insecure.

Conflict has also forced millions of people to abandon their homes and flee to neighboring countries. The Middle East currently has the largest refugee crisis in the world. Syrians have fled to Egypt, Iraq, Jordan, Lebanon, and Turkey, Yemenis have fled to neighboring countries in the Arabian Peninsula and Horn of Africa, and Iraqis have fled to Iran, Jordan, Lebanon, and Turkey.[18] Many of these people are living in overcrowded refugee camps that are ill-equipped to provide sufficient food and other basic services. The massive movement of people across borders has imposed enormous social, economic, and environmental costs on host countries and food insecurity among their own citizens has increased as a result.

Population increases also contribute to food insecurity in the Middle East. The total number of people living in the region has grown from 108 million in 1970 to 343 million today. Population growth rates are, on average, 1.8% compared to a global average of 1.2% and the highest population growth occurs in countries with the most constrained food systems.[19] Although fertility rates have fallen in many countries, overall population growth continues to be high due to the relatively low medium age of the region's people. Population growth is placing enormous demands on the region's natural resource base, especially its land and water resources.[20]

The Middle East has the lowest arable land per capita of any world region.[21] Eighty percent of the region is either arid or semi-arid and lands in these areas are largely unsuitable for food cultivation. The best areas for agriculture are in the Fertile Crescent, a semi-circular area from the Eastern Mediterranean to the Persian Gulf. The water and nutrients from the Euphrates, Jordan, and Tigris rivers that soak into the soil have created optimal farming conditions in parts of Iraq, Israel, Jordan, Lebanon, the Palestinian Territories, and Syria for centuries.[22] Increasing demands for water, however, have reduced the size of these rivers and much of the land in this area has been degraded. When farmers attempt to cultivate lands with little fertility, the soil loses even more of its capacity to retain water and nutrients. Desertification is most extensive in the western parts of the region, including large parts of Israel, Jordan, Lebanon, the

Palestinian Territories, Syria, and Turkey. Desertification is also occurring in Iran and Iraq. Because almost all of the region's fertile lands are being cultivated, the potential for horizontal expansion of agricultural output is minimal.

The Middle East also has severe shortages of water resources.[23] Per capita freshwater resources have decreased by two-thirds in the past forty years and are currently just one-sixth of the global average.[24] With approximately four and a half percent of the world's population, the region has less than two percent of the world's renewable freshwater. More than sixty percent of all people in the Middle East live in areas characterized by high surface water stress.[25] The largest rivers are fully exploited and unable to meet additional needs. The agriculture sector, which relies heavily on irrigation, consumes the vast majority of available freshwater in the region.[26] Extraction rates from groundwater aquifers are well beyond the rate of recharge and water tables are falling as much as two meters per year.[27]

Climate change has intensified natural resource scarcities and further constricted agricultural production in the Middle East.[28] The region is highly vulnerable to the negative consequences of a warmer climate. As extreme heat spreads across more land for longer periods, soil erosion and desertification increase. This is especially evident in the Fertile Crescent where water levels in the Euphrates, Jordan, and Tigris rivers have declined. Water and nutrients from these rivers are needed to maintain soil fertility. In addition, sea level rise is causing saline intrusion into previously fertile lands, especially in low lying agricultural lands of Kuwait, Oman, Qatar, and the United Arab Emirates. Declines in precipitation and more unpredictable rainfall patterns are lowering groundwater tables while higher temperatures and greater evaporation are drying up inland water bodies and reservoirs.[29] Rising ocean temperatures and ocean acidification are causing the loss of fish populations in the coastal waters of the Mediterranean and Arabian Seas.

Emergency Food Aid

Sectarian conflicts in the Middle East have dramatically increased the need for emergency food aid. Millions of people who have been internally displaced or become refugees are in desperate need of nutritional support. Hunger and malnutrition have increased exponentially in Syria,

Yemen, and Iraq. WFP has provided emergency food assistance to vulnerable communities in all three countries. The distribution of in-kind food aid is often carried out under extremely hazardous conditions and at considerable risk to the personal safety of humanitarian workers.

Emergency food aid is provided to over five million besieged and displaced Syrians.[30] Supplies typically arrive at Mediterranean ports and are transported overland through Lebanon or Turkey into Syria.[31] Land routes often go directly through conflict areas and highways are riddled with unexploded ordnance. When land routes are completely closed off, WFP relies on high altitude airdrops from cargo planes. These airdrops are also hazardous either because of anti-aircraft artillery or the sudden onset of dangerous weather conditions. WFP distributes food packets in all fourteen governorates of Syria. Each packet contains nutritionally enhanced commodities, including wheat flour fortified with a vitamin-mineral premix, iodized salt, and vegetable oil fortified with Vitamins A and D. The packets, which also include fortified date bars, milk, rice, chickpeas, lentils, white beans, and olive oil, are designed to feed a family of five for a month. Non-food items, such as hygiene kits and medical supplies, are also included. WFP distributes ready-to-eat (RTE) rations for displaced households in Northern Syria that do not have access to cooking facilities.[32] Children 6–23 months of age who exhibit signs of malnutrition are provided specialized lipid-based nutrient supplements. Pregnant and nursing women receive cash-based transfers to purchase fresh food, including fruits, vegetables, dairy products, and meat, from specially contracted shops.[33]

WFP also provides food aid to nearly twelve million people in Yemen.[34] The aid is either in-kind, with each family receiving a monthly ration of wheat flour, pulses, fortified vegetable oil, and iodized salt, or in the form of commodity vouchers that can be redeemed at authorized retailers. WFP also funds supplementary feeding programs that provide nutritional support to pregnant and nursing women and to children.[35] In-kind food aid is provided within the context of extreme insecurity. Trucks are often required to pay "custom taxes" to local militias at checkpoints along major highways and relief workers have been subject to threats, arbitrary arrest, and physical attacks. Fighting in and around the Red Sea ports of Hodeida and Saleef, where seventy percent of in-kind food aid arrives, has led to multiple closures of the ports and suspension of aid deliveries. Militias on all sides of the conflict have prevented aid from reaching certain areas of the country. Food aid has also been diverted to frontline combat units or sold on the black market. Lost or stolen food aid is common in areas controlled by Yemen's internationally recognized government as well as in the territories that are controlled by Houthi rebels.[36] In the rebel-held capital of Sana'a and the northern stronghold of Saada only about forty percent of food aid reaches eligible families.

Food aid to Iraq is mostly structured to meet the needs of people displaced by conflict. Monthly assistance is distributed in the form of either in-kind food rations or cash transfers. In-kind rations include ready-to-eat packets and food parcels for families that have access to cooking facilities. Micronutrient powders that can be added to food and fortified wheat flour to help combat Iron-Deficient Anaemia are distributed throughout the country. WFP also provides cash-based transfers to pregnant and nursing women as a means of improving their dietary diversity. Eligible women receive two vouchers per month, which can be used to purchase fresh food, including fruits, vegetables, and dairy products, from designated retailers. WFP has worked with the Iraqi government to digitize the public distribution system for food rations.

Food aid is also provided to millions of people who have abandoned their home countries.[37] Syrians who have fled to neighboring countries constitute the largest number of refugees. Syrians living in the Azraq refugee camp in Jordan receive commodity vouchers that can be redeemed at specially contracted shops. Open book accounting agreements with these retailers, which allow WFP personnel to monitor how the shops operate, help ensure nutritious food products are sold at competitive prices. WFP also opened two of its own supermarkets in Azraq camp. Eligible refugees redeem their vouchers by having their irises scanned and the transaction is then completed through blockchain technology. In the sprawling refugee camps in southeastern Turkey, electronic food cards are distributed which allow families to purchase food at participating stores.[38] WFP also constructed kitchens where meals are prepared for children who attend improvised schools in the camps.

WFP also assists Palestinians in those parts of Gaza and the West Bank where food insecurity rates are highest.[39] Residents of these areas receive both in-kind aid and electronic vouchers that can be used to purchase a variety of locally produced foods. Nutritional education workshops are offered to community groups to maximize the impact of the aid.[40] Participants in these workshops are trained in the preparation of nutritious foods as well as the prevention of infectious diseases. They are then asked to share this information with others in their home communities.

WFP supports school meal programs in most Middle Eastern countries. These programs have been especially critical for children impacted by conflict. In Syria, primary school children in more than a thousand schools across ten governorates are provided with a daily fortified date bar and a carton of milk. WFP also provides nutritious snacks to children who are no longer able to attend school but are participating in accelerated learning sessions. These sessions, which are co-sponsored with UNICEF, are designed to facilitate the eventual re-entry of children into regular schools. Parents who enroll their children in these sessions receive cash-based transfers for the purchase of food. WFP also provides school meals to children in food insecure regions of Yemen, as well as refugee children living in Egypt, Iran, Iraq, Jordan, and Lebanon. WFP has aided Middle Eastern countries in the administration of school meal programs. Teachers and canteen managers have been trained in a number of countries on the preparation, distribution, and storage of these meals. The Healthy Kitchen Project in Jordan, for example, links school meals with nutritional awareness and broader social protections.

Agricultural Productivity

While emergency food aid continues to be essential for large numbers of desperate people in the Middle East, multilateral assistance has also been structured to rebuild food production systems in the region. FAO has been especially engaged in aiding farmers adversely impacted by conflict. Cash-for-work programs have been established in those areas where civil conflict has subsided and farmers have returned to their fields. Work has focused on rehabilitating land and productive assets as well as repairing rural infrastructure. FAO has also provided technical assistance to support the clearing of munitions and mines from arable land.

Ensuring farmers have access to high yield seeds is a central component of these initiatives. In Iraq, FAO worked with officials from the Ministry of Agriculture to rehabilitate the country's seed industry. Equipment was provided to build seed testing laboratories and repair damaged research stations. FAO also helped draft the policy that established the parameters for further development of the seed industry in the country. In Lebanon, a seed bank supported by FAO has 350 vegetable seeds and 40 varieties of wheat seeds that have been sourced from throughout the Middle East. The seeds are distributed to farmers within Lebanon and in neighboring countries. For its part, IFAD worked with the International Center for

Agricultural Research in the Dry Areas (ICARDA) to develop improved varieties of medicinal and herbal seeds that were later distributed to small-scale farmers in the region. IFAD also provided support to the Department of Agriculture of Iran to expand plant breeding capabilities. Farmers who combined improved seeds with traditional varieties saw their yields increase and their crops become more resilient to heat and drought. The increased diversity of plant genes allowed crops to better adapt to weather and climate variability.[41]

The reconstruction of irrigation systems has also been an integral part of international assistance. In Iraq, FAO helped clean and restore irrigation canals that were damaged by conflict. An FAO-sponsored project in Jordan used solar power to lift harvested rainwater to farm fields. The project aided smallholder farmers and reduced groundwater overuse. In Lebanon, FAO worked with government officials to develop an action plan to improve water management practices. A project in the Palestinian Territories that rehabilitated water conveyance systems helped reduce water loss from leakages and damaged infrastructure. Small-scale farmers were able to avoid using untreated wastewater for irrigation. In Syria, FAO helped rehabilitate irrigation canals in Homs and Hama governorates that had been damaged by fighting. These areas include some of the country's most fertile lands and are critical for eventually rebuilding the agricultural sector. In Turkey, Farmers Field Schools introduced enhanced irrigation methods and promoted other water saving technologies. Similarly, an IFAD project in Jordan allowed farmers to draw upon water sources that had not been used previously for irrigation, such as salty, brackish, and mixed water. This reduced the vulnerability of farmers to drought and increased the supply of freshwater available for other purposes.

Extension services have also been funded through multilateral assistance. In Syria, FAO provided training in agro-processing, produce marketing, and nutrition-sensitive agriculture. FAO also trained Lebanese farmers in sustainable agriculture, including tree management, composting, and the production of organic pesticides and fertilizers. In Turkey, FAO trained farmers in horticultural practices, animal husbandry, greenhouse production, farm management, food storage, and post-harvest processes. FAO also helped develop the capacities of small-scale farmers in the Palestinian Territories in the use of modern production and harvesting technologies. FAO supports the development of micro-gardens in a number of Middle Eastern countries. These gardens allow people without access to agricultural land to cultivate vegetables, roots, tubers, and herbs in small spaces near their homes.

Support for farmers associations is also a component of external assistance. Focus is placed on strengthening the organizational and managerial capacity of these associations. IFAD worked with farmers associations in Iraq to augment their ability to undertake productive investments in both farm and non-farm income-generating activities. In Turkey, IFAD helped establish a number of village associations, including agricultural cooperatives, women's farming groups, water-users unions, and grazing associations. This work also addressed the central challenges that these groups face, including limited access to financial services, marketing opportunities, and advanced technologies. In Yemen, FAO helped reorganize the water user associations in the capital Sana'a to better regulate water consumption and conservation.

Rural Development

International assistance has also been allocated to support broader transformation of rural economies, although the range and number of projects supported have been limited. Emphasis is placed on the development and expansion of off-farm enterprises. In Iraq, for example, vulnerable households were aided in the development of greenhouses, backyard poultry industries, and cottage manufacturing. IFAD also assisted poor rural households develop small-scale agro-processing industries that diversify incomes away from a sole reliance on agriculture. An FAO project in Turkey also aided in the development of agro-processing industries.

Resources have also been extended to develop financial services. IFAD helped institute savings and credit associations for rural communities in a number of countries. This work is often carried out in countries where more traditional financial institutions have been disrupted by civil conflict. In Syria, for example, IFAD established a network of village credit funds that are housed in self-managed financial institutions. IFAD worked with intermediary institutions in Yemen to provide financial services to rural microfinance institutions and nongovernmental organizations. In Jordan, IFAD supported the expansion of rural financial services as well as helped form savings, credit, and microfinance groups.[42]

UN food agencies have also supported the construction and repair of rural infrastructure in the Middle East. Much of this work is carried out in areas where infrastructure has been damaged or destroyed by conflict. FAO-sponsored cash-for-work programs in Iraq and Yemen provide temporary employment for people in rural areas to work on the rehabilitation of agricultural infrastructure and communal assets, such as water catchments, canals, and river embankments. IFAD has also financed the building of rural roads in the West Bank to facilitate the transport of farm products to nearby markets.

Environmental Preservation

The preservation of natural resources is a core element of multilateral assistance to the Middle East. A number of projects have focused on the conservation of land. As noted above, Middle Eastern countries have very little arable land and the land that is available for cultivation is increasingly subject to soil erosion and desertification. IFAD has worked to rehabilitate and reclaim degraded land. A project on the West Bank helped increase land productivity through soil improvement techniques. IFAD also helped construct terraces and stone walls to reduce soil erosion in Turkey.[43]

The protection of freshwater resources frequently involves aiding local governments in the development of effective water management systems. FAO supported a regional initiative to strengthen national capacities to monitor transboundary surface and groundwater usage and formulate effective water management plans. A project in northwestern Iran introduced sustainable agricultural practices that lessen the need to draw water from Lake Urmia. The water level of this lake—which was once the largest inland lake in the Middle East—has dramatically decreased over the course of the past fifty years. The lake is now ten percent of its former size, largely as a result of persistent drought. In Jordan, IFAD funded a series of water harvesting projects that capture water resources before they evaporate. The projects significantly reduced groundwater use in the areas where they were implemented. IFAD supported a major watershed rehabilitation project in Turkey.[44]

UN food agencies have also addressed the challenges posed by climate change in the Middle East. Farmer Field Schools introduce Climate-Smart Agricultural technologies that are designed to reduce greenhouse gas emissions from agriculture, aquaculture, and livestock. FAO also contributed to the Palestinian Solar Initiative, with the goal of having renewable sources meet thirty percent of Gaza's energy needs by 2030. Climate change mitigation efforts have also sought to preserve forest resources. In Iran, FAO is working to strengthen national and local capacities in sustainable forest management. New mechanisms for forest restoration were also introduced in Lebanon, including the expansion of Stone-pine forests that provide essential environmental services in the country. FAO supported sustainable forest management and reforestation programs in Turkey.

UN agencies also strengthened resilience to the adverse impacts of climate change. FAO worked with Middle Eastern governments to integrate climate change adaptation strategies into the agricultural and rural development plans. Aid was also provided to help monitor emerging threats to food security. Advanced information on the severity of climatic changes, insect infestation, and crop diseases has been crucial for the development of adaptation strategies. The availability of reliable food security data has also helped community associations prepare for emerging threats. A joint FAO-IFAD project in the West Bank that improved weather forecasting services allowed farmers to better protect their crops and livestock. A similar project in Iraq strengthened national capacities to monitor climate change and issue early warning alerts to farmers.

Conclusion

Food insecurity has worsened in the Middle East over the course of the past three decades. Civil conflicts have caused massive damage to farms, crops, livestock, productive assets, irrigation systems, dams, and other rural infrastructure and millions of people have been forced to flee to other regions of their country or to neighboring countries. A number of additional factors, including poverty, inequality, public sector failures, and environmental decline, have intensified food deficits throughout the region. The Middle East has the lowest per capita arable land and freshwater resources of any world region and these resources are under extraordinary stress as a result of both population growth and climate change.

Emergency food aid to the Middle East has increased dramatically in recent years, largely due to protracted waves of sectarian conflict. Civil wars in Syria, Yemen, and Iraq have left millions of people almost completely dependent on external food aid. Although most resources are allocated to address these humanitarian emergencies, UN agencies also support a limited number of projects designed to build sustainable agricultural sectors and rural economies. Much of this work involves rehabilitating land, rebuilding irrigation systems, and repairing rural infrastructure. Resources are also allocated for the preservation of scarce natural resources, especially land and water resources. FAO and IFAD work to rehabilitate degraded land and strengthen water management capacities in the region. Climate-Smart Agriculture techniques are introduced to help mitigate the negative consequences of climate change.

As long as protracted conflicts continue to plague the Middle East, food aid will be imperative. The millions of people who have been displaced throughout the region, many of whom are currently living in refugee camps, are almost completely dependent on emergency food aid. WFP plays a critical role in coordinating the humanitarian response to these crises. External assistance is also needed to restore degraded lands, rebuild irrigation systems, repair rural infrastructure, and address the threats posed by environmental degradation. Building universal food security will require an effective and long-term partnership between Middle Eastern governments and multilateral institutions.

Notes

1. The Middle East is also referred to as the "Near East," "Western Asia," or "Southwest Asia."
2. The countries of the Arabian Peninsula and Persian Gulf with the highest per capita incomes include Kuwait, Qatar, Saudi Arabia, and the United Arab Emirates.
3. Malnutrition rates in the Middle East are almost certainly higher than reflected in these figures since civil conflicts have limited data availability in several countries. Detailed descriptions of food insecurity in the Middle East can be found in Amery 2019, Babar and Mirgani (eds.) 2014, Garduño-Diaz and Garduño-Diaz 2015, Kandeel 2014, Sabry 2015, and Solh 2016.
4. Concern Worldwide and Welthungerhilfe 2019.
5. Three of the countries with the highest levels of stunting in the world—Iraq, Turkey, and Yemen—are in the Middle East.
6. The Middle East is the most food dependent region in the world. See Le Mouël and Schmitt (eds.) 2018.
7. Gulf Cooperation Council (GCC) countries of Bahrain, Kuwait, Oman, Qatar, Saudi Arabia, and the United Arab Emirates are almost completely dependent on food imports.
8. Although ethnic and religious divisions can be traced back hundreds and even thousands of years, they were intensified after the First World

War when the British and French frequently exploited ethnic divisions to advance their own territorial interests.

9. The complex nature of gender dynamics and inequalities in the Middle East is examined by Ryan and Rizzo (eds.) 2019, Solati 2017, Meriwether and Tucker 2018, Pollard and Russell 2021, Bahramitash and Esfahani (eds.) 2016, and Motzafi-Haller (ed.) 2017.
10. Migrant laborers account for 51% of the population in Bahrain, 74% in Kuwait, 41% in Oman, 76% in Qatar, 32% in Saudi Arabia, and 88% in the United Arab Emirates.
11. Food and Agriculture Organization 2019d, p. 49.
12. Food and Agriculture Organization 2019d, p. 47.
13. Persian Gulf countries have leased or purchased land abroad in a wide range of countries including Argentina, Egypt, Ethiopia, India, Mauritania, Morocco, Namibia, Pakistan, Senegal, South Sudan, and Sudan. Food and Agriculture Organization 2019d, p. 22.
14. See de Elvira et al. (eds.) 2018, Kubbe and Varraich (eds.) 2019, and Ben Ali and Saha 2016 for analysis of variation in the nature and intensity of corruption among Middle Eastern countries.
15. See Kamrava (ed.) 2021, Elbadawi and Selim (eds.) 2016, and Ben Ali, Cockx, and Francken 2016 for application of the resource curse theory to the Middle Eastern context.
16. It is important to note that the Syrian civil war was preceded by a severe drought that devastated food production and caused approximately two million people to move from rural to urban areas. The lack of an effective public sector response to rising food insecurity contributed to the popular protests that ultimately culminated in the civil war. Food and Agriculture Organization 2018d, pp. 70–71.
17. Food insecurity in Yemen is greatest in the provinces of Hajjah, Hodeida, Sa'ada, and Taizz which have endured the highest levels of civil conflict.
18. Approximately five million Syrians have fled to neighboring countries. Syrian refugees in Lebanon equal nearly one-fourth of the country's pre-war population and Syrian refugees in Jordan equal nearly one-fifth of the country's pre-war population.
19. Although fertility rates have fallen during the past twenty-five years, total population is expected to increase in the Middle East from 343 million people today to 450 million people by 2050. Population growth has contributed to rapid urbanization. In 1900, less than ten percent of people in the Middle East lived in cities while today cities hold more than sixty percent of the region's population. Declining agricultural production and limited non-farm employment in rural areas continue to drive rural to urban migration throughout much of the region.

20. Engelmann 2016 and Pouran and Hakimian (eds.) 2019 offer detailed accounts of resource constraints and environmental degradation in the Middle East.
21. Arable land has fallen from 0.54 hectares per person in 1961 to 0.19 hectares per person in the region today.
22. The Fertile Crescent even extends as far as southeastern Turkey and the western part of Iran.
23. Ten of the seventeen most water scarce countries in the world are in the Middle East and over sixty million people lack access to safe drinking water. Hofste et al. 2019, p. 9. The scarcity of water resources in the Middle East is examined by Badran et al. (eds.) 2017, Brooks et al. 2019, Diep et al. 2017, and Zawahri 2019, and Keulertz and Woertz (eds.) 2017.
24. Nearly eighty percent of available freshwater in the Middle East is found in just four countries: Iran, Iraq, Syria, and Turkey.
25. The average renewable water share per capita in the Middle East is estimated to be 430 cubic meters, well below the internationally established water poverty line of 1,000 cubic meters per capita. World Bank 2018, pp. 11–14.
26. The agricultural sector consumes over eighty percent of the freshwater available in the Middle East. This percentage is especially high in Oman, Saudi Arabia, and Yemen.
27. Food and Agriculture Organization 2019d, p. 34. In Egypt, Gaza, Jordan, Saudi Arabia, Syria, and Yemen groundwater extraction rates are well beyond annual recharge rates.
28. See Rabinowitz 2020, Swain and Jägerskog 2016, Waha et al. 2017, and Ward and Ruckstuhl 2017 for analysis of the environmental impacts of climate change in the Middle East.
29. Over the past decade, nearly all regions of Iran have endured some level of drought. The drought that occurred in the Levant (especially Jordan, Lebanon, the Palestinian Territories, and Syria) between 1998 and 2012 is thought to have been the worst drought in the past nine centuries in this region. Sherwood 2017 offers detailed analysis of the relationship between climate change and water scarcity in the Middle East. See also World Bank 2018, pp. 16–17.
30. World Food Programme 2019a, pp. 43, 49–50.
31. Cross-border deliveries from Turkey are permitted under UN Security Council Resolutions 2165 in 2014 and 2449 in 2018.
32. The ready-to-eat rations include fava beans, chickpeas paste, canned chicken, canned tuna, vegetables, olive oil, pulses, juice, and dry thyme. When complemented with bread, these rations are designed to meet the needs of a family of five for a week. Once access to cooking facilities is restored, households are included in general food aid distributions.

33. WFP recently established a Protracted Relief and Recovery Operation (PRRO) in Syria that assists in re-establishing the livelihoods of people displaced or otherwise impacted by conflict. While an increasing number of people will transition to resilience building activities, the most vulnerable people continue to receive emergency food aid.
34. World Food Programme 2020b, p. 24; Food Security Information Network 2020, p. 7; World Food Programme 2019a, pp. 43, 50–51.
35. A biometric registration system is utilized to ensure the food aid reaches its intended beneficiaries.
36. Official lists of food aid beneficiaries in Yemen have been altered to give preferential access to the families of slain and wounded soldiers.
37. WFP support for refugees in the Middle East is typically coordinated with the United Nations High Commission for Refugees.
38. The food distribution programs in Turkey's refugee camps are carried out in partnership with the Turkish Red Crescent.
39. WFP works with the United Nations Relief and Works Agency (UNRWA), which assists Palestinian refugees obtain access to nutrition, healthcare, education, and other essential services.
40. The WFP's nutrition education programs in Gaza are undertaken in partnership with Ard Al Insan.
41. Food and Agriculture Organization 2018c, p. 102.
42. International Fund for Agricultural Development 2019a, p. 17.
43. International Fund for Agricultural Development 2018d, p. 14.
44. International Fund for Agricultural Development 2018d, p. 14.

CHAPTER 6

Asia

Asian countries have made advances in addressing food insecurity. Rapid economic growth during the course of the past three decades has lifted millions of people out of poverty and enhanced the overall nutritional well-being of poor communities. Increases in agricultural and aquacultural output have helped most countries in the region replace food deficits with food surpluses. At the same time, Asia remains home to the largest number of food-insecure people in the world. Nearly 500 million people, largely concentrated in South and Southeast Asia, struggle to meet their daily nutritional needs. Although this figure obviously reflects the immense size of Asia's overall population, it also points to the persistence of food insecurity in the region.

This chapter begins with a broad outline of hunger and malnutrition in Asia and then turns to the central causes of food insecurity. Emphasis is placed on the countries of South and Southeast Asia where malnutrition rates are highest.[1] A range of economic, political, and environmental factors undermine the nutritional well-being of millions of people throughout the region. Widespread poverty and rapid population growth, in particular, are placing enormous pressures on the natural environments and resources that are needed for sustainable food production. The last section reviews multilateral efforts to meet the nutritional needs of poor communities in Asia. While food aid is provided in emergency situations, especially in response to the natural disasters that frequently strike the

F. Adams, *The Right to Food*,
https://doi.org/10.1007/978-3-030-60255-0_6

region, most resources are invested in projects designed to improve agricultural productivity, promote rural development, and preserve natural environments.

Regional Context

Asia stretches from the eastern boundaries of the Middle East to the island and archipelago countries of the Pacific and is home to more than sixty percent of the world's people. The region is typically divided into three subregions. *East Asia*, which includes China, Japan, the Korean Peninsula, Mongolia, and Taiwan, has the highest average standards of living.[2] *South Asia*, which is bordered by the Himalayan Mountains to the north, Bay of Bengal to the east, Indian Ocean to the south, and Arabian Sea to the west, includes Afghanistan, Bangladesh, Bhutan, India, Maldives, Nepal, Pakistan, and Sri Lanka. Although South Asia occupies just five percent of the world's land area, it is home to nearly a quarter of the world's people. *Southeast Asia* includes the continental countries east of India and South of China (Cambodia, Lao PDR, Myanmar, Thailand, and Vietnam) as well as the countries of the South China Sea and Pacific Ocean (Brunei, Indonesia, Malaysia, Papua New Guinea, the Philippines, Singapore, and Timor-Leste).[3]

As noted above, Asian countries have made progress in improving food security. The devastating food shortages that once plagued this region have largely disappeared and a number of countries now produce annual food surpluses. Agricultural and aquacultural production has quadrupled over the course of the last half century.[4] Improved agricultural technologies, seed varieties, and irrigation systems have dramatically expanded crops and fish production is by far the largest of all world regions.[5] At the same time, food insecurity continues to be widespread. Nearly 500 million people struggle to meet their daily nutritional needs and twenty percent of all people are chronically malnourished.[6] This represents approximately half of all malnourished people in the world. Micronutrient deficiencies, especially Vitamin A, Iron, and Iodine deficiencies, are common throughout South and Southeast Asia. Food insecurity has actually increased in some of the poorest countries during the past two decades, especially in South Asia.[7] India has the largest number of malnourished people in the world while Afghanistan, Bangladesh, Nepal, Pakistan, and Sri Lanka also have high rates of food insecurity.[8] The Global Hunger Index lists six countries in Southeast Asia—Cambodia,

Indonesia, Lao PDR, Myanmar, the Philippines, and Timor-Leste—as having "serious" levels of malnutrition.[9]

Asia is also home to more than half of the world's malnourished children.[10] A large proportion of children in South and Southeast Asia do not consume the calories, vitamins, and minerals needed to ensure adequate physical and cognitive development. This results in high levels of stunting and wasting. Approximately seventy-seven million children under the age of five are stunted and fifty million children are wasted.[11] The diets of more than half of children between 6 and 23 months of age do not meet minimal diversity standards, which contributes to severe micronutrient deficiencies."[12] Child malnutrition is especially severe in South Asia where low levels of Vitamin A, Iron, Iodine, and Zinc are common.[13] Fifty-eight million children under five suffer from stunted growth.[14] This constitutes almost forty percent of all stunted children in the world. India alone has more than fifty million stunted children, roughly a third of all cases in the world. Thirty-four million children in South Asia are wasted.[15] Once again, this figure is highest in India where approximately twenty-five million children under five years of age are wasted.

Causes of Food Insecurity

Poverty is the single greatest cause of hunger and malnutrition in Asia. Although sufficient food is produced in most countries of the region to adequately feed all people, a significant share of the population is too impoverished to purchase the food that they need to maintain a healthy and active life. While economic growth has raised the incomes of some, many others have been left behind. At present, 750 million people in the region are impoverished. South Asian countries have the highest proportion of their population living in poverty. 530 million people in India, Afghanistan, Bangladesh, Nepal, Pakistan, and Sri Lanka live below their respective poverty lines and a third of all people in these countries live on less than two dollars a day. Southeast Asian countries, especially Cambodia, Indonesia, Lao PDR, Myanmar, the Philippines, Timor-Leste, and Vietnam, are also marked by widespread poverty. Because these people spend more than half of their incomes on food, they are highly vulnerable to sudden price increases.

Poverty rates are more than three times higher in rural areas than in urban areas and agricultural workers are over four times more likely to be poor than people employed in other sectors of the economy.[16]

The rural poor account for three-quarters of those living in extreme poverty throughout South and Southeast Asia. People in rural areas have less access to public services, including clean water, sanitation, electricity, healthcare, and education. Access to arable land is also limited. Tens of millions of landless people serve as migrant laborers without any form of steady employment or income. Inequalities in the ownership of land have intensified over time.[17] Land acquisitions by both domestic and foreign investors are forcing farmers off of lands that their families have worked collectively for generations. In Indonesia, Malaysia, and the Philippines, large tracts of land have been acquired for the production of biofuel crops, especially palm oil. Land acquisitions are also occurring at a rapid pace in Bangladesh, Cambodia, India, Lao PDR, and Nepal.

South and Southeast Asia are home to thousands of diverse ethnicities and food insecurity tends to be higher among minority groups.[18] Political parties often reflect ethnic identities and governments typically favor some groups over others. In general, minorities have less access to healthcare, education, employment, and land ownership than the population as a whole. Caste divisions are an especially powerful force in India and other parts of South Asia. Although no longer legal or sanctioned by governments, caste continues to exert enormous influence over almost every aspect of economic and social life, particularly within Hindu communities. Because people occupy specific places within a complex social hierarchy based on birth, caste plays a significant role in determining educational and employment opportunities, especially in small towns and rural villages where cultural traditions have changed little over time.[19] People who are members of so-called lower castes endure the highest levels of food insecurity.[20] Ethnic inequalities also account for differences in malnutrition rates in Southeast Asia.

Gender disparities also impact food insecurity in Asia.[21] Although there is considerable variation by country, economic status, region, and ethnicity, social and cultural norms generally favor men over women. A strong male preference, especially in South Asia, privileges boys over girls at an early age. This is evident with respect to childhood nutrition, healthcare, and education.[22] Early marriage and motherhood also limit opportunities for women. When women enter the labor force, they are typically relegated to lower paid work with fewer benefits and less security. Women are also responsible for the vast majority of unpaid labor. Although women shoulder almost half of all agricultural work, customary land rights and inheritance practices strongly favor men over women.

Public policies also contribute to food insecurity.[23] Public sector investments in agricultural and rural development typically lag behind investments in urban areas.[24] When investments are made in rural areas, large landowners tend to be the primary beneficiaries. Poorer farmers have little access to newer agricultural technologies, reliable irrigation systems, or extension services. Similar to other regions in the developing world, governments favor the cultivation of export crops, especially coconuts, palm oil, rubber, soybeans, sugarcane, and tea, over the cultivation of basic staples to meet domestic food needs.

Public sector corruption also undermines food security in South and Southeast Asia.[25] The Corruption Perceptions Index lists a number of countries among those perceived to have the highest levels of corruption.[26] The region is marked by low levels of transparency and accountability, weak regulation and enforcement frameworks, and limited judicial independence. Civil society organizations that challenge public sector corruption are routinely subject to state repression and judicial harassment. Corruption is most frequently manifest in cronyism and nepotism, with family members and associates of top government officials benefiting from privileged access to public sector resources. Embezzlement of state resources, kickbacks on government contracts, and bribes for the provision of public services are evident to varying degrees throughout the region. The diversion of public resources to private accounts limits the funds available for nutritional support programs or agrarian development.

Although civil conflict is less evident in Asia than in other regions of the developing world, Afghanistan and Myanmar constitute two notable exceptions. Four decades of foreign invasion and civil war have severely damaged food production in Afghanistan and left nearly five million people dependent on external aid.[27] The limited food that is produced within the country rarely reaches the poorest areas. Food insecurity is especially high for the millions of people who have been either internally displaced or forced to flee to neighboring countries.[28] In Myanmar, Rohingya Muslims have endured decades of discrimination and repression by the Buddhist majority. Although these people have had a presence in the country for centuries, they are often considered illegitimate migrants from neighboring Bangladesh. Rakhine state, home to the largest concentration of Rohingya people, is among the poorest areas in Southeast Asia. In recent years, massive human rights violations perpetrated by security forces have caused thousands of people to abandon their homes and depart for other parts of the country. In addition, more than a million

Rohingya have fled across the border to Bangladesh. Food insecurity has quadrupled for Rohingya communities in both Myanmar and Bangladesh since the most recent outbreak of sectarian violence.

Population growth is also a significant cause of food insecurity in Asia. Population pressures are especially evident in South Asia. With approximately 1.8 billion people, the sub-continent includes nearly a quarter of the world's people. Because South Asia occupies just five percent of the world's surface area, this is by far the most densely populated region in the world. Southeast Asian countries are also characterized by high levels of population density. With three percent of the world's surface area, the subregion has almost 700 million people or nearly nine percent of global population. Although birth rates have slowed in both South and Southeast Asia, they remain far above world averages.

Population growth is placing enormous stress on the region's natural resources.[29] In dryland regions, such as arid and semi-arid parts of Afghanistan, India, and Pakistan, much of the soil is subject to human-induced erosion and desertification. Commercial agriculture tends to use high levels of chemical fertilizers and pesticides that damage soil structures and disrupt the balance of nutrients. Poor irrigation systems cause widespread erosion, waterlogging, and salinization. These problems are especially evident in large parts of Bangladesh, India, Nepal, Pakistan, and Sri Lanka where monocropping of rice and wheat is common. Agricultural lands in the Mekong River Delta have been damaged by saltwater intrusion.

Asia is also experiencing a precipitous decline of freshwater resources. Unsustainable rates of water extraction, especially for agricultural production, have caused aquifers to be among the most stressed in the world. Water withdrawals for agriculture typically account for at least seventy percent of total freshwater use in South and Southeast Asia.[30] The discharge of agricultural, industrial, and household effluents has contaminated rivers and lakes in the region. Most wastes are dumped directly into water bodies without any form of treatment. As freshwater resources become heavily polluted, farmers increasingly tap into groundwater, further reducing the region's aquifers.

The rapid loss of forest resources is also evident in many Asian countries.[31] With the loss of approximately fifteen percent of forest cover since 2005, deforestation rates in Southeast Asia are among the highest in the world. The problem is most extensive in the Philippines and parts of Indonesia where over half of original forest cover has been lost. Cambodia and Lao PDR are also marked by high levels of forest loss. Deforestation is often driven by an ever-increasing need for agricultural land, especially for the cultivation of export crops. The expansion of palm oil production in particular has caused extensive deforestation in Indonesia, Malaysia, and the Philippines. Both legal and illegal logging operations are also major causes of forest loss in the region.

Fish populations have declined in many parts of South and Southeast Asia, most notably in the coastal waters of the Cambodia, Indonesia, the Philippines, and Vietnam. Much of this decline is due to overfishing. Governments in the region have limited capacities to monitor and prevent illegal fishing by large-scale commercial trawlers. The dumping of toxic wastes into coastal waters have also diminished marine fish populations. Inland fisheries have declined due to habitat loss, the drainage of wetlands, dam construction, and water pollution.

Asian countries are highly vulnerable to the adverse impacts of climate change.[32] Glaciers on the Tibetan plateau have been critical for feeding rivers in South and Southeast Asia for centuries. However, glacier melt due to warmer temperatures is reducing water supplies for people in Bangladesh, northern India, Nepal, and Pakistan. Water levels in the Indus and Ganges rivers have significantly declined. Similarly, the Mekong River, which stretches over four thousand kilometers from its source in the Tibetan highlands through China, Myanmar, Thailand, Lao PDR, Cambodia, and Vietnam before emptying into the South China Sea, is at its lowest level in a century. Rising sea levels are damaging freshwater resources, especially in the coastal parts of the Mekong Delta and the Bay of Bengal. Heatwaves have further reduced water availability for agriculture, livestock, and human consumption.

The increased intensity and frequency of natural hazards—including droughts, heatwaves, dust storms, typhoons, and cyclones—have been linked to the human-induced warming of the Earth's land and ocean temperatures.[33] Because most farming in South and Southeast Asia is dependent on rainfall, changes in precipitation patterns have disrupted agricultural production and food supplies. Drought and heatwaves have also crippled agricultural production in more arid and semi-arid parts of the region.[34] Drought has been especially intense in Afghanistan and parts of Bangladesh, India, Pakistan, and Sri Lanka.[35] Crops in these countries were already being grown close to their temperature tolerance limit prior to the onset of recent droughts.

Asian farmers rely on two monsoon systems to water their crops: the southwest monsoon (which occurs between April and September) and the northeast monsoon (which occurs between October and March). Monsoon patterns in the region have been less predictable in recent years. Warmer temperatures in the Indian Ocean are altering hydrological cycles, resulting in weaker southwest monsoons and less rainfall. When the monsoons fail, which occurred most recently in 2016 and 2017, the region's food output declines. Rice production, the most common staple in the region, is especially vulnerable to drops in precipitation. At other times, monsoons have produced much larger rainfall than normal. This has caused record flooding in parts of the region, especially in the Ganges Delta in South Asia and in the Mekong and Irrawaddy Deltas in Southeast Asia. Severe flooding in these areas has destroyed crops and damaged rural infrastructure. Monsoon rains have been especially destructive in Bangladesh where nearly two-thirds of all land is less than fifteen feet above sea level. Monsoon rains have submerged large parts of the country for extended periods. Similar flooding has caused catastrophic damage to rice crops in low-lying parts of India, Myanmar, Nepal, Pakistan, and Vietnam.[36]

Emergency Food Aid

Most emergency food aid to Asian countries is provided in response to natural disasters. WFP again serves as lead agency coordinating emergency logistics and communications among all humanitarian actors. The UN Humanitarian Air Service provides transportation for relief workers and mobile medical teams as well as the delivery of relief supplies. Humanitarian Response Facilities (HRF) have been constructed throughout the region to preposition emergency supplies. These facilities also serve as staging areas in the immediate aftermath of a natural disaster. WFP trains local officials in warehouse and facility management, humanitarian supply chain, and emergency response operations.

The Asian-Pacific region endures multiple named storms each year. In the last few years alone, major storms have caused significant damage in both South and Southeast Asia. Cyclones are especially common in the Bay of Bengal and have major impacts on eastern India, western Myanmar, and southern Bangladesh.[37] Typhoons are also increasingly common in the South China Sea, with the Philippines and Vietnam especially vulnerable.[38] WFP provides in-kind food aid, including nutrient-rich biscuits, wheat flour, pulses, lentils, rice, fortified vegetable oil, and iodized salt, in the aftermath of each disaster. The biscuits are especially useful since they are easy to transport and do not require cooking. Both WFP and FAO also provide humanitarian aid for the rehabilitation of agricultural lands and rural infrastructure.

The Asian-Pacific region is also highly vulnerable to earthquakes.[39] The 7.8 magnitude earthquake that struck central and western Nepal on April 25, 2015 killed 9000 people and displaced hundreds of thousands. The earthquake and subsequent aftershocks caused massive damage to homes, roads, bridges, communication networks, crops, and livestock. About half of all households in the six worst-affected districts lost virtually all of their stored rice, maize, wheat, and millet seeds. In the immediate aftermath of the earthquake, WFP undertook an assessment to determine the needs of affected populations, established a humanitarian staging area (HSA) next to the Kathmandu airport, deployed thirty-two mobile food storage units, and coordinated the transportation of relief materials. In-kind food aid was distributed to two million people along with medical supplies and shelter materials. Particular focus was placed on reaching female-headed households, pregnant women, children, and ethnic minorities. Emergency food supplies, including high energy biscuits, were brought in by air from warehouses in Bangladesh, Dubai, and Malaysia. Because roads and bridges had been damaged, helicopters were deployed to transport food to remote areas. Once the emergency phase of the operation ended, Food-for-Work programs were organized to support recovery and rebuilding efforts. Community infrastructures, including roads, bridges, storage facilities, and irrigation systems, were repaired and community gardens were reestablished.

On September 28, 2018, a 7.4 magnitude earthquake struck off the coast of Central Sulawesi, Indonesia. The earthquake triggered a multiple-wave tsunami that inundated mainland areas, including the provincial capital of Palu. The earthquake and tsunami killed approximately 4000 people, displaced hundreds of thousands, and damaged homes, buildings, infrastructure, and crops. Eighty percent of buildings in the north of the island were either significantly damaged or totally destroyed. In many areas the ground became so saturated that homes literally sunk into the mud. Once again, WFP played a lead role in coordinating the response to the disaster and providing immediate humanitarian relief.

WFP worked with the UN Humanitarian Response Depot in Subang, Malaysia to obtain storage equipment. Ten mobile storage units were deployed to aid the distribution of food, clean water, shelter materials, generators, and medical assistance. The Relief Item Tracking Application (RITA) system was deployed to coordinate the transportation and storage of humanitarian supplies and community kitchens were established to aid displaced populations. After the emergency phase of the operation was completed, FAO worked to restore the livelihoods of thousands of people dependent on agriculture and fishing. WFP also assisted with the design of six humanitarian hubs on each major island in the region that are designed to ensure supplies can reach people quickly in times of emergency.

WFP also provides emergency food aid to people displaced by conflict in Afghanistan and Myanmar. Delivery of food aid in Afghanistan is difficult due to widespread insecurity, unexploded ordnance, poor road conditions, and mountainous terrain in many parts of the country. It is especially challenging to access areas that are controlled by armed militias. Despite these obstacles, WFP has supported food-insecure communities in remote areas. A typical ration includes enough wheat flour, rice, lentils, pulses, yellow split peas, fortified vegetable oil, and iodized salt to feed a family of five for a week.

In Myanmar, food aid is provided to displace Rohingya communities in the states of Kachin, Rakhine, and Shan and to people who have fled to neighboring countries. As noted above, more than a million refugees have crossed into Bangladesh. Many of these people are living in the sprawling Cox's Bazar refugee camps, which are located in one of the poorest districts of Bangladesh. The make-shift camps are extremely crowded, poorly equipped, and subject to torrential rains. Refugees in these camps are increasingly desperate and largely dependent on humanitarian assistance.[40]

WFP has partnered with the United Nations High Commission for Refugees (UNHCR) to meet the immediate needs of Rohingya refugees.[41] Upon arrival, people are provided with cooked meals and micronutrient-fortified biscuits. WFP distributes monthly food rations that include rice, pulses, lentils, a nutrient-rich wheat soya blend, and fortified vegetable oil. Because firewood and cooking supplies are scarce, WFP and FAO provide fuel-efficient stoves that require forty percent less wood than traditional stone fire pits. WFP also distributes commodity vouchers to refugees that can be used to purchase nutritious foods from local shops. The vouchers are issued to the senior woman of each family and retailers are required to sell at least three items of fresh vegetables and fruits.

WFP also maintains nutrition centers within the refugee camps that provide counseling in food preparation, child feeding practice, and personal hygiene. Children under five are regularly assessed for malnutrition through close monitoring of their weight, height, and upper arm circumference. Disaster risk reduction activities are also organized within the camps. Refugees are provided commodity vouchers in return for work on infrastructure rehabilitation and risk mitigation projects. This work typically involves maintaining roads, constructing bridges, improving drainage channels, and stabilizing slopes in high risk areas. Rohingya refugees who return to their homes in Myanmar are provided food aid for up to six months to facilitate their resettlement.[42]

School meal programs are also supported in a number of Asian countries. In Cambodia, WFP provides a daily breakfast to pre-primary and primary school children across nine provinces. Local farmers produce most of the food under the Home Grown School Feeding Program. Children are also given take-home provisions if they maintain strong attendance records. In Lao PDR, WFP provides lunches to primary school students that typically include rice, canned fish, lentils, and a corn soya blend that is fortified with micronutrients. The program also supports school gardens that grow leafy green vegetables and herbs. In India, school meals are structured to address the micronutrient gaps that are most prevalent among children. Rice fortified with Iron has helped reduce anemia rates in the country and a micronutrient curry powder is sprinkled on the food.[43]

Enhancing local capacities to manage school meal programs is a core objective. WFP provides policy advice and technical assistance to government entities responsible for school meals.[44] In Lao PDR, WFP worked with the Ministry of Education to design a sustainable and nationally owned school lunch program. Emphasis was placed on building institutional capacity for program design, implementation, monitoring, and evaluation. WFP also trained members of the Lao Women's Union in food storage and preparation. This union now oversees school meal programs in most parts of the country. In India and Indonesia, WFP worked with provincial governments to formulate nutritional guidelines for school meals. FAO supports the Farm to School program in Bhutan where farmers are given essential inputs, including tools, greenhouses, irrigation facilities, and processing equipment, to help improve fruit and vegetable cultivation. These farmers are then linked with local schools, ensuring a regular supply of produce for daily meals. In Bangladesh, Myanmar, and Timor-Leste, WFP aided the transition to a nationally owned school meal program.[45]

WFP also supports broader nutritional education initiatives in a number of Asian countries. Because diets tend to be heavy in the consumption of carbohydrates, fat, and salt but low in the consumption of vegetables, fruits, and proteins, this has sometimes required challenging traditional eating habits.[46] Poor households often struggle to afford micronutrient-dense foods.[47] Dietary diversity is especially limited among infants and young children in many Asian countries.[48] WFP offers cooking demonstrations to parents on how to prepare nutritious meals with locally available foods. In India, WFP supported inclusion of nutritional counseling in the government's Targeted Public Distribution System (TPDS). WFP also helped improve the beneficiary registration system and create new bar-coded ration cards that enable families to collect their monthly entitlements of rice, wheat, and millet. In Timor-Leste, a nutritional supplement named Timor Vita is provided to pregnant and nursing women. The supplement is made from corn, green vegetables, carrots, sweet potatoes, soybeans, and eggs. In order to ensure the continued availability of Timor Vita, WFP contracted the private enterprise Timor Global to produce the supplement from locally available ingredients.[49] In Lao PDR, Farmer Nutrition Schools (FNS), jointly sponsored by WFP and IFAD, enhance knowledge of nutrient-rich crops, post-harvest handling, and food preservation. Participants are asked to share their knowledge with others in their communities.

Agricultural Productivity

While emergency food aid continues to be provided to Asian countries, especially in response to natural disasters, most of the work of the UN food agencies is in the form of broader food assistance. Raising agricultural productivity has been a central objective. In Bangladesh and Cambodia, IFAD-supported projects introduced high-yield seed varieties and enhanced seed management techniques. IFAD also worked with the RAK College of Agriculture in India to produce improved varieties of pigeon pea, chickpeas, and lentils. In Lao PDR and Vietnam, IFAD introduced seeds that had been treated with biofungicides as a means of reducing the spread of soil-borne diseases. IFAD assisted community groups in Nepal to produce improved seed varieties for beans, groundnuts, soybeans, and lentils. In Myanmar and Vietnam, FAO helped refine many local rice varieties that were subsequently made available to small-scale farmers.

Assistance is also provided for the construction of irrigation systems, with IFAD again playing the lead role. In Myanmar, IFAD worked with the Ministry of Agriculture to improve the supply of water to farms and household gardens. Air compressors and water pumps were adapted for small-scale irrigation schemes. Similar irrigation projects were supported in Lao PDR and Nepal. In Indonesia, an IFAD project improved water delivery systems and raised the capacity of water user associations to better manage irrigation systems. IFAD partnered with FAO to aid Afghan farmers in the regions of Jalalabad, Kunduz, and Mazar rehabilitate irrigation systems that had been damaged by conflict. Community development councils were then established to manage the irrigation systems.[50] These projects helped increase the cultivation of wheat, a crop that is critical for food security and rural livelihoods in the country, by reducing the loss of water from seepage and evaporation. Water management projects were also supported in drought-affected areas, especially the provinces of Badhis, Ghor, and Herat. In Pakistan, an FAO-sponsored project repaired fifty water harvesting structures, increasing the availability of water for vegetable cultivation.

Food assistance has also included the provision of extension services to small-scale farmers and rural communities. The FAO's Regional Rice Initiative focuses on improving the efficiency and sustainability of rice production. Farmer Field Schools introduce sustainable rice ecosystem approaches that increase output while preserving natural resources. Laotian farmers were trained in the cultivation of more profitable crops, such as coriander and tomato. Emphasis was placed on ensuring product quality as farmers transitioned to the cultivation of non-traditional crops. In Sri Lanka, FAO introduced improved pest management strategies to combat Fall Armyworm without relying on hazardous pesticides. Integrated pest management to reduce post-harvest losses was also a central component of the instruction provided by Farmer Field Schools in Cambodia.

IFAD has also been engaged in the provision of extension services. In Bangladesh and Indonesia, IFAD helped farmers upgrade agricultural practices, diversity crops, and improve animal husbandry. Knowledge

Centers were established in Myanmar to aid farmers grow higher quality produce and adapt to new markets. In Nepal, IFAD worked with remote mountain communities to increase the cultivation of high value crops, such as apples, ginger, and turmeric. The initiative targeted small-scale farmers, especially so-called low-caste Dalits, indigenous groups, and women. Cellars to store produce were also built that allowed farmers to market their goods at higher prices later in the year. In Bangladesh, IFAD supported the production of a small fish called Mola which is rich in Calcium, Iron, Vitamin A, and Zinc. IFAD aided the cultivation of agricultural commodities in Myanmar that better respond to market demands and generate higher profits. Training focused on cost-effective ways to modernize production techniques. In Afghanistan, IFAD provided training in livestock and poultry husbandry.[51]

Rural Development

UN food agencies have also worked to support broader transformation of rural economies in Asia. In Afghanistan, for example, emergency food aid for people displaced by conflict is linked to vocational training programs. Participants are trained in a range of skills including carpentry, handicrafts, carpet weaving, and food processing. An IFAD project in the Philippines helped diversify sources of income for rural communities by establishing partnerships with private sector actors. In India, FAO helped strengthen employment-generating agribusinesses. IFAD also promoted marine-based enterprises and initiatives to enhance the efficiency of fisheries in Indonesia.[52]

The expansion of financial services in rural areas is also prioritized, with much of this work sponsored by IFAD. The FinServAccess initiative has increased the availability of rural financial services for smallholder producers and agro-entrepreneurs throughout South and Southeast Asia. The Microfinance for Marginal and Small Farmers Project in Bangladesh introduced a credit system for farming communities. This project was later scaled up to a national program. IFAD also aided vulnerable families living on river islands to obtain land titles. With land as collateral, these families are now able to access credit and acquire labor-saving machinery, including small irrigation pumps and rice threshers.[53] IFAD also supported a women's development fund for microfinance in Vietnam.[54] In Sri Lanka, rural financing was provided for small businesses engaged in green tea and rubber production. The Program for Increasing

Sustainable Finance, jointly funded by IFAD and the government of Pakistan, linked the microfinance sector with commercial banks to ensure the rural poor had access to financial services. In the Philippines, IFAD and the Asian Development Bank (ADB) co-financed a project that lent money to local groups seeking to build community-owned businesses. Farmers in Cambodia were trained in financial literacy and received small loans to develop agrobusinesses. Rural women in India were organized into self-help groups to establish small enterprises and obtain credit.[55] IFAD also expanded financing for small- and medium-sized enterprises in Myanmar, Nepal, and Indonesia.

Aiding small-scale farmers gain access to wider markets is also a component of rural development strategies. In Lao PDR, FAO became directly engaged in facilitating a contract between local farmers and a socially responsible export company. Project participants are now cultivating a wider range of crops and their commodities are reaching high value overseas markets. Similarly, IFAD built commercial relations between small-scale farmers and market intermediaries in India that helped farmers reach broader markets. In Thailand, IFAD aided groundnut producers in meeting the quality control standards of local and regional markets. Similarly, an IFAD-supported project in the Philippines helped farmers better meet market demand by improving the quality of the goods they produced. Emphasis was placed on post-harvest management and the use of modern processing facilities.

Environmental Preservation

Promoting the sustainable use of natural resources is an integral part of multilateral assistance to Asian countries. Environmental preservation projects have been supported throughout the region. In Lao PDR, FAO provides training to farmers in environmentally sustainable agricultural practices and soil conservation. The training has helped farmers not only preserve soils but also produce more nutritious crops. Farmer Field Schools in Afghanistan introduced Conservation Agriculture practices, including crop rotation and the planting of green gram, cowpeas, okra, and other legume cereal crops. These crops raise nitrogen content in soils, especially if plant residues are also used for mulching.[56] Farmers Field Schools in Sri Lanka helped reduce land degradation while increasing the output of smallholder farmers.

UN agencies have also worked to preserve water resources in Asia. FAO aided farming communities in Cambodia and Nepal to develop watershed management plans. Vegetation and trees were planted near streams, rivers, mangrove forests, marshes, and estuaries. Farmers were also trained in techniques for watershed management, water resource preservation, and ecosystem health.[57] In Myanmar, FAO replenished an aquifer and rehabilitated tube wells used for irrigation. Food-for-Work schemes in Bangladesh contributed to the construction of two small dams by local communities. The dams improve the harvesting of monsoon rains and ensure year-round access to water in a region that typically has water shortages during the winter months. IFAD worked with local communities in Indonesia to develop village-based coastal management plans. In India, IFAD promoted sustainable agriculture and farming practices that use water more efficiently.

United Nations food agencies have also supported forest preservation projects in Asia. FAO serves as the Secretariat for the Asia-Pacific Forestry Commission (APFC) which promotes regional cooperation in forest conservation and facilitates the exchange of best practices on forest management. FAO has also provided technical assistance in sustainable forest management to governments throughout the region, with emphasis placed on developing tools and methodologies to monitor forest loss. In India, FAO helped establish forest management groups in rural communities. These groups help reduce reliance on jhum—a slash and burn agricultural method—which contributes to deforestation.[58] The project also aided communities improve soil health by promoting agroforestry and the cultivation of horticultural crops. In Cambodia, FAO helped map the country's forest resources. The project, which collected data on the size, species, and carbon content of forests, was part of a larger public sector initiative to reduce carbon emissions from deforestation and forest degradation. In Indonesia and the Philippines, FAO provided assistance for planting food crops on firebreaks which increased crop output while reducing the risk of forest fires.

Assistance has also been provided to expand fisheries. FAO established a Regional Fisheries Livelihood Programme (RFLP) for South and Southeast Asia to foster more sustainable fishing practices. In Indonesia, IFAD provided coastal communities with fishing gear and motorized engines that made it possible to access high value fish further from the coast. The project also included the distribution of cooler boxes to store fresh fish and the construction of processing warehouses. In Bangladesh, IFAD partnered with WorldFish to increase the breeding of small nutrient-rich fish. A series of projects in the Philippines introduced resource management and environmental protection practices in coastal communities that prevent overfishing, protect marine ecosystems, and improve coastline infrastructure. Community-based IUU fishing reporting systems were also introduced in a number of countries.[59]

Meeting the challenges posed by climate change is also a central component of multilateral assistance to Asian countries. The reduction of greenhouse gas emissions is at the forefront of these efforts. Community forest monitoring programs are included as part of the Reducing Emissions from Deforestation and Forest Degradation (REDD+) initiative. FAO worked with the government of Bhutan to train forestry managers in sustainable forest management and carbon stock measurement. In Indonesia, FAO and the Ministry of Marine Affairs jointly implemented a project to preserve aquatic biodiversity. The project increased carbon sequestration, flood control, and other ecosystem services.[60] FAO aided Vietnam's Green Growth Strategy by promoting the use of renewable energy, establishing a GHG inventory system, and developing a domestic carbon market.

Programs have also been structured to build resilience to the adverse impacts of climate change. Farmer Field Schools introduced techniques to increase crop production while simultaneously strengthening resilience to climate change. Emphasis is placed on crop diversification, ecological pest management, and the preservation of biodiversity. In the Philippines, farmers were introduced to new crop management strategies that reduce the risks associated with extreme weather events. In Lao PDR, cost-effective measures to reduce the impact of climate change on wetlands ecosystems were introduced. FAO funded the distribution of seed varieties that can tolerate heat, flooding, drought, saline intrusion, and unpredictable rainfall in a number of Asian countries. The promotion of Conservation Agriculture, which emphasizes minimum soil disturbance, permanent soil cover, and crop rotation, also helps build resilience to climate change.

IFAD has supported a number of similar initiatives. In India, IFAD invested in climate-resilient technologies that improve soil health, increase water conservation, enhance pest management, and expand agroforestry. Small-scale farmers are encouraged to adopt drought-tolerant crop varieties and diversify their cropping systems in order to increase resilience to climatic changes. In the Mekong Delta of Vietnam, an IFAD project promoted climate-smart agricultural value chains. Farmers were taught environmentally safe production methods and water-saving irrigation techniques.[61] IFAD's Climate Change Adaptation Fund supports farmers who adopt practices that strengthen resilience to the adverse impacts of climate change.[62]

Disaster preparedness efforts have also been supported throughout South and Southeast Asia. In the Philippines, WFP helped strengthen the offices responsible for natural hazards mitigation. This included building national capacities to use meteorological forecasting information for emergency preparedness. Training was also provided to local officials on hazard analysis, early warning systems, and the construction of flood prevention infrastructure. In Lao PDR, WFP helped establish early warning systems and coordinate multi-stakeholder emergency responses. WFP partnered with the National Agricultural Research Institute to provide real-time weather forecasting and Farmer Field Schools disseminated agroclimatic information to help mitigate risks to food security. A project that was co-sponsored with the government of Bangladesh enhanced the resilience of rural communities to climate shocks. Participants built community assets in exchange for food aid.[63]

FAO also supports disaster preparation efforts. In Lao PDR, FAO worked with the Ministry of Agriculture to provide disaster risk reduction and management training. The training improved the resilience of agricultural communities to natural disasters. FAO subsequently supported implementation of the country's Plan of Action for Disaster Risk Reduction Management in Agriculture. In Cambodia, the Philippines, and Vietnam, FAO supported projects to ensure climatic forecasts and early warning systems are available in rural communities. An FAO project in Bangladesh helped build weatherproof infrastructure to improve the resilience of rural communities in flood-prone regions. A similar project in Myanmar enhanced the capacity of local and regional authorities in disaster preparedness and recovery.

Conclusion

Asia is home to half of all food-insecure people in the world. Nearly 500 million people, largely concentrated in South and Southeast Asia, struggle to meet their daily nutritional needs and food insecurity has actually increased in some of the poorest countries since the turn of the century. Poverty is the single greatest cause of hunger and malnutrition in Asia.

Millions of people are unable to purchase sufficient quality food to maintain a healthy and active life. Poverty rates are three times higher in rural areas than in urban areas and the rural poor account for three-quarters of those living in extreme poverty. Access to arable land is limited and inequalities in land ownership have intensified over time. Public sector investment tends to privilege large landowners over small-scale farmers. Poorer farmers rarely have access to newer technologies, reliable irrigation systems, or extension services. Population growth and climate change are placing extreme pressures on the natural resources needed for sustainable food production.

Although United Nations food agencies provide food aid in response to natural disaster or civil conflict, most allocations are in the form of broader food assistance. FAO and IFAD both work to raise agricultural productivity in South and Southeast Asia. This includes the distribution of high-yield seeds and the introduction of enhanced seed management techniques. Assistance is also been provided for the construction of irrigation and water delivery systems. Farmer Field Schools work with small-scale farmers to upgrade agricultural practices and improve animal husbandry. Broader rural development is also a core component of external assistance. UN food agencies support the development of non-farm enterprises, provision of financial services, and expansion of rural markets. FAO and IFAD also provide training on environmentally safe agricultural practices, including soil conservation, water preservation, and the sustainable use of forest resources.

Although the countries of South and Southeast Asia have made advances in food and nutritional security, the need for international assistance remains imperative. UN food agencies can play an especially proactive role in raising agricultural productivity. Poorer farmers will need greater access to quality seeds, advanced technologies, and improved irrigation systems. External assistance can also promote broader transformation of rural areas. The rural poor, who constitute seventy-five percent of those living in extreme poverty, should have wider access to off-farm employment, financial services, and commercial markets. Meeting the long-term needs of rapidly growing populations in South and Southeast Asia will also require the conservation and effective use of land, water, forests, and fisheries. Productive investments, training programs, and extension services will continue to be essential for building sustainable food systems in the region.

Notes

1. The Global Hunger Index scores for most countries in South and Southeast Asia are considered "serious." Concern Worldwide and Welthungerhilfe 2019.
2. Because the East Asian countries have lower rates of hunger and malnutrition than elsewhere in the region, they are not included in this chapter. China, Japan, South Korea, and Taiwan make annual contributions to international food assistance programs.
3. A number of smaller Pacific island countries are also considered part of the Asian region. However, because these countries are not major recipients of international food assistance, they are also not included in this chapter.
4. For example, India is now self-sufficient in the production of rice and wheat.
5. Asia accounts for ninety percent of worldwide aquacultural production. World Resources Institute 2018, p. 41.
6. The Asia–Pacific region is home to well over half of all people worldwide who do not obtain sufficient dietary energy to maintain normal, active, and healthy lives. Food and Agriculture Organization 2019h, p. v.
7. For detailed description of food insecurity in South Asia see Akhtar 2016, Galistcheva 2018, Harding et al. 2018, and Hossain 2014.
8. With 190 million food insecure people, India ranks 102 out of 117 countries on the 2019 Global Hunger Index. Concern Worldwide and Welthungerhilfe 2019.
9. Concern Worldwide and Welthungerhilfe 2019. See Haddad et al. 2015 and Davila et al. 2018 for analysis of food insecurity in Southeast Asia.
10. Food and Agriculture Organization 2018e, p. 7.
11. Food and Agriculture Organization 2019h, p. 6. One half of all children under five in the world who are stunted and two-thirds of all children under five who are wasted live in Asia. Food and Agriculture Organization 2019h, pp. 7–8.
12. Food and Agriculture Organization 2019h, p. v.
13. Vitamin A and Iron deficiencies are highest in Bangladesh, Bhutan, India, and Nepal.
14. Food and Agriculture Organization 2019h, p. 6.
15. Of the thirty-four million children who are wasted in Asia, 11.7 million suffer from Severe Acute Malnutrition. Food and Agriculture Organization 2019h, pp. 7–9.
16. Food and Agriculture Organization 2018e, p. 1.
17. In India, for example, five percent of farm households own nearly sixty percent of the country's arable land.
18. Scholarship on ethnic conflict in South and Southeast Asia is extensive. See especially Phadnis and Ganguly 2015, Sachdeva et al. (eds.) 2019, Shani and Kibe (eds.) 2019, Suryadinata 2015, and Yoshino (ed.) 2019.

19. It is important to note that secular education and growing urbanization have weakened caste-based discrimination to some extent, especially in areas where people of different castes share living and working environments.
20. Social divisions between Hindus and Muslims also play a role in unequal distributions of income, resources, and services in South Asian countries.
21. Scholarship on gender relations in South and Southeast Asia is also extensive. See especially Alston (ed.) 2016, Bhagowati 2014, Channa 2013, Fernandes (ed.) 2018, Huang and Ruwanpura (eds.) 2020, Hussein (ed.) 2018, Joshil and Brassard (eds.) 2020, and Parker et al. (eds.) 2017.
22. Iron Deficiency Anemia, which affects 400 million women of reproductive age in Asia, is the leading cause of maternal mortality. Fifty percent of all pregnant women and one-third of women of reproductive age in South Asia suffer from Anemia. Food and Agriculture Organization 2019h, p. 18.
23. Most countries in South and Southeast Asia have redistributive programs aimed at improving food security. India's Targeted Public Distribution System (TPDS), for example, is the world's largest food distribution program. However, these programs typically focus on improving daily caloric consumption rather than ensuring a nutritionally balanced diet.
24. Food and Agriculture Organization 2018e, p. 1.
25. dela Rama and Rowley (eds.) 2017, Gong and Scott (eds.) 2016, Piliavsky (ed.) 2014, and Rajan 2020 examine the causes and socioeconomic consequences of corruption in Asia.
26. Transparency International, 2019. Afghanistan, Bangladesh, Cambodia, Lao PDR, Myanmar, Nepal, Pakistan, Papua New Guinea, and the Philippines have the lowest CPI rankings in South and Southeast Asia.
27. Food Security Information Network 2020, p. 7.
28. Persistent drought has further compromised food security in Afghanistan, especially in the northern and western regions of the country.
29. See James (ed.) 2019 for a collection of papers that consider the relationship between population growth and environmental degradation in Asia. The pressures placed on the natural resources of Asian countries as a result of population growth and other factors are also outlined in Hirsch 2016, Kukreja (ed.) 2019, and United Nations Environmental Programme 2015.
30. There has also been a precipitous decline of wetlands areas in South and Southeast Asia. See Intergovernmental Panel on Climate Change, 2019b.
31. Forests occupy approximately twenty-five percent of the total land area in Asia. Sudhakar et al. 2018 examine contemporary pressures on forest resources in South Asia.
32. Asian Development Bank 2017 offers a comprehensive analysis of the impact of climate change on the standard of living in Asia. See also Alam

et al. (eds.) 2018, Barua et al. 2018, Chou et al. 2020, Filho (ed.) 2015, Koh (ed.) 2015, Majaw 2020, Srivastava 2020, and Vachani and Usmani (eds.) 2014.

33. Food and Agriculture Organization 2019h, p. 36.
34. For analysis of the impact of climate change on land in South Asia see Dissanayake et al. 2017.
35. Drought has caused a steep decline in rice production in Pakistan's Sindh province.
36. Food and Agriculture Organization 2018c, p. 63. Many densely populated Asian cities, including Bangkok, Chennai, Dhaka, Ho Chi Minh City, Karachi, Kolkata, Jakarta, Manila, Mumbai, and Yangon, are highly vulnerable to sea level rise and extreme weather events.
37. The most severe cyclones in South Asia in recent years include Fani 2019, Vardah 2020, and Amphan 2020.
38. Recent typhoons in the South China Sea include Damrey 2017, Mangkhut 2018, Kammuri 2019, and Vongfong 2020.
39. The countries of South and Southeast Asia are located above complex geological plate structures. In South Asia, friction between the Indian and Eurasian plates causes earthquakes in Bangladesh, Bhutan, India, Nepal, and Pakistan. In Southeast Asia, the Eurasian, Philippine, and Australian plates continually rub against each other on the ocean floor. Earthquakes in this region pose the added risk of causing powerful tsunamis.
40. According to the WFP's Refugee Influx Emergency Vulnerability Assessment (REVA), over eighty percent of Rohingya refugees in Bangladesh are dependent on humanitarian assistance to meet their daily food needs.
41. World Food Programme 2019a, p. 45.
42. WFP has worked with World Vision and the Rahmonya Peace Foundation on the resettlement of Rohingya refugees to Myanmar.
43. WFP also supports sizable school meal programs in Bangladesh, Bhutan, Myanmar, Nepal, and the Philippines.
44. World Food Programme 2019a, p. 53.
45. World Food Programme 2019a, p. 53.
46. Food and Agriculture Organization 2018e, p. 15.
47. Food and Agriculture Organization 2018e, p. 15.
48. Food and Agriculture Organization 2019h, p. 15.
49. The WFP's food assistance initiatives in Timor-Leste are carried out in partnership with CARE International.
50. International Fund for Agricultural Development 2019a, p. 9.
51. International Fund for Agricultural Development 2018d, p. 6.
52. International Fund for Agricultural Development 2018d, p. 5.
53. International Fund for Agricultural Development 2018d, p. 5.
54. International Fund for Agricultural Development 2019a, p. 8.
55. International Fund for Agricultural Development 2019a, p. 8.

56. FAO also provided technical assistance to the government of Afghanistan to develop the country's Land Resources Information Management System (LRIMS).
57. Much of the funding for these water conservation activities in Asia was provided by the Global Environmental Fund (GEF).
58. The practice of Jhum can actually improve soil fertility in the short-term because it leaves a nutrient-rich layer of ash. However, the nutrients are depleted in three to five years and soils lose their fertility. Farmers then move to new areas and repeat the process, further expanding deforestation.
59. The FAO's community-based IUU fishing reporting system has been adopted in Cambodia, Indonesia, Papua New Guinea, the Philippines, Sri Lanka, Thailand, Timor-Leste, and Vietnam.
60. This project in Indonesia also received support from Global Environmental Fund (GEF).
61. International Fund for Agricultural Development 2019a, p. 7.
62. International Fund for Agricultural Development 2019a, p. 7.
63. Food and Agriculture Organization 2018c, p. 109.

CHAPTER 7

Conclusion

Although access to safe, sufficient, and nutritious food is among the most fundamental of all human rights, millions of people continue to suffer from hunger and malnutrition. This book examined food insecurity in the developing world and the global campaign to meet the nutritional needs of poor communities. The United Nations and three of its affiliated agencies—the World Food Programme, Food and Agriculture Organization, and International Fund for Agricultural Development—have been at the forefront of this campaign.

As noted in the introduction and reiterated throughout this book, the causes of hunger and malnutrition are complex and vary considerably among the regions and countries of the developing world. At the same time, a number of common factors can be identified and these factors generally interact in ways that compound and intensify food insecurity. More than a billion people are so impoverished that meeting their nutritional needs is a daily struggle. Governments have generally not used public resources to effectively reduce poverty or address the root causes of hunger and malnutrition. Public sector investments in social protection programs, agricultural productivity, or rural development are nowhere close to what is needed to effectively combat food insecurity. In fact, governments are often part of the problem rather than the solution. Agricultural policies typically favor the cultivation of cash crops for export over basic staples for domestic consumption and public resources are frequently lost to mismanagement or corruption. Civil conflicts in

F. Adams, *The Right to Food*,
https://doi.org/10.1007/978-3-030-60255-0_7

many parts of the developing world, especially in sub-Saharan Africa and the Middle East, cause immense damage to agricultural sectors, rural infrastructure, local economies, and people's lives. The natural resources needed for sustainable food production, especially land, water, forests, and fisheries, are under extreme pressures, and these pressures are intensified by climatic changes. There are also components of the world economy—the unequal trade in agricultural commodities, dominance of global agribusinesses, transnational land acquisitions, illegal fishing, and external debt—that undermine food security across the developing world.

Hunger and malnutrition pose enormous challenges for the world community. Given the size, scope, and complexity of these challenges, it would be easy to despair. Yet over the course of the past half century very real progress has been achieved in the campaign for universal food security. As chronicled in Chapter 2, the United Nations played a lead role in ensuring access to safe, sufficient, and nutritious food is universally recognized as a fundamental human right. The right to food regime is a powerful instrument that both international institutions and societal groups can use to hold governments accountable for their actions. UN agencies have also provided both food aid and food assistance throughout the developing world. Chapters 3–6 reviewed the work of WFP, FAO, and IFAD in Latin America, Africa, the Middle East, and Asia. While emergency food aid is distributed in times of crisis, UN agencies also provide broader food assistance to each region of the developing world to address the underlying causes of food insecurity.

The contemporary challenge is to build on the progress that has been achieved to further reduce hunger and malnutrition. This will require rethinking some of our past policies and developing innovative approaches to solve new problems. Multilateral efforts are needed to help meet emergency food needs, increase agricultural productivity, promote rural development, and preserve natural resources. Global food security requires substantial and sustained progress in each of these areas. This chapter offers a series of recommendations for improving and strengthening both food aid and food assistance in the years to come.

Emergency Food Aid

Food aid remains imperative in response to natural hazards or civil conflicts. When local food supplies have been destroyed or are beyond the reach of desperate and displaced communities, food aid is absolutely essential. At the same time, such aid must be carefully-crafted and well-executed to avoid causing more harm than good. Although the provision of surplus grains to poor countries may be carried out with the best of intentions, this can actually undermine the goal of achieving food security in the developing world. Local farm economies are adversely impacted by foreign grains being freely distributed in domestic markets and small-scale farmers can be driven out of business altogether. Food aid can also lessen incentives for both public and private investment in domestic agriculture. With fewer farmers, less agrarian investment, and declining output, these countries risk becoming even *more* dependent on external sources of food.

Food aid can be structured in ways that do not undermine domestic agriculture or harm local farmers. When in-kind food aid is provided, local and regional purchases (LRP) should be utilized whenever possible. Food is often available in a country, just not in specific areas. If severe food shortages preclude local purchases, food should be obtained from neighboring countries in the region. LRP aid farmers in the developing world, increase incentives to invest in domestic agriculture, and help build national capacities. Cash-based transfers or commodity vouchers to obtain locally produced food achieve these same objectives. LRP also avoid the costs associated with purchasing, transporting, and distributing food from donor countries.[1] Because food-deficit areas can be hard to reach due to poor infrastructure, adverse weather conditions, harsh terrain, or insecurity, delivering food to these areas is often much more difficult than simply purchasing the food in nearby markets. When in-kind food aid is provided, it should be fortified with vitamins and minerals to ensure the highest nutritional content possible.[2] The provision of therapeutic foods is crucial for people who are unable to digest traditional meals. Coupling food aid with nutritional education is a cost-effective way of improving community health and food safety.

Meeting the nutritional needs of pregnant and nursing women is essential for both mother and child. Consumption of micronutrients, especially Calcium, Folic Acid, Iodine, Iron, Zinc, and Vitamins A, C, and D is critically important throughout pregnancy. Women who are nursing infants also need nutritional support for an extended period. The World Health Organization recommends initiation of breastfeeding within one hour of birth, exclusive breastfeeding for the first six months of life, and continued breastfeeding for up to two years of age or beyond, accompanied by solid foods. Breastmilk includes virtually all of the vitamins, minerals, and enzymes required for a baby's physical and cognitive growth and the antibodies needed to protect against infectious diseases. The frequency and severity of upper respiratory infections, ear infections, and even chronic conditions such as asthma and allergies are significantly reduced when infants are breastfed. Breastfeeding also reduces the risk of diabetes, meningitis, pneumonia, and some forms of cancer later in life. Women also benefit from nursing their infants since it replenishes Iron lost during pregnancy, promotes uterine contraction, helps prevent postpartum hemorrhage, and may even reduce the risk of contracting serious illnesses later in life, including breast cancer, cardiovascular disease, diabetes, hypertension, osteoporosis, and ovarian cancer. Ensuring nursing mothers have access to nutritious food must be a central component of all food aid programs.

School meals are a powerful instrument for improving childhood nutrition. Well-designed and carefully-targeted meals, which are fortified with essential vitamins and minerals, are beneficial in a number of respects.[3] Children are assured at least one nutritious meal each day and their ability to concentrate on their studies improves. School meals also raise attendance rates by reducing illness-related absences and giving parents an additional incentive to ensure their children attend school. Purchasing food for school meals from local markets benefits smallholder farmers in the community. The inclusion of multiple food groups, especially fruits, vegetables, and dairy products, can help diversify local agriculture and promote healthy eating habits.

Agricultural Productivity

Food assistance can also enhance agricultural productivity in the developing world. Increasing the quantity, quality, and range of foods that are available in domestic markets is essential for achieving food security. This will also improve household incomes in rural areas through forward and backward linkages between the farm and non-farm sectors. As noted by FAO, agricultural growth is twice as effective in reducing poverty as growth in other sectors of the economy.[4] Supporting local agricultural production reduces vulnerability to global price increases for imported grains and other food commodities.

Given the scarcity of land and water resources in many parts of the developing world, the potential for horizontal expansion of food output is limited.[5] Future increases in output will largely depend on raising agricultural productivity per unit of land and water. Emphasis should be placed on aiding smallholder farmers improve crop and livestock productivity. Training and extension services should be designed to ensure farmers have access to new knowledge and technologies. Mobile and Internet services can be used to share information with farmers in remote areas who are difficult to reach through traditional methods.

The introduction of hydroponics and aquaponics can be especially useful for countries with limited water resources. Hydroponics, which involves growing crops in water rather than soil, actually requires less water than traditional agriculture because water is kept where it is needed rather than draining away. Plants obtain nutrients from special solutions that are added to the water. Light, temperature, and water supply can be more precisely controlled and there is less need for chemical fertilizers, herbicides, and pesticides. Aquaponics combines the principles of hydroponics and aquaculture to create a single integrated system for food cultivation. Fish in an aquaculture tank eat food and excrete waste, which is converted by bacteria into nutrients. Once the water from an aquaculture tank is transferred to a hydroponics tank, plants are able to consume the nutrients needed for optimal growth. Because the plants help purify the water, it can be transferred back to the aquaculture tank. This process can be repeated continuously without requiring the discharge of water. Aquaponics can produce more food, including grains, fruits, vegetables, and fish, than traditional approaches while using far less water and artificial chemicals.

Advances in biotechnology can also boost agricultural output. Plant breeding is an effective means of expanding the genetic base of cropping systems.[6] Crops can be genetically modified (GM) to increase their resilience to insects, disease, weeds, and climatic changes. The biofortification of seeds increases the micronutrient content of crops.[7] GM crops also reduce production costs and ensure more consistent food supplies.[8] Such crops are more environmentally sustainable since they require fewer chemical inputs.[9]

Although advances in biotechnology can play an important role in increasing agricultural productivity, it will be important to avoid repeating the errors of the Green Revolution. Between the 1950s and 1970s the introduction of high-yield, disease-resistant hybrid seeds for major cereal crops, especially maize, rice, and wheat, dramatically increased agricultural output in some parts of the developing world.[10] Cereal production more than doubled between 1955 and 1975 in the areas where these seeds were introduced. However, most of the benefits of this increased output accrued to wealthy farmers with the greatest access to land and capital. These farmers were able to purchase the more expensive seeds, as well as the synthetic fertilizers, herbicides, and pesticides that were needed for these seeds to flourish. Wealthier farmers also had greater access to irrigation. Small-scale farmers, on the other hand, found it harder to obtain the seeds and other needed inputs. Those who took out loans to make these purchases often accumulated such large debts that they were eventually forced to sell their lands. Land ownership became more concentrated and poverty rates increased. Moreover, as the larger farms began to rely on higher levels of mechanization, employment opportunities in rural areas decreased. Although food production per person expanded, this did not result in corresponding improvements in food security. Green Revolution techniques, especially monoculture agriculture and the heavy use of agrochemicals, led to unsustainable levels of natural resource exploitation. Soil fertility was reduced and water tables fell.

Advances in biotechnologies must be introduced in ways that ensure small-scale farmers are the primary beneficiaries and natural resources are more carefully preserved. It will be important to identify how well scientific advances perform under small-farm conditions with limited mechanical equipment and irrigation. Small-scale farmers must also be able to retain traditional knowledge of genetic resources and be guaranteed the right to use, exchange, and sell farmed-saved seeds. Intellectual property laws and certification schemes must be structured to protect the rights of these farmers.[11]

Food assistance should also expand irrigation systems in the developing world. While access to irrigation almost always raises agricultural productivity, this does not necessarily require large-scale investments, aquifer depletion, or increased use of fossil fuels. A number of low-cost, environmentally safe methods can be utilized. Drip irrigation simply requires a network of perforated tubes linked to a water source, treadle pumps can draw water through a hose from a well or stream, and shallow tube wells and boreholes with submersible pumps can irrigate sizable areas at minimal cost. With appropriate treatment, wastewater can be used to provide irrigation. Solar-powered pumps can produce high quality energy for irrigation at near zero marginal costs and electronic sensors can ensure optimal moisture levels in fields.

It will also be important to ensure that the food produced is fully utilized through the introduction of improved preservation, storage, and distribution technologies. International assistance should ensure small-scale farmers have access to hermetic storage containers and metallic silos that guard against insects, mold, moisture, and rodents. Farmers and fishers can also reduce post-harvest loss through greater access to drying and threshing equipment, enhanced processing facilities, and refrigeration units.

Securing access to land is vital for rural communities. As noted in the introductory chapter and described in the regional chapters, the unequal distribution of land and the increasingly common practice of large-scale land acquisitions are major causes of food insecurity in the developing world. Strengthening land rights and undertaking land reform can help correct past injustices and substantially improve the nutritional well-being of rural households.[12] When smallholder farmers have secure access to land, their output expands and income increases. Digitized registration systems should be introduced to update land records and provide title guarantees to farmers in those countries where property rights are weak. Collective registration of communal and customary lands is essential for the long-term well-being of rural communities. International institutions can also help ensure land acquisitions include fair compensation to displaced communities, job creation, infrastructural improvements, and environmental protections. The negotiation process must be fully transparent and include representatives from the communities most directly impacted.

Increasing fish production will also enhance food security in the developing world. Inland freshwater aquaculture can improve nutrition and expand income opportunities for rural households. Aquaculture produces fewer environmental costs than the production of other animal source foods. Investments should also be made to aid coastal fishing communities. It will be important to ensure artisanal fishers have the equipment and supplies needed to support themselves and their families. International assistance should be structured to combat illegal fishing. Joint monitoring, surveillance, and enforcement mechanisms are needed to protect fish populations in the exclusive economic zones (EEZ) of developing countries. Multilateral assistance can help ensure catches are limited to levels that allow fish populations to regenerate, fishing is restricted during breeding times, and aquatic habitats are protected.[13] Marine Protected Areas (MPA), where fishing is completely prohibited, should be established in those areas where rapid declines in fish populations have been identified. When properly monitored, MPA have been an effective tool for ensuring the recovery of fish stocks.[14]

Rural Development

Food assistance must also be structured to support broader transformation of rural economies in the developing world.[15] Programs that promote income-generating opportunities in agro-processing and the wider non-farm economy are needed to reduce rural poverty and inequality. The expansion of financial services in rural areas is essential. Small-scale farmers and non-farm workers must have secure ways to save money, protect assets, transfer funds, purchase insurance, and obtain credit at reasonable interest rates. Access to credit creates opportunities to expand rural enterprises. Cooperatives and postal banks can assist people in remote areas who lack access to traditional financial institutions. Microfinance, which provides small loans without requiring collateral, can aid people who do not have significant assets or formal financial ties. Insurance products help safeguard against crop losses due to natural hazards or adverse weather events.

Improvements in rural infrastructure are also imperative. Rural areas often lack adequate clean water, sanitation, storage facilities, communications services, energy sources, and transportation systems. Investments in all of these areas will expand economic opportunities and enhance the quality of life for rural communities. Simply improving road linkages between rural and urban areas aids small-scale farmers by reducing the costs of inputs, improving market access, and facilitating interaction with extension agents.

Rural development initiatives should place special focus on improving the lives of women. Although women play a major role in food production, processing, and marketing, they endure higher levels of food insecurity than men. Women have less access to the resources needed to be productive, including quality seeds, tools, technology, training, and extension services. Most significantly, women's ability to own land is restricted in much of the developing world. While the proportion of women who are heads of rural households has increased, women continue to own less than five percent of all agricultural land. Without land tenure, women have lower incomes and less access to credit. In the non-farm economy, women are relegated to lower-paid jobs with few legal or social protections.

International assistance must promote gender equality and the empowerment of women.[16] In-kind food aid, cash-based transfers, and commodity vouchers can be structured to ensure women are the primary beneficiaries. It will also be important to ensure women have access to the resources needed to be successful. Microfinance, which has been a catalyst for female empowerment in a number of countries, must be made more widely available. Small loans can help women establish or expand businesses that generate independent sources of income.[17] As the income of women increases, the nutritional well-being of rural communities improves since women are more likely to spend additional income on food and other necessities for their families. Gender mainstreaming in the design and implementation of all food assistance initiatives is essential to ensure these programs are fully responsive to the needs of women.[18]

Environmental Preservation

International assistance must also be structured to promote the sustainable management of natural resources in the developing world. Environmental preservation is critical for increasing agricultural productivity and ensuring the vibrancy of rural economies. This includes protecting land, water, forests, and fisheries, as well as crafting effective responses to the challenges posed by climate change.

Farmer Field Schools should more fully incorporated the principles of agroecology into their training programs. Agroecology offers an alternative approach to food production from that of industrial agriculture. The latter relies on large-scale monoculture, extensive tilling of fields, and the heavy use of chemical inputs. Although this approach can increase total output in the short-term, the ecological costs are high. Industrial agriculture damages soils, depletes water resources, and releases harmful effluents into the environment. Natural resources are often exploited beyond their capacity to regenerate. Industrial agriculture also contributes to deforestation, habitat destruction, biodiversity loss, and high levels of greenhouse gas emissions.

Agroecology, on the other hand, incorporates ecological principles into the design and management of food systems.[19] By adapting to natural conditions and cycles, farmers create synergies between agricultural production and ecological processes. Minimal soil disturbance is especially important. Rather than tilling fields, seeds are inserted directly into undisturbed soil. Farmers are also encouraged to diversify their crop varieties through intercropping and multiyear crop rotations. Planting cover crops during the off-season helps build soil health by preventing erosion, replenishing soil nutrients, and reducing weeds. Composts that incorporate organic matter from crop residues can be used to maintain the fertility and water-holding capacity of soils and the construction of terraces and windbreaks reduces soil erosion.[20] Agroforestry, the mixing of trees and shrubs into farming operations, provides shade, shelter, and nutrients to better protect crops, soil, and water sources. Natural fertilizers and biological pest control techniques can be used in place of chemical inputs.

Agroecological approaches will help ensure a long-term balance between food production and the sustainability of natural resources. The organic structure, nutrient content, and overall fertility of soils will improve. In addition to nitrogen, phosphorus, and potassium, healthy soils require the restoration of depleted carbon. Higher organic carbon in soils increases nutrient and water intake by plants, reduces soil erosion, and better conserves land and water resources.[21] Agroecology also lowers the risks of pests and disease, helps preserve biodiversity, and reduces the burning of fossil fuels.

The sustainable use of freshwater and marine resources is especially important. Freshwater ecosystems, such as lakes, rivers, wetlands, and estuaries, are increasingly polluted by agricultural runoff, the toxic wastes of factories and mines, and untreated sewage. Urban runoff is contaminating coastal marine resources. International assistance can help protect water resources and promote sustainable water use. New methods can be adopted to increase water availability, including rainwater harvesting, wastewater recycling, and desalination. Reservoirs, farm ponds, and check dams can store water in rainy seasons for use during dry seasons. By using water resources more efficiently, water tables can gradually be restored.

Multilateral assistance should also be structured to improve forest management and conservation. As noted earlier, healthy forests support a range of ecological functions that are critical for food security. Forests help purify the air, store carbon, replenish soils, regulate water cycles, protect watersheds, and preserve biodiversity. Responsible forest management necessitates expanding protected areas. Reforestation programs can also be an important part of this process provided a diverse range of trees are planted that enhance biodiversity and carbon sequestration. Support for the natural reforestation of marginal or abandoned agricultural land is also imperative.[22] The Reduce Emissions from Deforestation and Forest Degradation (REDD+) initiative of the UN promotes the conservation of tropical forests. Developing countries can draw on these funds to support programs that preserve and expand their forest resources.

International assistance should also address the threats posed by climate change. The Earth's air, surface, and ocean temperatures are projected to rise between 1.5 and 2.5 degrees centigrade by 2100. Temperature increases have already caused massive disruptions to food systems throughout the developing world. While climate change will have differential impacts on food production depending on a multitude of location-specific factors, international assistance must be crafted to both mitigate the central causes of climate change and help communities adapt to climate-induced environmental threats.

Food production contributes roughly a third of all greenhouse gas emissions. The promotion of Climate-Smart Agriculture (CSA) and agroecology will reduce these emissions. Restoring degraded soils and sequestering carbon will lower levels of atmospheric carbon dioxide. No till farming, which allows carbon to be stored in soils, not only combats an important source of climate change but increases the resilience of soils to temperature changes. Investments in renewable energy sources, especially solar and wind power, also contribute to reduced emissions. Since forests have an enormous capacity to sequester carbon, sustainable forest management is imperative.[23]

Local communities will also need to build resilience to the environmental threats caused by climate change. International assistance can help devise and implement adaptation strategies through policy advice, technical assistance, and capacity development. Disaster risk management must be incorporated into all policies and programs. Vulnerability mapping can help predict localized impacts of climate change and enhance emergency preparedness. Technical assistance, including the provision of geographic information system (GIS) and remote sensing technologies, can strengthen risk monitoring, early warning systems, and vulnerability reduction mechanisms.

The Road Forward

Achieving universal food security is among the greatest challenges in the world today. One of the central themes of this book is that hunger and malnutrition cannot be adequately addressed solely at the local and national levels. Limited resources in the world's poorest countries, the interdependence of food systems, and the global nature of environmental threats necessitate a coordinated response by the international community. Food aid remains essential in times of emergency while food assistance is needed to promote agricultural productivity, rural development, and environmental preservation. *Global governance is essential for global food security.*

Advocating a collective response to the problems of hunger and malnutrition is not meant to suggest that the same approaches should be applied throughout the developing world. International agencies must tailor their programs to the specific context and needs of each country. A range of factors, including economic conditions, demographic pressures, cultural practices, geographic features, and environmental constraints, must be considered in the design and implementation of assistance programs. These factors not only vary among countries but can vary among regions within the same country.

It will be important to ensure the regular monitoring and evaluation of food assistance programs. A standardized method for collecting information about the performance of all activities should be utilized throughout the lifespan of a specific initiative. This information should then be used to assess the relevance, impact, efficiency, effectiveness, and sustainability of the initiative. Monitoring and evaluation must be conducted by independent evaluators to ensure the impartiality and credibility of the process. Monitoring and evaluation are essential for assessing the effectiveness of an intervention and making necessary adjustments during project implementation. This will improve the effectiveness of ongoing projects and enhance the design of future initiatives.

Effective coordination between international and domestic actors is also imperative. This includes UN agencies, other multilateral institutions, national and local governments, the private sector, producer cooperatives, and civil society organizations. Achieving food security necessitates building effective partnerships among all relevant actors. Such partnerships will maximize the gains that can be achieved from the expertise and resources of a diverse range of institutions while avoiding duplication or working at cross-purposes. Effective coordination will also allow for scaling-up projects to benefit larger numbers of target populations.

The participation of civil society organizations is especially important. When local communities are involved in the design, implementation, monitoring, and evaluation of development projects, success rates increase and the projects are more likely to continue after external assistance ends. The participation of community groups is critical to ensuring the relevance, ownership, and sustainability of all initiatives. The inclusion of civil society groups also helps build local capacities. Poor people must be able to exercise control over their communities and direct the development process in their interests. This will create more self-reliant communities that have the resources and capabilities necessary to meet their nutritional needs on a long-term basis.

These principles are reflected in the movement for "food sovereignty" which prioritizes meeting the nutritional needs of local communities over supplying food to distant markets.[24] The food sovereignty movement works to strengthen smallholder agriculture, artisanal-fishing, pastoralist-led grazing, and food production systems that are socially and environmentally sustainable.[25] The movement "... puts those who produce, distribute, and consume food at the heart of food systems and policies rather than the demands of markets and corporations."[26] Food sovereignty thus represents an alternative vision to the agro-industrial model of large-scale production for global markets.[27] Emphasis is placed on locally-oriented, small-scale food production for domestic consumption and ensuring lands, waters, seeds, livestock, and biodiversity are in the hands of those who produce food in local communities.[28]

Our world clearly has the resources and capacity to construct a global food system that is economically viable, socially just, culturally appropriate, and environmentally sustainable. This requires supporting small-scale, autonomous, and ecologically-sound agricultural and rural development initiatives that empower poor communities throughout the developing world. We all share a common interest in a world without hunger and we can all contribute to making this vision a reality.

Notes

1. The storage, transportation, and distribution of overseas in-kind food aid typically constitute about twenty-five percent of the total costs of such aid.
2. For example, flour can be fortified with Folic Acid, Iron, Niacin, Riboflavin, Thiamine, and Zinc; sweet potatoes, rice, and legumes can be fortified with Iron and Zinc; maize can be fortified with Vitamin A and Zinc; and cassava and sorghum can be fortified with Amino Acids.
3. It is especially important to fortify school meals with Vitamins A, B, and D, Folic Acid, Iodine, Iron, and Zinc.
4. Food and Agriculture Organization 2019d, p. 49.
5. The limited potential for horizontal expansion of agricultural output is especially true if developing countries seek to preserve their forest areas and savannas. World Resources Institute 2018, p. 8.

6. At least half of all gains in agricultural productivity can be attributed to the use of improved crop varieties. World Resources Institute 2018, p. 24. The Global Partnership Initiative for Plant Breeding Capacity Building (GIPB) is an alliance dedicated to enhancing sustainable food security through improved plant breeding and delivery systems. The CGIAR Consortium of International Agricultural Research Centers works to improve global nutrition through research on agriculture, crop breeding, livestock husbandry, agroforestry, and aquaculture.
7. New Rice for Africa (NERICA) is an example of a high yield variety that has increased rice output in a number of African countries. The International Rice Research Institute identifies genes for tolerance to submergence, salinity, and drought conditions and then transfers the genes to high-yield breeding lines.
8. Genetic modification involves inserting the genes from one plant into another plant. CRISPR, a genetic engineering technique where the genomes of living organisms are modified, (gene editing), is much more precise than traditional plant breeding techniques. It can be used to develop climate, insect, and disease-resistant crops with enhanced nutritional value that require minimal fertilizers and pesticides. World Resources Institute 2018, p. 24.
9. Although concerns have been raised regarding the safety and environmental impact of genetically-modified crops, little empirical evidence has been generated to support these concerns. The World Resources Institute found no evidence that GM crops have directly harmed human health. World Resources Institute 2018, p. 24.
10. High-yield varieties were later developed for barley, beans, cassava, chickpeas, lentils, millet, potatoes, and sorghum.
11. The right to use, exchange, and sell farm-saved seeds is included in Article 9 of the *International Treaty on Plant Genetic Resources for Food and Agriculture*. The treaty was a response to attempts by multinational agribusinesses to replace native seeds with commercial varieties that farmers would be required to purchase each year.
12. The International Land Coalition (ILC) is a global alliance of over two hundred intergovernmental and nongovernmental organizations working to secure land rights for those who live on and from the land in the developing world, especially small-scale farmers, indigenous peoples, pastoralists, and women.
13. World Resources Institute 2018, p. 40.
14. Foreign fishing vessels can be outfitted with tracking devices to prevent entry into Marine Protected Areas.
15. As FAO notes, "[r]ural transformation and agricultural transformation support each other. The growth of off-farm incomes through rural transformation supports agricultural transformation by providing demand for

agricultural products. Agricultural transformation, in turn, supports rural transformation by providing demand for off-farm inputs (such as seeds, machinery, and technical expertise) and marketing and transportation services." Food and Agriculture Organization 2019d, p. 45.

16. Research on the link between gender equality and food security includes Bellows et al. (eds.) 2017, de Schutter 2013a, Njuki et al. (eds.) 2016, Sachs (ed.) 2019, and Schmidt 2018.
17. At the same time, safeguards need to be put in place to ensure microfinance loans remain in the hands of women, are at low interest rates, and do not lead to the accumulation of unsustainable debts.
18. The Women's Empowerment in Agriculture Index (WEAI), which was formulated by the International Food Policy Research Institute (IFPRI) and the Oxford Poverty and Human Development Initiative, can be utilized to help structure international food assistance programs. The index measures women's overall empowerment in the agricultural sector, with emphasis placed on control over income, ownership of land and other assets, access to credit and extension services, and participation in decision-making.
19. There is an extensive and continually expanding literature on agroecology. Among the most important contributions in recent years include Gliessman 2015, Nooy van Tol 2016, Vandermeer and Perfecto 2017, Shiva 2016, Bohlen 2009, Giraldo 2019, Benkeblia (ed.) 2015, 2018, Snapp and Pound (eds.) 2017, Brescia (ed.) 2017, Steier and Cianci (eds.) 2019, Mossi et al. (eds.) 2020, Altieri and Nicholls 2021, Rosset and Altieri 2017, Hilmi 2017, Pimbert (ed.) 2018, and Sahn 2015.
20. Parties to the 1994 *United Nations Convention to Combat Desertification* (UNCCD) agreed to reduce desertification and restore degraded land. The convention includes national targets based on the level of erosion in each country with an overall goal of achieving land degradation neutrality (LDN) by 2030. UN 1994.
21. Food and Agriculture Organization 2019e, p. 56.
22. World Resources Institute 2018, p. 35.
23. Conversely, when forests are destroyed or converted for other uses, they emit sequestered carbon into the atmosphere.
24. The concept of "food sovereignty" was developed by the international movement La Via Campesina. The movement brings together peasants, small-scale farmers, landless people, indigenous people, migrants and agricultural workers in an attempt to influence global agricultural policy. It includes 164 local and national organizations in 73 countries. The World Development Movement, Food First Information and Action Network (FIAN), and the International Planning Committee on Food Sovereignty also work to promote a more just, equitable, and sustainable global food system.

25. The Forum for Food Sovereignty 2007, p. 1.
26. Forum for Food Sovereignty 2007, p. 1. The *Declaration of Nyéléni* defined food sovereignty as the "… right of peoples to healthy and culturally appropriate food produced through ecologically sound and sustainable methods, and their right to define their own food and agriculture systems." Forum on Food Sovereignty, 2007, p. 1. Other important documents in the food sovereignty movement include Forum on Food Sovereignty 2002, La Via Campesina, 2003; World Development Movement, 2012; and International Land Coalition, May 2011.
27. Detailed description and analysis of the food sovereignty movement can be found in Andrée et al. (eds.) 2014, Claeys 2015, Cohen (ed.) 2020, Constance et al. (eds.) 2018, Desmarais et al. 2010, Edelman 2017, Herrera and Lau (eds.) 2015, Holt-Giménez et al. (eds.) 2017, Mayer and Anderson (eds.) 2020, McMichael 2009b, Pefecto et al. 2019, Schanbacher 2019, Shattuck et al. (eds.) 2018, Tilzey 2018, Trauger (ed.) 2015, Trauger 2017, and Wittman 2009, 2015.
28. The Forum for Food Sovereignty 2007, p. 1.

Bibliography

Acar, Sevil. (2017) *The Curse of Natural Resources: A Developmental Analysis in a Comparative Context*. New York: Palgrave Macmillan.

Achebe, Nwando and Claire Robertson (eds.) (2019) *Holding the World Together: African Women in Changing Perspective*. Madison: University of Wisconsin Press.

Adunbi, Omolade. (2015) *Oil Wealth and Insurgency in Nigeria*. Bloomington: Indiana University Press.

African Union. (2001a) *New Partnership for African Development*. Addis Ababa: African Union.

African Union. (2001b) *Maputo Declaration on Agriculture and Food Security*. Assembly/AU/Decl.7(II). Addis Ababa: African Union.

African Union. (2003) *Comprehensive Africa Agriculture Development Program*. Addis Ababa: African Union.

African Union. (2014) *Malabo Declaration on Accelerated Agricultural Growth and Transformation for Shared Prosperity and Improved Livelihoods*. Addis Ababa: African Union.

African Union. (2015a) *Agenda 2063: The Africa We Want*. Addis Ababa: African Union.

African Union. (2015b) *Africa Regional Nutrition Strategy for 2016–2025*. Addis Ababa: African Union.

Agang, Sunday Bobai, Pregala Pillay, and Chris Jones. (2019) *A Multidimensional Perspective on Corruption in Africa*. Newcastle upon Tyne, UK: Cambridge Scholars Publishing.

Akhtar, Saeed. (2016) "Malnutrition in South Asia—A Critical Reappraisal," *Critical Reviews in Food Science and Nutrition*, 15, 14: 2320–2330.

F. Adams, *The Right to Food*,
https://doi.org/10.1007/978-3-030-60255-0

Akombi, Blessing J., Kingsley E. Agho, Dafna Merom, Andre M. Renzaho, and John J. Hull. (2017) "Child Malnutrition in Sub-Saharan Africa: A Meta-Analysis of Demographic and Health Surveys (2006–2016)," *PLoS One* 12, 5, eø177338.

Alam, Mozaharul, Jeongho Lee, and Puja Sawhney (eds.) (2018) *Status of Climate Change Adaptation in Asia and the Pacific*. Cham, Switzerland: Springer.

Aleman, Julie C., Marta A. Jarzyna, and A. Carla Staver. (2018) "Forest Extent and Deforestation in Tropical Africa Since 1990," *Nature Ecology and Evolution*, 2: 26–33.

Allan, John Anthony, Martin Keulertz, Suvi Sojamo, and Jeroen Warner (eds.) (2013) *Handbook on Land and Water Grabs in Africa: Foreign Direct Investment and Food and Water Security*. New York: Routledge.

Alston, Margaret (ed.) (2016) *Women, Political Struggles and Gender Equality in South Asia*. New York: Palgrave Macmillan.

Altieri, Miguel and Clara L. Nicholls. (2021) *Agroecology for Sustainable and Resilient Farming*. New York: Routledge.

Amery, Hussein A. (2019) "Food Security in the Middle East," in Anders Jägerskog, Michael Schulz, and Ashok Swain (eds.), *Routledge Handbook on Middle East Security*. New York: Routledge: 182–198.

Amundsen, Inge (ed.) (2019) *Political Corruption in Africa: Extraction and Power Preservation*. Cheltenham, UK: Edward Elgar Publishers.

Andrée, Peter, Jeffrey Ayres, Michael J. Bosia, and Marie-Josée Massicotte (eds.) (2014) *Globalization and Food Sovereignty: Global and Local Change in the New Politics of Food*. Toronto: University of Toronto Press.

Arellano-Gault, Davíd. (2019) *Corruption in Latin America*. New York: Routledge.

Armenteras, et al. (2017) "Deforestation Dynamics and Drivers in Different Forest Types in Latin America," *Global Environmental Change*, 46: 139–147.

Asian Development Bank. (2017) *A Region at Risk: The Human Dimensions of Climate Change in Asia and the Pacific*. Manila: Asian Development Bank.

Auty, Richard M. and Haydn I. Furlonge. (2018) *The Rent Curse: Natural Resources, Policy Choice, and Economic Development*. Oxford: Oxford University Press.

Babar, Zahra and Suzi Mirgani (eds.) (2014) *Food Security in the Middle East*. Oxford: Oxford University Press.

Badran, Adnan, Sohail Murad, Elias Baydoun, and Nuhad Daghir (eds.) (2017) *Water, Energy and Food Sustainability in the Middle East*. Cham, Switzerland: Springer.

Bahramitash, Roksana and Hadi Salehi Esfahani (eds.) (2016) *Political and Socio-Economic Change in the Middle East and North Africa: Gender Perspectives and Survival Strategies*. New York: Palgrave Macmillan.

Ballard, Terri J., Anne W. Kepple, and Carlo Cafiero. (2013) "The Food Insecurity Experience Scale: Development of a Global Standard for Monitoring Hunger Worldwide," Technical Paper, Version 1.1, Rome: Food and Agriculture Organization.

Barker, David, Ducan McGregor, and Kevon Rhiney. (2017) *Global Change and the Caribbean: Adaptation and Resilience*. Kingston: University of the West Indies Press.

Barua, Anamika, Vishal Narain, and Sumit Vij. (2018) *Climate Change Governance and Adaptation: Cases from South Asia*. Boca Raton: CRC Press.

Bellows, Anne C., Flavio L. S. Valente, Stefanie Lemke, and María Daniela Núñez Burbano de Lara (eds.) (2017) *Gender, Nutrition, and the Human Right to Adequate Food: Toward an Inclusive Framework*. New York: Routledge.

Ben Ali, Mohamed Sami, Lara Cockx, and Nathalie Francken. (2016) "The Middle East and North Africa: Cursed by Natural Resources?," in Mohamed Sami Ben Ali (ed.) *Economic Development in the Middle East and North Africa: Challenges and Prospects*. New York: Palgrave Macmillan: 71–94.

Ben Ali, Mohamed Sami, and Shrabani Saha. (2016) "Corruption and Economic Development," in Mohamed Sami Ben Ali (ed.) *Economic Development in the Middle East and North Africa: Challenges and Prospects*. New York: Palgrave Macmillan: 133–154.

Benkeblia, Noureddine (ed.) (2015) *Agroecology, Ecosystems, and Sustainability*. Boca Raton: CRC Press.

Benkeblia, Noureddine (ed.) (2018) *Climate Change and Crop Production: Foundations for Agroecosystem Resilience*. Boca Raton: CRC Press.

Berck, Cyndi Spindell, Peter Berck, and Salvatore Di Falco (eds.) (2018) *Agricultural Adaptation to Climate Change in Africa: Food Security and a Changing Environment*. New York: Routledge.

Besada, Hany Gamil (ed.) (2016) *Governing Natural Resources for Africa's Development*. New York: Routledge.

Bhagowati, Surajit Kumar. (2014) *Women in Southeast Asia*. New Delhi: New Century Publications.

Bohlen, Patrick J. (2009) *Sustainable Agroecosystem Management: Integrating Ecology, Economics and Society*. Boca Raton: CRC Press.

Brescia, Steven (ed.) (2017) *Fertile Ground: Scaling Agroecology from the Ground Up*. Oakland, CA: Food First Books.

Briend, A., T. Khara, and C. Dolan. (2015) "Wasting and Stunting—Similarities and Differences: Policy and Programmatic Implications," *Food Nutrition Bulletin*, 36, 1, Supplemental: 15–23.

Brooks, David B., Julie Trottier, and Giulia Giordano. (2019) *Transboundary Water Issues in Israel, Palestine and the Jordan River Basin*. Cham, Switzerland: Springer.

Cafiero, Carlo, Sara Viviani, and Mark Nord. (2018) *Food Security Measurement in a Global Context: The Food Insecurity Experience Scale*. Rome: Food and Agriculture Organization.

Carney, Megan A. (2015) *The Unending Hunger: Tracing Women and Food Insecurity Across Borders*. Oakland, CA: University of California Press.

Channa, Subhadra Mitra. (2013) *Gender in South Asia: Social Imagination and Constructed Realities*. Cambridge: Cambridge University Press.

Christoplos, Ian (ed.) (2015) *New Challenges to Food Security: From Climate Change to Fragile States*. New York: Routledge.

Chou, Kuei-Tien, Koichi Hasegawa, Dowan Ku, and Shu-Fen Kao. (2020) *Climate Change Governance in Asia*. New York: Routledge.

Chuku, Gloria (ed.) (2015) *Ethnicities, Nationalities, and Cross-Cultural Representations in Africa and the Diaspora*. Durham, NC: Carolina Academic Press.

Claeys, Priscilla. (2015) *Human Rights and the Food Sovereignty Movement: Reclaiming Control*. New York: Routledge.

Cohen, Marc J. (ed.) (2020) *Advances in Food Security and Sustainability*. Amsterdam: Academic Press.

Committee on World Food Security. (2009) *Reform of the Committee on World Food Security*. 35th Session, October 14, 15, and 17. Agenda Item III. CFS: 2009/2 Rev. 2. Rome: Food and Agriculture Organization.

Committee on World Food Security. (2012) *Global Strategic Framework for Food Security and Nutrition*. Rome: Food and Agriculture Organization.

Committee on World Food Security. (2017) *Global Strategic Framework for Food Security and Nutrition*. Rome: Food and Agriculture Organization.

Community of Latin American and Caribbean States. (2014) *Food Security, Nutrition and Hunger Eradication Plan*. Caracas: Community of Latin American and Caribbean States.

Conceicão, P., Sebastian Levine, Michael Lipton, and Alex Warren-Rodríguez. (2016) "Toward a Food Secure Future: Ensuring Food Security for Sustainable Human Development in Sub-Saharan Africa," *Food Policy*, 60: 1–9.

Concern Worldwide and Welthungerhilfe. (2019) *Global Hunger Index 2019*. Dublin, Ireland and Bonn, Germany: Concern Worldwide and Welthungerhilfe.

Constance, Douglas H., Jason T. Konefal, and Maki Hatanaka (eds.) (2018) *Contested Sustainability: Discourses in the Agrifood System*. New York: Routledge.

Cotula, Lorenzo. (2013) *The Great African Land Grab? Agricultural Investments and the Global Food System*. London: Zed Books.

Cresswell Riol, Katharine S.E. (2017) *The Right to Food Guidelines, Democracy and Citizen Participation: Country Case Studies*. New York: Routledge.

Darkoh, Michael and Apollo Rwomire (eds.) (2018) *Human Impact on Environment and Sustainable Development in Africa*. New York: Routledge.

Davila Cisneros, Frederico, Robert Dyball, and Jennifer Marie Amparo. (2018) "Transdisciplinary Research for Food and Nutrition Security: Examining Research-Policy Understandings in Southeast Asia," *Environmental Development*, 28: 67–82.

Davis, Kyle F., Paolo D'Odorico, and Maria Christina Rulli. (2014) "Land Grabbing: A Preliminary Quantification of Economic Impacts on Rural Livelihoods," *Population and Environment*, 36: 180–192.

Debnath, Deepayan and Suresh Chandra Babu (eds.) (2019) *Biofuels, Bioenergy and Food Security: Technology, Institutions and Policies*. Washington, DC: International Food Policy Research Institute.

Deininger, Klaus, Sara Savastano, and Fang Xia. (2017) "Smallholders' Land Access in Sub-Saharan Africa: A New Landscape," *Food Policy*, 67: 78–92.

de Elvira, Laura Ruiz, Christoph H. Schwarz, and Irene Weipert-Fenner (eds.) (2018) *Clientelism and Patronage in the Middle East: Networks of Dependency*. New York: Routledge.

dela Rama, Marie and Chris Rowley (eds.) (2017) *The Changing Face of Corruption in the Asia Pacific: Current Perspectives and Future Challenges*. Amsterdam: El Sevier.

Delgado, Luisa E. and Víctor H. Marín. (2019) *Socio-Ecological Systems of Latin America: Complexities and Challenges*. Cham, Switzerland: Springer.

de Schutter, Olivier. (2013a) *Gender Equality and Food Security: Women's Empowerment as a Tool Against Hunger*. Rome: Food and Agriculture Organization.

de Schutter, Olivier. (2013b) "The Reform of the Committee on World Food Security: The Quest for Coherence in Global Governance," Louvain: Catholic University of Louvain. Center for the Philosophy of Law. CRIDHO Working Paper 2013/8.

de Schutter, Olivier and Kaitlin Y. Cordes (eds.) (2011) *Accounting for Hunger: The Right to Food in the Era of Globalisation*. Oxford: Hart Publishing.

Desmarais, Annette, Netti Wiebe, and Hannah Wittman. (2010) *Food Sovereignty: Reconnecting Food, Nature and Community*. San Francisco: Food First Books.

Diep, Loan, Tim Hayward, Anna Walnycki, Marwan Husseiki, and Linus Karlsson. (2017) "Water, Crises and Conflict in MENA," London: International Institute for Environment and Development, Working Paper.

Dissanayake, Asafu-Adjaye, and Mahadeva. (2017) "Addressing Climate Change Cause and Effect on Land Cover and Land Use in South Asia," *Land Use Policy*, 67: 352–366.

Djenontin, Ida Nadia S., Samson Foli, and Leo C. Zulu. (2018) "Revisiting the Factors Shaping Outcomes for Forest and Landscape Restoration in Sub Saharan Africa," *Sustainability*, 10, 4: 906–1030.

Du Toit, Brian M. (ed.) (2019) *Ethnicity in Modern Africa*. New York: Routledge.

Dzanku, Fred Mawunyo. (2019) "Food Security in Rural Sub-Saharan Africa: Exploring the Nexus Between Gender, Geography and Off-farm Employment," *World Development*, 113: 26–43.

Edelman, Marc. (2017) *Critical Perspectives on Food Sovereignty: Global Agrarian Transformations*. New York: Routledge.

Elbadawi, Ibrahim and Hoda Selim (eds.) (2016) *Understanding and Avoiding the Oil Curse in Resource-Rich Arab Economies*. Cambridge: Cambridge University Press.

Engelmann, Kurt. (2016) *Rural Development in Eurasia and the Middle East: Land Reform, Demographic Change, and Environmental Constraints*. Seattle: University of Washington Press.

Fernandes, Leela (ed.) (2018) *Routledge Handbook of Gender in South Asia*. New York: Routledge.

Filho, Walter Leal (ed.) (2015) *Climate Change in the Asia-Pacific Region*. Cham, Switzerland: Springer.

Filho, Walter Leal (ed.) (2017) *Climate Change Adaptation in Africa: Fostering Resilience and Capacity to Adapt*. Cham, Switzerland: Springer.

Filho, Walter Leal and Leonardo Esteves de Freitas (eds.) (2018) *Climate Change Adaptation in Latin America: Managing Vulnerability, Fostering Resilience*. Cham, Switzerland: Springer.

Fombad, Charles M. and Nico Steytler. (2020) *Corruption and Constitutionalism in Africa*. Oxford: Oxford University Press.

Food Aid Committee. (1995) *Food Aid Convention*. London: Food Aid Committee Secretariat.

Food Aid Committee. (1999) *Food Aid Convention*. London: Food Aid Committee Secretariat.

Food and Agriculture Organization. (1974) *Report of the World Food Conference*. E/CONF.65/20. Rome: Food and Agriculture Organization, November 5–16.

Food and Agriculture Organization. (1996a) *Rome Declaration on World Food Security*. The World Food Summit Rome: Food and Agriculture Organization.

Food and Agriculture Organization. (1996b) *World Food Summit Plan of Action*. Rome: Food and Agriculture Organization.

Food and Agriculture Organization. (2002) *Declaration of the World Food Summit: Five Years Later*. Rome: Food and Agriculture Organization.

Food and Agriculture Organization. (2005a) *Voluntary Guidelines to Support the Progressive Realization of the Right to Adequate Food in the Context of National Food Sovereignty*. Adopted by the 127th Session of the FAO Council, November 2005. Rome: Food and Agriculture Organization.

Food and Agriculture Organization. (2005b) *Hunger-Free Latin American and Caribbean 2025 Initiative*. Rome: Food and Agriculture Organization.

Food and Agriculture Organization. (2008) *Integrated Food Security Phase Classification*. Rome: Food and Agriculture Organization.

Food and Agriculture Organization. (2009) *Declaration of the World Summit on Food Security*. Rome: Food and Agriculture Organization.

Food and Agriculture Organization. (2012) *Voluntary Guidelines on the Responsible Governance of Tenure of Land, Fisheries and Forests in the Context of National Food Security*. Rome: Committee on World Food Security, Food and Agriculture Organization.

Food and Agriculture Organization. (2014a) *The Right to Food within the International Framework of Human Rights and Country Constitutions*. Rome: Food and Agriculture Organization.

Food and Agriculture Organization. (2014b) *The Right to Food: Past Commitment, Current Obligation, Further Action for the Future: A Ten Year Retrospective on the Right to Food Guidelines*. Rome: Food and Agriculture Organization.

Food and Agriculture Organization. (2014c) *Right to Food Handbooks*. Rome: Food and Agriculture Organization.

Food and Agriculture Organization. (2014d) *Principles for Responsible Investment in Agriculture and Food Systems*. Rome: Food and Agriculture Organization.

Food and Agriculture Organization. (2015a) *Voluntary Guidelines for Protecting the Rights and Improving the Livelihoods of Marine and Inland Fisheries and Fish Workers Within the Context of Sustainable Fish Management*. Rome: Food and Agriculture Organization.

Food and Agriculture Organization. (2015b) *The Framework for Action for Food Security and Nutrition in Protracted Crises*. Rome: Food and Agriculture Organization.

Food and Agriculture Organization. (2016) *Voluntary Guidelines for Agro-Environmental Policies in Latin America and the Caribbean*. Santiago: Food and Agriculture Organization.

Food and Agriculture Organization. (2017) *Yearbook of Forest Products 2017*. Rome: Food and Agriculture Organization.

Food and Agriculture Organization. (2018a) *Achieving Zero Hunger in Africa by 2025: Taking Stock of Progress*. Rome: Food and Agriculture Organization.

Food and Agriculture Organization. (2018b) *Recent Report on Food Security in Asia*. Rome: Food and Agriculture Organization.

Food and Agriculture Organization. (2018c) *State of Food Security and Nutrition in the World 2018—Building Climate Resilience for Food Security and Nutrition*. Rome: Food and Agriculture Organization.

Food and Agriculture Organization. (2018d) *The State of Food and Agriculture 2018—Migration, Agriculture and Rural Development*. Rome: Food and Agriculture Organization.

Food and Agriculture Organization. (2018e) *Asia and the Pacific—Regional Overview of Food Security and Nutrition 2018: Accelerating Progress Toward the SDGs*. Bangkok: Food and Agriculture Organization.

Food and Agriculture Organization. (2019a) *State of Food and Agriculture 2019: Moving Forward on Food Loss and Waste Reduction*. Rome: Food and Agriculture Organization.

Food and Agriculture Organization. (2019b) *State of Food Security and Nutrition in the World 2019: Safeguarding Against Economic Slowdowns and Downturns*. Rome: Food and Agriculture Organization.

Food and Agriculture Organization. (2019c) *Enhancing the Contributions of Small-Scale Fisheries to Food Security and Sustainable Livelihoods*. Rome: Food and Agriculture Organization.

Food and Agriculture Organization. (2019d) *Near East and North Africa—Regional Overview of Food Security and Nutrition 2018: Rural Transformation—Key for Sustainable Development in the Near East and North Africa*. Cairo: Food and Agriculture Organization.

Food and Agriculture Organization. (2019e) *Africa—Regional Overview of Food Security and Nutrition 2018: Addressing the Threat from Climate Variability and Extremes for Food Security and Nutrition*. Accra: Food and Agriculture Organization.

Food and Agriculture Organization. (2019f) *FAO School Food and Nutrition Framework*. Rome: Food and Agriculture Organization.

Food and Agriculture Organization. (2019g) *Latin America and the Caribbean—Regional Overview of Food Security and Nutrition 2018: Inequality and Food Systems*. Santiago: Food and Agriculture Organization.

Food and Agriculture Organization. (2019h) *Asia and the Pacific—Regional Overview of Food Security and Nutrition 2019: Placing Nutrition at the Centre of Social Protection*. Bangkok: Food and Agriculture Organization.

Food and Agriculture Organization. (2020a) *Climate Change and Food Security*. Rome: Food and Agriculture Organization.

Food and Agriculture Organization. (2020b) *Global Forest Resources Assessment 2020*. Rome: Food and Agriculture Organization.

Food and Agriculture Organization. (2020c) *State of the World's Forests 2020*. Rome: Food and Agriculture Organization.

Food and Agriculture Organization. (2020d) *State of World Fisheries and Aquaculture 2020*. Rome: Food and Agriculture Organization.

Food and Agriculture Organization. (2020e) *Global Information and Early Warning System*. Rome: Food and Agriculture Organization.

Food and Agriculture Organization. (2020f) *Incorporating Climate Considerations into Agricultural Investment Programmes.* Rome: Food and Agriculture Organization.

Food and Agriculture Organization. (2020g) *Coastal Fisheries Initiative: Promoting Sustainable Fisheries in Coastal Areas.* Rome: Food and Agriculture Organization.

Food and Agriculture Organization. (2020h) *Gender in Food and Nutrition Security.* Rome: Food and Agriculture Organization.

Food and Agriculture Organization. (2020i) *Africa—Regional Overview of Food Security and Nutrition 2019: Containing the Damage of Economic Slowdowns and Downturns to Food Insecurity in Africa.* Accra: Food and Agriculture Organization.

Food and Agriculture Organization. (2020j) *Latin America and the Caribbean—Regional Overview of Food Security and Nutrition 2019: Towards Healthier Food Environments That Address All Forms of Malnutrition.* Santiago: Food and Agriculture Organization.

Food and Agriculture Organization and the Pan American Health Organization. (2017) *Panorama of Food Security and Nutrition in Latin America and the Caribbean 2017.* Rome: Food and Agriculture Organization and the Pan American Health Organization.

Food and Agriculture Organization and World Food Programme. (2019) *Monitoring Food Security in Countries with Conflict Situations.* Rome: Food and Agriculture Organization and World Food Programme.

Food and Agriculture Organization and the World Health Organization. (1992) *World Declaration and Plan of Action for Nutrition.* Rome: Food and Agriculture Organization.

Food and Agriculture Organization and the World Health Organization. (2014a) *Conference Outcome Document: Rome Declaration on Nutrition.* Second International Conference on Nutrition. ICN2 2014/2, November 19–21. Rome: Food and Agriculture Organization.

Food and Agriculture Organization and the World Health Organization. (2014b) *Conference Outcome Document: Framework for Action.* Second International Conference on Nutrition. ICN2 2014/3, Corr. 1, November 19–21. Rome: Food and Agriculture Organization.

Food Security Information Network. (2018) *2018 Global Nutrition Report.* Rome: Food Security Information Network.

Food Security Information Network. (2020) *2020 Global Report on the Food Crisis: Joint Analysis for Better Decisions.* Rome: Food Security Information Network.

Forum on Food Sovereignty. (2002) *Declaration of the NGO Forum at the FAO Summit Rome + 5.* Rome: Forum on Food Sovereignty.

Forum on Food Sovereignty. (2007) *Declaration of Nyéléni*. Nyéléni Village, Sélingué, Mali: Forum on Food Sovereignty.

Fouilleux, Eve, Nicolas Bricas, and Arlene Alpha. (2017) "Feeding 9 Billion People: Global Food Security Debates and the Productionist Trap," *Journal of European Public Policy*, 24, 11: 1658–1677.

Friedmann, Harriet. (2005) "From Colonialism to Green Capitalism: Social Movements and the Emergence of Food Regimes," in Frederick. H. Buttel and Philip D. McMichael (eds.) *New Directions in the Sociology of International Development: Research in Rural Sociology and Development*. Amsterdam: Elsevier: 227–264.

Galicia, Luis, et al. (2016) "Tackling Malnutrition in Latin America and the Caribbean: Challenges and Opportunities," *Revista Panamericana de Salud Publica*, 40, 2: 138–146.

Galistcheva, Natalia V. (2018) *Food Security in South Asia: Major Challenges and Solutions*. Vestnik MGIMO-Universiteta, 58, 1: 148–168.

Garduño-Diaz, Sara D. and Philippe Y Garduño-Diaz. (2015) "Food Security in the Middle East and North Africa," *International Journal of Nutrition and Food Engineering*, 9, 1: 47–50.

Giraldo, Omar Felipe. (2019) *Political Ecology of Agriculture: Agroecology and Post-development*. Cham, Switzerland: Springer.

Gliessman, Stephen R. (2015) *Agroecology: The Ecology of Sustainable Food Systems*. Boca Raton: CRC Press.

Gong, Ting and Ian Scott (ed.) (2016) *Routledge Handbook of Corruption in Asia*. New York: Routledge.

Grove, Richard and George Adamson. (2017) *El Niño in World History*. New York: Palgrave Macmillan.

Haddad, Lawrence, Lisa Cameron, and Inka Barnett. (2015) "The Double Burden of Malnutrition in Southeast Asia and the Pacific: Priorities, Policies and Politics," *Health Policy and Planning*, 30, 9: 1193–1206.

Harding, Kassandra L., Víctor M. Aguayo, and Patrick Webb. (2018) "Hidden Hunger in South Asia: A Review of Recent Trends and Persistent Challenges," *Public Health Nutrition*, 21, 4: 785–795.

Haslam, Paul A. and Pablo Heidrich (eds.) (2016) *The Political-Economy of Natural Resources and Development: From Neoliberalsim to Resource Nationalism*. New York: Routledge.

Hassan, Areej (ed.) (2016) *Food Security and Child Malnutrition: The Impact on Health, Growth, and Well-Being*. Boca Raton, FL: CRC Press.

Hendrix, Cullen S. and Marcus Noland. (2014) *Confronting the Curse: The Economics and Geopolitics of Natural Resource Governance*. Washington, DC: Paterson Institute for International Economics.

Herrera, Rémy and Kin Chi Lau (eds.) (2015) *The Struggle for Food Sovereignty: Alternative Development and the Renewal of Peasant Societies Today*. London: Pluto Press.

High Level Task Force on Global Food and Nutrition Security. (2008) *Comprehensive Framework for Action*. Rome: Food and Agriculture Organization.

High Level Task Force on Global Food and Nutrition Security. (2010) *Updated Comprehensive Framework for Action*. Rome: Food and Agriculture Organization.

Hilmi, Angela. (2017) *Agroecology: Reweaving a New Landscape*. New York: Palgrave Macmillan.

Hirsch, Philip. (2016) *Routledge Handbook of the Environment in Southeast Asia*. New York: Routledge.

Hofste, Rutger Willem, Paul Reig, and Leah Schleiter. (2019) *17 Countries Home to One-Quarter of the World's Population, Face Extremely High Water Stress*. Washington, DC: World Resources Institute.

Holt-Giménez, Eric, et al. (eds.) (2017) *Food Sovereignty: Convergence and Contradictions, Conditions and Challenges*. New York: Routledge.

Hope, Elizabeth Thomas (ed.) (2016) *Climate Change and Food Security: Africa and the Caribbean*. New York: Routledge.

Hope, Kempe Ronald. (2017) *Corruption and Governance in Africa*. New York: Palgrave Macmillan.

Hossain, Mahabub. (2014) "Food Security in South Asia: Status, Challenges and Policy Considerations," *World Food Policy*, 1, 2: 108–123.

Huang, Shirlena and Kanchana N. Ruwanpura (eds.) (2020) *Handbook on Gender in Asia*. Cheltenham, UK: Edward Elgar.

Human Rights Commission. (1987) *The Right to Adequate Food as a Human Right*. New York: United Nations.

Human Rights Commission. (2002) *Report of the Special Rapporteur on the Right to Food*. New York: United Nations.

Human Rights Council. (2007) *Mandate of the Special Rapporteur on the Right to Food*. New York: United Nations.

Human Rights Council. (2008a) *The Right to Food*. Res. 7/14. 40th Meeting, New York: United Nations, March 27.

Human Rights Council. (2008b) *Promotion and Protection of all Human Rights, Civil, Political, Economic, Social, and Cultural Rights, Including the Right to Development. Report of the Special Rapporteur on the Right to Food*. Jean Ziegler, Human Rights Council, 7th Session, United Nations General Assembly, A/HRC/7/5.

Human Rights Council. (2015) *Promotion and Protection of all Human Rights, Civil, Political, Economic, Social, and Cultural Rights, Including the Right to Development*. United Nations General Assembly Resolution A/HRC/28/L.16.

Human Rights Council. (2019) *The Right to Food*. United Nations General Assembly Resolution A/HRC/40/L.12, New York: United Nations.

Humphreys, Macartan, Jeffrey D. Sachs, and Joseph E. Stiglitz (eds.) (2007) *Escaping the Resource Curse*. New York: Columbia University Press.

Hussein, Nazia (ed.) (2018) *Rethinking New Womanhood: Practices of Gender, Class, Culture and Religion in South Asia*. New York: Palgrave Macmillan.

Intergovernmental Panel of Experts on Climate Change. (2018) *Global Warming of 1.5 C*. Geneva: Intergovernmental Panel on Climate Change.

Intergovernmental Panel of Experts on Climate Change. (2019a) *Climate Change and Land*. Geneva: Intergovernmental Panel on Climate Change.

Intergovernmental Panel of Experts on Climate Change. (2019b) *The Ocean and Cryosphere in a Changing Climate*. Geneva: Intergovernmental Panel on Climate Change.

International Food Policy Research Institute. (2020) *2020 Global Food Policy Report: Building Inclusive Food Systems*. Washington, DC: International Food Policy Research Institute.

International Fund for Agricultural Development. (2016) *IFAD Strategic Framework 2016–2025: Enabling Inclusive and Sustainable Rural Transformation*. Rome: International Fund for Agricultural Development.

International Fund for Agricultural Development. (2017a) *Inclusive Finance and inclusive Rural Transformation*. Research Series Issue 10. Rome: International Fund for Agricultural Development.

International Fund for Agricultural Development. (2017b) *Measuring Women's Empowerment in Agriculture: A Streamlined Approach*. Rome: International Fund for Agricultural Development.

International Fund for Agricultural Development. (2018a) *Agents of Rural Change: The IFAD Story*. Rome: International Fund for Agricultural Development.

International Fund for Agricultural Development. (2018b) *Sustainable Rural Transformation in Asia and the Pacific*. Rome: International Fund for Agricultural Development, December.

International Fund for Agricultural Development. (2018c) *IFAD's Support for Land and Natural Resource Tenure Security: West and Central Africa*. Rome: International Fund for Agricultural Development.

International Fund for Agricultural Development. (2018d) *Annual Report 2017*. Rome: International Fund for Agricultural Development.

International Fund for Agricultural Development. (2018e) *Effective Rural Development: IFAD's Evidence-Based Approach to Managing for Results*. Rome: International Fund for Agricultural Development.

International Fund for Agricultural Development. (2018f) *Sustainable Rural Transformation in the Asia and the Pacific Region*. Rome: International Fund for Agricultural Development.

International Fund for Agricultural Development. (2018g) *Asia's Rural-Urban Disparity in the Context of Growing Inequality.* Rome: International Fund for Agricultural Development.

International Fund for Agricultural Development. (2018h) *IFAD's Support for Land and Natural Resource Tenure Security.* Rome: International Fund for Agricultural Development.

International Fund for Agricultural Development. (2018i) *Farmers Organizations in Africa*. Rome: International Fund for Agricultural Development.

International Fund for Agricultural Development. (2019a) *Annual Report 2018.* Rome: International Fund for Agricultural Development.

International Fund for Agricultural Development. (2019b) *Inclusive Financial Services for the Poor.* Rome: International Fund for Agricultural Development.

International Fund for Agricultural Development. (2019c) *2019 Annual Report on Results and Impact of IFAD Operations.* Rome: International Fund for Agricultural Development, Independent Office of Evaluation.

International Fund for Agricultural Development. (2019d) *The Food Loss Reduction Advantage: Building Sustainable Food Systems.* Rome: International Fund for Agricultural Development.

International Fund for Agricultural Development. (2019e) *The Fisheries and Aquaculture Advantage: Fostering Food Security and Nutrition, Increasing Incomes and Empowerment*. Rome: International Fund for Agricultural Development.

International Fund for Agricultural Development. (2019f) *Climate Action Report 2019.* Rome: International Fund for Agricultural Development.

International Fund for Agricultural Development. (2020) *IFAD and Farmers' Organizations—Partnership in Progress 2016–2019.* Rome: International Fund for Agricultural Development.

International Land Coalition. (2011) *Tirana Declaration.* Rome: International Land Coalition.

James, Helen (ed.) (2019) *Population, Development and the Environment: Challenges to Achieving the Sustainable Development Goals in the Asia Pacific*. New York: Palgrave Macmillan.

Joshil, Divya Upadhyaya and Caroline Brassard (eds.) (2020) *Urban Spaces and Gender in Asia*. Cham, Switzerland: Springer.

Kaag, Mayke and Annelies Zoomers (eds.) (2014) *The Global Land Grab: Beyond the Hype*. London: Zed Books.

Kamrava, Mehran (ed.) (2021) *The "Resource Curse" in the Persian Gulf*. New York: Routledge.

Kandeel, Amal A. (2014) "Food Insecurity: The Basic Threat in an Overburdened Region," *Middle East Policy*, 21, 4: 84–91.

Kent, George. (2005) *Freedom From Want: The Human Right to Adequate Food.* Washington, DC: Georgetown University Press.

Kent, George (ed.) (2008) *Global Obligations for the Right to Food*. Lanham, MD: Rowman & Littlefield.

Keulertz, Martin and Eckart Woertz (eds.) (2017) *The Water-Energy-Food Nexus in the Middle East and North Africa*. New York: Routledge.

Knuth, Lidija and Margret Vidar. (2011) *Constitutional and Legal Protection of the Right to Food Around the World*. Rome: Food and Agriculture Organization.

Koh, Kheng-Lian (ed.) (2015) *Adaptation to Climate Change: ASEAN and Comparative Experiences*. Singapore: World Scientific Publishing Company.

Konte, Maty and Nyasha Tirivayi (eds.) (2020) *Women and Sustainable Human Development: Empowering Women in Africa*. New York: Palgrave Macmillan.

Kubbe, Ina and Aiysha Varraich (eds.) (2019) *Corruption and Informal Practices in the Middle East and North Africa*. New York: Routledge.

Kukreja, Sunil (ed.) (2019) *Southeast Asia and Environmental Sustainability in Context*. Lanham: Lexington.

Kuwornu, John K.M. (ed.) (2018) *Climate Change and Sub-Saharan Africa: The Vulnerability and Adaptation of Food Supply Chain Actors*. Wilmington, DE: Vernon Press.

La Via Campesina. (2003) *People's Food Sovereignty—WTO Out of Agriculture*. Harare: La Via Campesina.

Le Billon, Philippe. (2013) *Fueling War: Natural Resources and Armed Conflicts*. New York: Routledge.

Le Mouël and Bertrand Schmitt (eds.) (2018) *Food Dependency in the MENA Region*. Cham, Switzerland: Springer.

Lindsay, Abby. (2018) "Water and Climate in Latin America," *Journal of Environmental Studies and Sciences*, 8, 4: 435–440.

Lorenzo, Cristian (ed.) (2020) *Latin America in Times of Global Environmental Change*. Cham, Switzerland: Springer.

Mailey, John R. (2017) *The Anatomy of the Resource Curse: Predatory Investment in Africa's Extractive Industries*. Washington, DC: African Center for Strategic Studies.

Majaw, Baniateilang. (2020) *Climate Change in South Asia: Politics, Policies, and the SAARC*. New York: Routledge.

Manners, Rhys and Consuelo Varela-Ortega. (2017) "Analysing Latin American and Caribbean Forest Vulnerability from Socio-Economic Factors," *Journal of Integrative Environmental Sciences*, 14, 1: 109–130.

Margulis, Matias E. (2013) "The Regime Complex for Food Security: Implications for the Global Hunger Challenge," *Global Governance*, 19, 1: 53–67.

Matondo, Jonathan I., Berhanu F. Alemaw, and Jean Pierre Sandwidi (eds.) (2017) *Climate Variability and Change in Africa: Perspectives, Experiences and Sustainability*. Cham: Switzerland, Springer.

Mayer, Tamar and Molly D. Anderson (eds.) (2020) *Food Insecurity: A Matter of Justice, Sovereignty, and Survival*. New York: Routledge.

Mazumdar, Aparajita. (2015) *The Right to Food: An International Organization Perspective*. Riga, Latvia: Scholars Press.

McCauley, John F. (2017) *The Logic of Ethnic and Religious Conflict in Africa*. Cambridge: Cambridge University Press.

McMichael, Philip. (2009a) "A Food Regime Genealogy," *Journal of Peasant Studies*, 36, 1: 139–169.

McMichael, Philip. (2009b) "Food Sovereignty, Social Reproduction, and the Agrarian Question," in Haroon Akram-Lodhi (ed.) *Peasants and Globalization*. New York: Routledge: 288–312.

Meriwether, Margaret L. and Judith E. Tucker. (2018) *A Social History of Women and Gender in the Modern Middle East*. New York: Routledge.

Mosley, Paul. (2017) *Fiscal Policy and the Natural Resource Curse: How to Escape from the Poverty Trap*. New York: Routledge.

Mossi, Alelemir Jose, Claudia Petry, and Francisco Wilson (eds.) (2020) *Agroecology: Insights, Experiences and Perspectives*. Hauppauge, NY: Nova Science Publishers.

Motzafi-Haller, Pnina (ed.) (2017) *Women in Agriculture in the Middle East*. New York: Routledge.

Munyai, Anzanilufuno. (2020) *Overcoming the Corruption Conundrum in Africa*. Newcastle upon Tyne, UK: Cambridge Scholars Publishing.

Murshed, Syed Mansoob. (2018) *The Resource Curse*. Newcastle upon Tyne, UK: Agenda Publishing.

Nasong'o, Wanjala S. (ed.) (2016) *The Roots of Ethnic Conflict in Africa: From Grievance to Violence*. New York: Palgrave Macmillan.

Nhamo, Godwell and Caiphas Chekwoti (eds.) (2014) *Land Grabs in a Green African Economy: Implications for Trade, Investment, and Development Policies*. Pretoria: African Institute of South Africa.

Niles, Meredith T. and Jonathan D. Salerno. (2018) "A Cross-Country Analysis of Climate Shocks and Smallholder Food Insecurity," *PLoS One*, 13, 2: 1–14.

Njuki, Jemimah, John R. Parkins, and Amy Kaler (eds.) (2016) *Transforming Gender and Food Security in the Global South*. New York: Routledge.

Nooy van Tol, Jelleke de. (2016) *Transition to Agro-Ecology: For a Food Secure World*. Bloomington, IN: Authorhouse.

Okech, Awino (ed.) (2020) *Gender, Protest and Political Change in Africa*. New York: Palgrave Macmillan.

Okonjo-Iweala, Ngozi. (2018) *Fighting Corruption is Dangerous: The Story Behind the Headlines*. Cambridge: Massachusetts Institute of Technology Press.

Ordway, Elsa M., Gregory P. Asner, and Eric F. Lambin. (2017) "Deforestation Risk Due to Commodity Crop Expansion in Sub-Saharan Africa," *Environmental Research Letters*, 12, 4: 1–13.

Organization for Economic Cooperation and Development/Food and Agriculture Organization. (2018) *OECD-FAO Agricultural Outlook 2018–2027*. Paris: Organization for Economic Cooperation and Development.

Palmer, Lisa. (2017) *Hot, Hungry Planet: The Fight to Stop a Global Food Crisis in the Face of Climate Change*. New York: St. Martin's Press.

Papyrakis, Elissaios. (2018) *The Resource Curse Reexamined: The Role of Extractive Industry in Development*. New York: Routledge.

Papyrakis, Elissaios (ed.) (2019) *Why Does Development Fail in Resource Rich Economies: The Catch 22 of Mineral Wealth*. New York: Routledge.

Paquet, Laura. (2017) *The Environment of Contemporary Africa*. New York: Cavendish Square.

Parker, Lyn, Laura Dales, and Chie Ikeya (eds.) (2017) *Contestations over Gender in Asia*. New York: Routledge.

Pendrill, Florence and U. Martin Persson. (2017) "Combining Global Land Cover Datasets to Quantify Agricultural Expansion into Forests in Latin America: Limitations and Challenges," *PLoS One*, 12, 7: 1–21.

Perfecto, Ivette, John Vandermeer, and Angus Wright. (2019) *Nature's Matrix: Linking Agriculture, Biodiversity Conservation and Food Sovereignty*. New York: Routledge.

Perkins, Patricia E. (ed.) (2015) *Water and Climate Change in Africa*. New York: Routledge.

Phadnis, Urmila and Rajat Ganguly. (2015) *Ethnicity and Nation-Building in South Asia*. Los Angeles: Sage.

Piliavsky, Anastasia (ed.) (2014) *Patronage as Politics in South Asia*. Cambridge: Cambridge University Press.

Pimbert, Michel P. (ed.) (2018) *Food Sovereignty, Agroecology and Biocultural Diversity: Constructing and Contesting Knowledge*. New York: Routledge.

Pinto, Juliet, Paola Pradoo, and J. Alexander Tirado-Alcaraz. (2017) *Environmental News in South America: Conflict, Crisis and Contestation*. New York: Palgrave Macmillan.

Pollard, Lisa and Mona L. Russell. (2021) *History, Women and Gender in the Modern Middle East: From Orientalism to the Arab Spring*. New York: Routledge.

Pouran, Hamid and Hassan Hakimian (eds.) (2019) *Environmental Challenges in the MENA Region*. London: Gingko Press.

Pritchard, Bill, Heather MacKay, and Christopher Turner. (2017) "Special Issue Introduction: Geographical Perspectives on Food and Nutrition Insecurity in the Global South," *Geographical Research*, 55, 2: 127–130.

Quisumbing, Agnes R., Ruth Suseela Meinzen-Dick, and Jemimah Njuki (eds.) (2019) *2019 Annual Trends and Outlook Report: Gender Equality in Rural Africa: From Commitments to Outcomes*. Washington, DC: International Food Policy Research Institute.

Rabinowitz, Dan. (2020) *The Power of Deserts: Climate Change, the Middle East, and the Promise of a Post-Oil Era*. Stanford: Stanford University Press.

Rajan, Sudhir Chella. (2020) *A Social Theory of Corruption: Notes from the Indian Subcontinent*. Cambridge, MA: Harvard University Press.

Reyer, Christopher P. O., Sophie Adams, and Torsten Albrecht, et al. (2017) "Climate Change Impacts in Latin America and the Caribbean and their Implications for Development," *Regional Environmental Change*, 17, 6: 1601–1621.

Rieff, David. (2015) *The Reproach of Hunger: Food, Justice and Money in the Twenty-First Century*. New York: Simon and Schuster.

Robins, Nicholas A. and Barbara J. Fraser. (2020) *Landscapes of Inequity: Environmental Justice in the Andes-Amazon Region*. Lincoln: University of Nebraska Press.

Rodríguez Goyes, David, Hanneke Mol, and Niger South (eds.) (2017) *Environmental Crime in Latin America: The Theft of Nature and the Poisoning of Land*. New York: Palgrave Macmillan.

Roessler, Philip. (2016) *Ethnic Politics and State Power in Africa*. Cambridge: Cambridge University Press.

Rosset, Peter M. and Miguel A. Altieri. (2017) *Agroecology: Science and Politics*. Warwickshire, UK: Practical Action Publishing.

Rossi, Maximo, Gastón Ares, and Zuleika Ferre. (2017) "Socio-Economic Determinants of Hunger in Latin American Countries," Working Paper No. 1017, Orebro University School of Business.

Rotberg, Robert I. (ed.) (2019) *Corruption in Latin America: How Politicians and Corporations Steal from Citizens*. Cham, Switzerland: Springer.

Ryan, J. Michael and Helen Rizzo (eds.) (2019) *Gender in the Middle East and North Africa: Contemporary Issues and Challenges*. Boulder: Lynne Rienner.

Sabry, Sarah. (2015) "Food Security in the Middle East," *Journal of Agrarian Change*, 15, 4: 611–613.

Sachdeva, Vivek, Queeny Pradhan, and Anu Venugopalan (eds.) (2019) *Identities in South Asia: Conflicts and Assertions*. New York: Routledge.

Sachs, Carolyn E. (ed.) (2019) *Gender, Agriculture and Agrarian Transformations: Changing Relations in Africa, Latin America and Asia*. New York: Routledge.

Sahn, David E. (2015) *The Fight Against Hunger and Malnutrition: The Role of Food, Agriculture, and Targeted Policies*. Oxford: Oxford University Press.

Sangmpan, S.N. (2017) *Ethnicities and Tribes in Sub-Saharan Africa: Opening Old Wounds*. New York: Palgrave Macmillan.

Schanbacher, William. (2019) *Food as a Human Right: Combatting Global Hunger and Forging a Path to Food Sovereignty*. Santa Barbara, CA: Praeger.

Schmidt, Lisa. (2018) *Food Security and the Crisis of the New Millennium: Empowering Women as a Tool to Achieve Food Security*. Norderstedt, Germany: GRIN Verlag.

Schubert, Jon, Ulf Engel, and Elísio Macamo (eds.) (2018) *Extractive Industries and Changing State Dynamics in Africa: Beyond the Resource Curse*. New York: Routledge.

Sen, Amartya. (1981) *Poverty and Famines: An Essay on Entitlement and Deprivation*. Oxford: Oxford University Press.

Shani, Giorgio and Takashi Kibe (eds.) (2019) *Religion and Nationalism in Asia*. New York: Routledge.

Shattuck, Annie, Christina Schiavoni, and Zoe Van Gelder (eds.) (2018) *The Politics of Food Sovereignty: Concept, Practise and Social Movements*. New York: Routledge.

Sherwood, Leah. (2017) *Climate Change and Water Resources in the MENA Region: Looking at Adaptive Governance*. Abu Dhabi: Trends Research and Advisory.

Shiva, Vandana. (2016) *Who Really Feeds the World? The Failures of Agribusiness and the Promise of Agroecology*. Berkeley, CA: North Atlantic Books.

Smith, Michael D. and Birgit Meade. (2019) *Who Are the World's Food Insecure? Identifying the Risk Factors of Food Insecurity Around the World*. Washington, DC: United States Department of Agriculture, Economic Research Service.

Smith, Michael D., Matthew P. Rabbitt, and Alisha Coleman-Jensen. (2017) "Who Are the World's Food Insecure? New Evidence from the Food and Agriculture Organization's Food Insecurity Experience Scale," *World Development*, 93: 402–412.

Smith, Michael D., Woubet Kassa, and Paul Winters. (2017) "Assessing Food Insecurity in Latin America and the Caribbean Using FAO's Food Insecurity Experience Scale," *Food Policy*, 71: 48–61.

Snapp, Sieglinde and Barry Pound (eds.) (2017) *Agricultural Systems: Agroecology and Rural Innovation for Development*. London: Academic Press.

Solati, Fariba. (2017) *Women, Work, and Patriarchy in the Middle East and North Africa*. New York: Palgrave Macmillan.

Solh, Mahmoud. (2016) "The Outlook for Food Security in the Middle East and North Africa," in Alberto Garrido and Ayman Rabi (eds.) *Managing Water in the 21st Century: Challenges and Opportunities*. Proceedings of the 8th Rossenberg International Forum on Water Policy, Oakland: University of California: 95–119.

Srivastava, Ravindra Kumar. (2020) *Managing Urbanization, Climate Change and Disasters in South Asia*. Cham, Switzerland: Springer.

Steier, Gabriela and Alberto Giulio Cianci (eds.) (2019) *Environmental Resilience and Food Law: Agrobiodiversity and Agroecology*. Boca Raton: CRC Press.

Sudhakar Reddy, Saranya, et al. (2018) "Assessment and Monitoring of Deforestation and Forest Fragmentation in South Asia Since the 1930s," *Global Planetary Change*, 161: 132–148.

Suryadinata, Leo. (2015) *The Making of Southeast Asian Nations: State, Ethnicity, Indigenism, and Citizenship*. London: World Scientific Publishing.

Swain, Ashok and Anders Jägerskog. (2016) *Emerging Security Threats in the Middle East: The Impact of Climate Change and Globalization*. Lanham: Rowman & Littlefield.

Tambo, Justice A. and Johnathan Mockshell. (2018) "Differential Impacts of Conservation Agriculture Technology Options on Household Income in Sub-Saharan Africa," *Ecological Economics*, 151c: 95–105.

Telles, Edward. (2014) *Pigmentocracies: Ethnicity, Race and Color in Latin America*. Chapel Hill: University of North Carolina Press.

Tilzey, Mark. (2018) *Political Ecology, Food Regimes, and Food Sovereignty: Crisis, Resistance and Resilience*. New York: Palgrave Macmillan.

Tobias, Joseph Nangombe Tobias. (2019) *The Inevitability of Corruption in Africa*. Norderstedt, Germany: GRIN Verlag.

Transparency International. (2019) *Corruption Perceptions Index*. Berlin: Transparency International Secretariat.

Trauger, Amy (ed.) (2015) *Food Sovereignty in International Context: Discourse, Politics and Practice of Place*. New York: Routledge.

Trauger, Amy. (2017) *We Want Land to Live: Making Political Space for Food Sovereignty*. Athens, GA: University of Georgia Press.

Tumushabe, Jennifer Turyatemba. (2018) "Climate Change, Food Security and Sustainable Development in Africa," in Samuel Ojo Oloruntoba and Toyin Falola (eds.) *The Palgrave Handbook of African Politics, Governance and Development*. New York: Palgrave Macmillan: 853–868.

Uchendu, Florence N. (2018) "Hunger Influenced Life Expectancy in War-Torn Sub-Saharan African Countries," *Journal of Health, Population and Nutrition*, 37: 11–15.

Udogu, E. Ike. (2018) *The Issue of Political Ethnicity in Africa*. New York: Routledge.

United Nations. (1948) *Universal Declaration of Human Rights*. General Assembly Resolution 217A, New York: United Nations.

United Nations. (1965) *International Convention on the Elimination of All Forms of Racial Discrimination*. General Assembly Resolution 2106 (xx), New York: United Nations.

United Nations. (1966) *International Covenant on Economic, Social and Cultural Rights*. General Assembly Resolution 2200A (XXI), New York: United Nations.

United Nations. (1974) *Universal Declaration on the Eradication of Hunger and Malnutrition*. General Assembly Resolution 3348. New York: United Nations.

United Nations. (1983) *The Right to Adequate Food as a Human Right*. New York: United Nations, Special Rapporteur on the Right to Food.

United Nations. (1986) *Declaration on the Right to Development*. General Assembly Resolution 41/128, New York: United Nations.

United Nations. (1987) *Resolution 90 of the Economic and Social Council of the United Nations*. New York: United Nations.

United Nations. (1989) *Convention on the Rights of the Child*. General Assembly Resolution 44/25. New York: United Nations.

United Nations. (1990) *Plan of Action of the World Summit for Children*. New York: United Nations.

United Nations. (1994) *United Nations Convention to Combat Desertification*. United Nations General Assembly, A/AC 241/27. New York: United Nations.

United Nations. (1999) *The Right to Adequate Food: General Comment Number 12*. Committee on Economic, Social and Cultural Rights. E/C.12/1999/5. New York: United Nations.

United Nations. (2000a) *United Nations Millennium Declaration*. New York: United Nations.

United Nations. (2000b) *Millennium Development Goals*. New York: United Nations.

United Nations. (2002a) *Johannesburg Declaration on Sustainable Development*. World Summit on Sustainable Development. A/Conf.199/20. New York: United Nations.

United Nations. (2002b) *Plan of Implementation of the World Summit on Sustainable Development*. A/Conf.199/20. New York: United Nations.

United Nations. (2003) *Monterrey Consensus of the International Conference on Financing for Development*. Adopted March 22, 2002. New York: United Nations.

United Nations. (2008) *Doha Declaration on Financing for Development*. A/Conf.212/L.1/Rev.1* Adopted December 9, 2008. New York: United Nations,

United Nations. (2010) *The Right to Adequate Food*. Office of the High Commissioner for Human Rights. Fact Sheet #34. New York: United Nations.

United Nations. (2012) *Food Assistance Convention*. New York: United Nations.

United Nations. (2015a) *World Water Development Report 2015*. New York: United Nations.

United Nations. (2015b) *Transforming Our World: The 2030 Agenda for Sustainable Development*. General Assembly Resolution A/RES/70/1. New York: United Nations.

United Nations. (2016) *World Water Development Report 2016*. New York: United Nations.

United Nations. (2017) *Global Governance for Nutrition and the Role of the United Nations Standing Committee on Nutrition*. New York: United Nations.

United Nations Children's Fund. (1990) *World Declaration on the Survival, Protection, and Development of Children and a Plan of Action*, World Summit for Children. Adopted September 29–30, New York: United Nations Children's Fund.

United Nations Children's Fund. (2019) *The State of the World's Children*. New York: United Nations Children's Fund.

United Nations Children's Fund, World Health Organization, World Bank Group. (2019) *Levels and Trends in Child Malnutrition*. New York: United Nations Children's Fund.

United Nations Committee on Economic, Social and Cultural Rights. (1999) *General Comment Number 12*. Adopted at the Twentieth Session of the Committee on Economic, Social and Cultural Rights on 12 May 1999. E/C.12/1999/5 New York: United Nations.

United Nations Economic Commission for Africa. (2017) *Economic Report on Africa 2017: Urbanization and Industrialization for Africa's Transformation*. Addis Ababa: United Nations Economic Commission for Africa.

United Nations Economic Commission for Africa. (2019) *Economic Report on Africa 2019: Fiscal Policy for Financing Sustainable Development in Africa*. Addis Ababa: United Nations Economic Commission for Africa.

United Nations Economic Commission for Latin America and the Caribbean. (2018a) *Malnutrition Among Children in Latin America and the Caribbean*. Santiago: United Nations Economic Commission for Latin America and the Caribbean.

United Nations Economic Commission for Latin America and the Caribbean. (2018b) *Social Panorama of Latin America 2018*. Santiago: United Nations Economic Commission for Latin America and the Caribbean.

United Nations Economic Commission for Latin America and the Caribbean. (2019) *Social Panorama of Latin America 2019*. Santiago: United Nations Economic Commission for Latin America and the Caribbean.

United Nations Economic and Social Commission for Asia and the Pacific. (2019) *Economic and Social Survey of Asia and the Pacific 2019: Ambitions for Growth*. Bangkok: United Nations Economic and Social Commission for Asia and the Pacific.

United Nations Economic and Social Commission for Asia and the Pacific. (2020) *Economic and Social Survey of Asia and the Pacific 2020: Toward Sustainable Economies*. Bangkok: United Nations Economic and Social Commission for Asia and the Pacific.

United Nations Economic and Social Commission for Western Asia. (2019) *Tracking Food Security in the Arab Region*. Beirut: United Nations Economic and Social Commission for Western Asia.

United Nations Environmental Programme. (2015) *Keeping Track of Our Changing Environment in Asia and the Pacific*. New York: United Nations.

Vachani, Sushil and Jawed Usmani (eds.) (2014) *Adaptation to Climate Change in Asia*. Cheltenham, UK: Edward Elgar.

Vakis, Renos, Jamele Rigolini, Leonardo Lucchetti. (2016) *Chronic Poverty in Latin America and the Caribbean*. Washington, DC: World Bank.

Vandermeer, John and Ivette Perfecto. (2017) *Ecological Complexity and Agroecology*. New York: Routledge.

Van Nieuwland, Marla. (2020) *Examining the Natural Resource Curse: Why do States Fail?* Norderstedt, Germany: GRIN Verlag.

von Bennewitz, Eduardo. (2017) "Land Tenure in Latin America: From Land Reform to Counter-Movement to Neoliberalism," *Acta Universitatis Agriculturae et Silviculturae Mendelianae Brunensis*, 65, 5: 1793–1798.

Von Oppeln-Bronikowski, Constanze. (2011) "Moving from Food Aid to Food Assistance," *International Journal for Rural Development*, 21, 3: 32.

Waha, Katharina, et al. (2017) "Climate Change Impacts in the Middle East and Northern Africa (MENA) Region and their Implications for Vulnerable Population Groups," *Regional Environmental Change*, 17: 1623–1638.

Wambogo, Edwina A., Hala Ghattas, Kenneth L. Leonard, and Nadine R. Sahyoun. (2018) "Validity of the Food Insecurity Experience Scale for Use in Sub-Saharan Africa and Characteristics of Food Insecure Individuals," *Current Developments in Nutrition*, 2, 9: 1–10.

Wane, Njoki Nathani. (2019) *Gender, Democracy and Institutional Development in Africa*. New York: Palgrave Macmillan, 2019.

Ward, Christopher and Sandra Ruckstuhl. (2017) *Water Security, Climate Change, and Conflict in the Middle East: Securing Livelihoods, Building Peace*. London: I. B. Tauris.

Williams, Aled and Philippe Le Billon. (2017) *Corruption, Natural Resources and Development: From Resource Curse to Political Ecology*. Northampton, MA: Edward Elgar Publishers.

Wise, Tim A. (2019) *Eating Tomorrow: Agribusiness, Family Farmers and the Battle for the Future of Food*. New York: The New Press.

Wittman, Hannah. (2009) "Reworking the Metabolic Rift: Via Campesina, Agrarian Citizenship, and Food Sovereignty," *Journal of Peasant Studies*, 36, 4: 805–826.

Wittman, Hannah. (2015) "From Protest to Policy: The Challenges of Institutionalizing Food Sovereignty," *Canadian Food Studies*, 2, 2: 174–182.

Wolford, Wendy, Saturnino M. Borras Jr., Ruth Hall, Ian Scoones, and Ben White (eds.) (2013) "Governing Global Land Deals: The Role of the State in the Rush for Land," *Development and Change*, 44, 2: 189–210.

World Bank. (2018) *Beyond Scarcity: Water Scarcity in the Middle East and North Africa*. MENA Development Report, Washington, DC: World Bank.

World Development Movement. (2012) *Transforming Our Food System: The Movement for Food Sovereignty*. London: World Development Movement.

World Food Council. (1988) *Beijing Declaration*. Rome: Food and Agriculture Organization.

World Food Council. (1989) *Program of Co-operative Action 1989*. Rome: Food and Agriculture Organization.

World Food Programme. (2015a) *Food in an Uncertain Future: The Impacts of Climate Change on Food Security and Nutrition in the Middle East and North Africa*. Rome: World Food Programme.

World Food Programme. (2015b) *Strengthening National Safety Nets—School Feeding: WFP's Evolving Role in Latin America and the Caribbean*. Rome: World Food Programme.

World Food Programme. (2016) *Global School Feeding Sourcebook*. Rome: World Food Programme.

World Food Programme. (2017a) *Smart School Meals: Nutrition—Sensitive National Programs in Latin America and the Caribbean*. Rome: World Food Programme.

World Food Programme. (2017b) *Strategic Plan 2017–2021*. Rome: World Food Programme.

World Food Programme. (2017c) *World Food Assistance 2017: Taking Stock and Looking Ahead*. Rome: World Food Programme.

World Food Programme. (2018a) *WFP and Climate Change: Helping Countries Increase Climate Resilience to Achieve Zero Hunger*. Rome: World Food Programme.

World Food Programme. (2018b) *Home-Grown School Feeding Resource Framework*. Rome: World Food Programme.

World Food Programme. (2018c) *Annual Performance Report for 2017*. Rome: World Food Programme, June.

World Food Programme. (2018d) *World Food Assistance 2018: Preventing Food Crises*. Rome: World Food Programme.

World Food Programme. (2018e) *WFP and Food Fortification*. Rome: World Food Programme.

World Food Programme. (2019a) *Annual Performance Report for 2018*. Rome: World Food Programme.

World Food Programme. (2019b) *School Feeding Contribution to the SDGs: Strategic Evaluation*. Rome: World Food Programme.

World Food Programme. (2019c) *Impact of School Feeding Programs*. Rome: World Food Programme.

World Food Programme. (2019d) *Evaluation of WFP's Capacity to Respond to Emergencies*. Rome: World Food Programme.

World Food Programme. (2019e) *World Food Programme—Emergency Response and Preparedness*. Rome: World Food Programme.

World Food Programme. (2019f) *Innovating for Climate Resilience in Latin America and the Caribbean*. Rome: World Food Programme.

World Food Programme. (2019g) *Two Years On—WFP Rohingya Refugee Response*. Rome: World Food Programme.

World Food Programme. (2019h) *Climate Risk Financing: Early Response and Anticipatory Actions for Climate Hazards*. Rome: World Food Programme.

World Food Programme. (2020a) *The Power of Gender Equality for Food Security*. Rome: World Food Programme.

World Food Programme. (2020b) *Annual Performance Report for 2019: Briefing to the Executive Board*. Rome: World Food Programme.

World Food Programme. (2020c) *A Chance for Every Schoolchild—WFP School Feeding Strategy 2020 - 2030*. Rome: World Food Programme.

World Food Programme and Food and Agriculture Organization. (2020) *Monitoring Food Security in Countries with Conflict Situations*. Rome: World Food Programme and Food and Agriculture Organization.

World Resources Institute. (2018) *Creating a Sustainable Food Future: Synthesis Report*. Washington, DC: World Resources Institute.

Yacob-Haliso, Olajumoke, Toyin Falola, and Kenneth Kalu (eds.) (2018) *Africa's Big Men: Predatory State-Society Relations in Africa*. New York: Routledge.

Yoshino, Kosaku (ed.) (2019) *Consuming Ethnicity and Nationalism: Asian Experience*. New York: Routledge.

Zawahri, Neda A. (2019) "The Multidimensional Aspect of Water Security in the Middle East and North Africa," in Anders Jägerskog, Michael Schulz, and Ashok Swain (eds.) *Routledge Handbook on Middle East Security*. New York: Routledge: 168–181.

Ziegler, Jean, Christophe Golay, Claire Mahon, and Sally-Anne Way. (2011) *The Fight for the Right to Food: Lessons Learned*. New York: Palgrave Macmillan.

Zinyengere, Nkulumo, Theobald Frank Theodory, Million Gebreyes, and Chinwe Ifejika Speranza (eds.) (2017) *Beyond Agricultural Impacts: Multiple Perspectives on Climate Change and Agriculture in Africa*. London: Academic Press.

Index

F. Adams, *The Right to Food*,
https://doi.org/10.1007/978-3-030-60255-0

The manufacturer's authorised representative in the EU is Springer Nature Customer Service Centre GmbH, Europaplatz 3, 69115 Heidelberg, Germany. If you have any concerns regarding our products, please contact ProductSafety@springernature.com

Printed and bound by CPI Group (UK) Ltd, Croydon, CR0 4YY
30/09/2026
02225461-0003